I AM
JOHN GALT

I AM
JOHN GALT

Today's Heroic Innovators
Building the World
and the
Villainous Parasites
Destroying It

DONALD L. LUSKIN
ANDREW GRETA

WILEY

John Wiley & Sons, Inc.

Published by John Wiley & Sons, Inc., Hoboken, New Jersey.
Published simultaneously in Canada.

Limit of Liability/Disclaimer of Warranty: While the publisher and authors have used their best
efforts in preparing this book, they make no representations or warranties with respect to the
accuracy or completeness of the contents of this book and specifically disclaim any implied warranties
of merchantability or fitness for a particular purpose. No warranty may be created or extended by
sales representatives or written sales materials. The advice and strategies contained herein may not
be suitable for your situation. You should consult with a professional where appropriate. Neither the
publisher nor authors shall be liable for any loss of profit or any other commercial damages, including
but not limited to special, incidental, consequential, or other damages.

AYN RAND® is a registered mark of the Estate of Ayn Rand.

For general information on our other products and services or for technical support, please contact
our Customer Care Department within the United States at (800) 762-2974, outside the United States
at (317) 572-3993 or fax (317) 572-4002.

Wiley also publishes its books in a variety of electronic formats. Some content that appears in print
may not be available in electronic books. For more information about Wiley products, visit our web
site at www.wiley.com.

Library of Congress Cataloging-in-Publication Data:

Luskin, Donald L.
    I am John Galt : today's heroic innovators building the world and the villainous parasites
destroying it / Donald L. Luskin and Andrew Greta.
        p. cm.
    Includes index.
    ISBN 978-1-118-01378-6 (hardback); 978-1-118-10096-7 (ebk.); 978-1-118-10097-4 (ebk.);
    978-1-118-10098-1 (ebk.)
        1. Entrepreneurship—Biography.   2. Creative ability in business.   3. Self-esteem.
    I. Greta, Andrew.   II. Title.
    HC29.L87   2011
    338'.040922—dc22

                                                                                    2011010991

Printed in the United States of America

10 9 8 7 6 5 4 3 2 1

To Christine, Roark, and Roark
—Don

To my wife Emily, and daughter Lucy
—Andrew

Contents

I AM
JOHN GALT

Introduction

Who is John Galt? Ayn Rand asked that question over and over as a catchphrase in *Atlas Shrugged*, one of the bestselling and most inspiring novels of all time. The question was a cry of despair in a desperate time not unlike our own—the equivalent of "What's the use?" More precisely, it meant "Where are the great men and women who could inspire us?" That's a question many are asking today. The world portrayed in *Atlas Shrugged* is racked by a pervasive economic and social crisis—its eerie similarity to our own real world today is one of the reasons it is selling more copies than ever, 50 years after it was first published.

Your personal answer to Rand's question could be "*I* am John Galt." Yes, *you*, the person reading these words now in an increasingly quaint hard copy, or on your handheld digital reading device. *You* can be one of the epic heroes of Rand's books—like John Galt himself, her greatest hero—the ones who fight despair, overcome relentless opposition, and lift the world out of desperation.

We think that's the real secret explaining why Rand's fiction—*Atlas Shrugged* (1957), but also *The Fountainhead* (1943), *We the Living* (1936), and *Anthem* (1938)—are so timeless. Simply stated: they are inspiring. Rand set out to portray ideal men and women, and she did.

The heroes and heroines of her novels are individualists, innovators, and iconoclasts. They are achievers—in business, in the arts, and in love. Their ordeals are the ones that all potentially great people face. What's special about them is that in the course of Rand's novels, they discover and put to work core philosophies—life strategies, really—that lead ultimately to triumph.

You can do it, too. Our proof is the heroes we portray in this book. They faced all the same challenges you do. And yet they made themselves great by following the same life strategies that Rand's heroes did—some of them quite self-consciously, others without having ever even heard of Rand as far as we know. This book shows you what their life strategies—their philosophies—are, and how they map with great precision to the philosophies of Rand's heroes.

Yes, the world portrayed in Rand's books was the world of the industrial era—when leading-edge technologies were railroads and steel mills. Today's Randian heroes run software companies, not railroads. They manufacture semiconductors, not steel. But the principles of success are the same. The philosophy is the same, and Rand laid it all out more than 50 years ago.

Unfortunately, Rand's villains are alive and well in today's world, too. We portray them here as proof that collectivism, self-abnegation, envy, power lust, and, most tellingly, the corrupt alliance of business and government are all strategies for personal ruin. And they spill over into horrific consequences for the world. As you'll see, the economic paroxysm that rocked the world late in the first decade of the 2000s was caused specifically by individuals operating perfectly in the mode of Rand's parasitic villains.

So as another timeless book puts it, our real world and Rand's fictional world are both the best of times and the worst of times. Our heroes have created personal wealth never before seen in history by creating technological marvels that were thought, just a few years ago, to be impossibilities found only in science fiction. Our villains very nearly succeeded in bringing the world economy to its knees. Such is the power of one's personal philosophy. Such is the power of your choice.

Whom do you choose to be like? Do you want to be like Bill Gates? Gates is reviled as a monopolist and a plutocrat akin to Rand's hero Henry Rearden, the steel tycoon. His own government came within inches of branding him a criminal and breaking up his company.

If you agree he's a hero, you need to read this book to learn what he did to became one. If you think he's a villain, you *urgently* need to read this book—we'll show you that his greatness is to be celebrated, not feared. Do you want to be like Steve Jobs? He dropped out of school to follow his professional passion like Rand's hero Howard Roark. Even after he became rich and famous, over and over again Jobs risked his fortune on new and untried technologies—just because he thought they were so damn cool. Now his company is one of the most valuable on the planet. Yet he's widely regarded as a pirate who steals the ideas of others, and an autocratic son of a bitch entirely incapable of working with people. If you agree that he's a hero, maybe one of the reasons is that you're reading this on an iPad—one of Jobs's many magical innovations that have transformed our culture. If you think he's a villain, go out and get an iPad—it might change your mind.

Maybe you'd like to be Paul Krugman. He's a media darling and widely known academic much like Rand's villain Ellsworth Toohey. He's also a rabid partisan who, in the vivid words of one critic, pulls his so-called facts from "a database somewhere in his lower intestine."[1] He has discredited himself among serious thinkers and brought dishonor to the once-great newspaper on whose opinion pages his politicized deceptions appear. He's also a socialist who is willing to destroy as many lives as necessary to deliver the United States into collectivism. If you've experienced a visceral revulsion when reading a Krugman column or seeing him on the Sunday morning talk shows, we'll help you understand your intuition that he is a villain. If he's a hero in your mind, then you shouldn't be afraid to read what we have to say about him—but we might change your mind.

Does all this strike you as a strange conception of "heroes" and "villains"? Maybe when you think of a hero, you think of someone like "Sully"—Chesley Sullenberger, the US Airways pilot who saved 155 passengers by successfully landing a disabled plan in the Hudson River. Sully isn't a titan of business. He's not rich. Yet we emphatically believe he is a hero, and we suspect Ayn Rand would, too. Why? Because Sully's performance in those fateful few minutes in January 2009 was a tour de force of sheer ability, the bravura performance of a highly skilled and courageous man motivated by a single purpose, doing battle with chaos—and winning. What Sully has in common with Bill Gates, Steve Jobs, and the other heroes we talk about in this book is competence, courage, and purpose. *That's* what makes a hero.

Maybe when you think of a villain (and let's leave out overt monsters like, say, Adolf Hitler) you think of a corrupt politician like Richard Nixon or a crook like Bernard Madoff. Who could disagree with that? Ayn Rand certainly demonstrated that evil could exist at the highest levels of government and in business as well. We'll meet real-world villains of both types in this book. But Rand's novels focused primarily on that special brand of evil that is carried out under the high-minded slogans of altruism. The real-world villains you'll meet in this book all have one thing in common: No matter how rabid their lust for power, no matter how voracious their appetite for unearned wealth, and no matter how many lives they have to destroy in the process, their villainy is all carried out in the name of selfless service to others.

Real-life Randian heroes and villains are among us. If you so choose, you can live your life such that you can truly say, "I am John Galt." This book shows you how.

The Books That Changed Our World

To Ayn Rand fans, her books, characters, and philosophy need no introduction. If you are new to Rand, let us introduce her.

Ayn Rand is one of the best-selling novelists of all time. *Atlas Shrugged* has sold over 7 million copies since its 1957 publication, with a record 500,000 copies in 2009 alone. Of the Modern Library Reader's List of 100 Best Novels, Rand's titles hold four of the top eight positions, with *Atlas Shrugged* at #1 and *The Fountainhead* at #2.[2] In a survey by the Library of Congress and the Book of the Month Club, respondents ranked *Atlas Shrugged* second only to the Bible when asked what book had made the biggest impact on their lives.[3]

The *New York Times* has called *Atlas Shrugged* "one of the most influential business books ever written." The *Chicago Tribune* called it "the boldest affirmation of the gospel of free enterprise ever attempted in fiction."[4] Its ongoing popularity is an astonishing achievement for a literary franchise that has produced no new content since Rand's death in 1982, and for a book that was derided as too long, too intellectual, and too politically conservative.

References to Rand's work continually crop up in popular culture ranging from *Mad Men* to *Mad* magazine. There's even a video game saturated with Rand references, including cigarettes branded with gold dollar signs and the ever-present question, "Who is Atlas?"

But Rand has something deeper to offer. Her books are sought out for their enduring practical and philosophical content by readers eager to learn how to live a more successful life. Rand's work has inspired lives and helped create the society, politics, economics, law, and culture we live in today.

Former Federal Reserve chair Alan Greenspan and the eminent economist Milton Friedman (both of whom we'll examine in detail in this book), as well as Supreme Court Justice Clarence Thomas and House Budget Committee chair Paul Ryan all count themselves among Rand's devotees. It's far more than just conservative political figures, though. Whole Foods Market founder John Mackey, former BB&T chief executive John Allison (whom we'll also examine), Dallas Mavericks owner Mark Cuban, baseball's "Iron Man" Cal Ripken, actor Vince Vaughn, magician Penn Jillette, actress Angelina Jolie, and even Hillary Clinton have all said publicly that Rand has been an inspiration.

Beyond Political Labels

Do you have to be a political conservative to be a real-life Ayn Rand hero? Hardly! Rand used the word *conservative* as an insult. But then again, she did the same thing with the word *liberal*. When it came to politics, she was maddeningly hard to pin down—and very resistant to being labeled.

That said, she is probably associated more with so-called conservative ideas than with so-called liberal ones. And with *Atlas Shrugged* selling better than ever, the political right has been quick to claim that it's because of politics. The right's story is that the Great Recession that rocked the globe in 2008 and 2009 was caused entirely by government meddling in the economy, and that Ayn Rand's masterwork amounts to a prediction of that, made more than a half century ago.

This is a misreading of Rand, and the political left should be the first to say so. In fact, Rand has always offered as much to liberals as she has to conservatives.

For starters, it's much too simple to say that *Atlas Shrugged* is a parable of the destructive effects of government intervention, a black-and-white world in which businesspeople are heroes and public servants are villains. In fact, the primary villain in *Atlas Shrugged* is a businessman, railroad executive James Taggart. There are villainous politicians, to be sure, but for the most part they are portrayed as passive bumblers. The government's most destructive acts are carried out at the behest of Taggart and his cronies, not for ideological motives.

Yes, many of the heroes of *Atlas Shrugged* are businessmen. But that is only to say that the key dynamic animating the story's action is the conflict between good businessmen and bad businessmen.

Even the heroic businessmen in *Atlas Shrugged* are portrayed as flawed and conflicted individuals. They are not examples of "an ideal man," the projection of which was for Rand the "motive and the purpose of my writing."[5] That honor belongs to John Galt, a humble inventor. (Liberals take note: In *Atlas Shrugged* Galt invents a motor that requires no energy—what would now be called green technology.)

The same distinction shows up with a vengeance in *The Fountainhead*, Rand's first major novel. The ideal man is Howard Roark, an art-for-art's-sake architect. Ultrarich newspaper tycoon Gail Wynand is portrayed in heroic terms, prefiguring some of the industrial giants who will later populate *Atlas Shrugged*. But Wynand is a tragic hero who makes the error of pursuing wealth for the sake of power over other people—as in fact many highly achieved businesspeople do. In the closing scenes of the book Wynand commits suicide, declaring his entire life to have been a failure.

It's ironic to see the political right overlooking these realities in order to embrace Rand. Until now conservatives have despised her. So if my enemy's enemy is my friend, then Rand is a friend to liberals.

Rand was a militant atheist, and that has always been an irreconcilable difference with the conservative movement, given its coalition with the Christian church. Rand never even tried to be conciliatory on the subject. When she first met William F. Buckley Jr., the founding father of modern conservatism and a devout Catholic, she reportedly proclaimed in her heavy Russian accent, "Mr. Buckley, you arrrr too intelligent to believe in Gott!"[6]

Buckley himself used to repeat that story, and denied any animosity about Rand's atheism. But when it came time in 1957 for Buckley's highly influential conservative magazine *National Review* to review the newly published *Atlas Shrugged*, it was worse than a pan—it was a smear. The review was by conservative icon Whittaker Chambers, the ardent anticommunist—who also happens to have been an ardent Christian.

Chambers portrayed *Atlas Shrugged* as a call for totalitarianism by big business, with "the Sign of the Dollar, in lieu of the Sign of the Cross."[7] To anyone who had read the book, such an idea was preposterous to the point of slander. But reviews are intended for people who haven't read the book. This review was intended so that no conservative ever would. It didn't quite work *that* well, but it set the tone for half a century for how conservatives would regard the ideas of Ayn Rand.

But while conservatives have despised Rand, she often despised them right back. She loathed Dwight Eisenhower. And in 1975 she wrote, "I urge you, as emphatically as I can, not to support the candidacy of Ronald Reagan."[8]

Issues always made the difference. Rand endorsed Richard Nixon in 1968 because he supported abolition of the military draft—and Rand was especially proud of her protégé Alan Greenspan serving on Nixon's Gates Commission, whose findings led to today's all-volunteer army. Rand opposed Reagan on his antiabortion stance. She was ardently prochoice, saying five years before *Roe v. Wade*, "Abortion is a moral right—which should be left solely to the woman involved. An embryo *has no rights*."[9]

These weren't the only times Rand took positions that didn't exactly ingratiate her to the right. She was an early opponent of the Vietnam War, once saying, "It is as irrational and immoral as any public act in our history."[10] As an individualist who insisted on seeing people as individuals, she declared, "I am an enemy of racism,"[11] and she advised opponents of school busing, "If you object to sending your children to school with black children, you'll lose for sure because right is on the other side."[12]

Rand's own life story ought to ingratiate her to the left. As a woman alone, an immigrant arriving penniless in the United States, not speaking English—if she were to show up today rather than in 1925, modern liberals would give her a driver's license and register her to vote.

Rand ridiculed feminism as a "phony movement" and once described herself as "a male chauvinist."[13] Yet she lived as a poster child for feminism, utterly defying gender stereotypes. She rose from poverty to become an enormously powerful intellectual influence upon the culture, a very rare achievement for a woman in the 1940s and the 1950s. She is believed to have had an abortion in the early 1930s.[14] She was the family breadwinner throughout her life. In late middle age, she became enamored of a much younger man and made up her mind to have an affair with him—having in advance duly informed her husband and his wife. Conservatives don't do things like that (or at least they say they don't).

In some sense Rand's novels are feminist fantasies, as Camille Paglia, a postmodern critic embraced by liberal academics, has pointed out. *We the Living*, *The Fountainhead*, and *Atlas Shrugged* are all told primarily from the viewpoint of female characters. *Atlas Shrugged*, in particular, is built around the extraordinarily capable railroad executive Dagny Taggart and her struggles with her corrupt and incompetent brother James, the railroad president. She's the female who deserves the man's job, but doesn't have it because she's a woman; he's the man who has the job because he's a man, but doesn't deserve it.

So don't let politics get in your way of learning from the heroes who embody Ayn Rand's philosophy. Political labels are products of the collective; you are an individual, as Rand was, and don't have to be bound by them.

Objectivism 101

The standard of value for Rand's Objectivist ethics is human life, or correspondingly, those things required for human survival. She correctly observes that, unlike other members of the animal kingdom, humans are not endowed with innate physical traits or complex behavioral instincts to ensure their continuation on the earth. We must clothe ourselves, arrange shelter, and obtain food for our sustenance through choice and action.

The basic survival tool and competitive advantage we have at our command is the human mind and our ability to reason. Since everything we need to live must be discovered by our own minds and produced by our own efforts, the essential means of life are thinking and productive work. That which supports the life of a rational, thinking, working human being is good; that which opposes or negates it is evil.

It follows that the individual mind is the root of all value that is produced or ever existed. No amount of brutish, mindless labor could perform a set of physical motions and create a nuclear reactor, or even a wheel and axle. No amount of randomly placed machinery could assemble itself into a productive assembly line, and no sack of rice could exist if someone didn't first think, reason, and figure out the fundamentals of agriculture by using their own brainpower. There is no such thing as a collective mind. All value distills down to the individual.

But no man is an island. Humans come together into societies for mutual benefit, including group protection and division of labor, which allows members to develop specialized skills that can exceed the productive value of an individual generalist. Yet any time people come together in a civilization, there are those who seek to profit by taking the production of others rather than by freely and voluntarily trading the products of their own efforts with others in fair exchange.

According to Ayn Rand, there are two potential violators of a human's rights: criminals and the government. Outright thievery is condemned across all cultures. Tribal raids for the purpose of sacking and looting the resources of a neighboring clan are generally absent from developed societies. Yet governmental looting is alive and well; the looters have just gotten more sophisticated. Through the promotion of various philosophies of altruism that teach that individual advancement is ignoble and that self-sacrifice is noble, siphoning of individual production by government is not only rationalized, but portrayed as a moral good.

After all, who wouldn't deem it desirable to lift the poor out of poverty, to grant health care to all people, and to help the helpless? It's not for our benefit; it's for the public good (the "public" in this case being some sort of mythical entity with a superior claim over any individual member of it).

For the altruist, the beneficiary of an action is the only measure of moral value. As long as that beneficiary is someone other than you, it must be good. Selfishness, they say, is an evil. We must not live for ourselves, but for our fellow man.

Objectivists would agree that eliminating hunger and poverty would be a good thing. The difference is that Randians ask the next logical question that the collectivists conveniently ignore: "At what cost in terms of human freedom?" Shall we forcibly confiscate property from some to dole it out to others? Should we enslave some workers to support the nonworking? What about imprisoning those who resist in order to force compliance with the social good as determined by a supposedly benevolent dictator? All have been tried throughout modern history in the name of greater social progress. Some exist today to various extents—even in the United States.

These are all forms of collectivism, and they are made possible by mystical philosophies such as altruism. Their opposite is individualism, which is made possible by reason-based philosophies such as Objectivism.

Rand, rather controversially, uses the word *selfishness* to capture the virtues that lead to individualism and freedom. She means "selfish" in the sense of one's personal rights, defended and exercised in one's rational self-interest over the course of an entire life. This is not the same as the collectivist's derisive depiction of the "selfish" man as a hedonistic brute who seeks only the whims and pleasures of the moment and who, in the end, is no better than a marauder, seizing from others whatever he wishes. For Rand, that describes the collectivist, who has no respect for the rights of others—even though he calls himself an altruist. Selfishness in the Randian sense implies deriving your survival and your happiness from achieving command over nature, not over other people.

It means gaining the skills needed to engage in productive work while honing one's rational mind to inform well-reasoned decisions. It means providing for ourselves through our own efforts and not expecting others to live in support of us. It also means living with the consequences of our actions—reaping the gain from favorable outcomes while shouldering the loss from downside risks.

Collectivists believe the world is like a zero-sum poker game with a fixed amount of chips on the table. Wealth exists in the economy as a fixed-size pool to divvy up. If someone gains a larger share, it must be at the expense of another. The collectivist's goal—at least the stated goal—is to ensure "fairness" by forcibly penalizing the productive "rich" and giving the proceeds to the unproductive "poor." Since they see wealth as fixed, then it follows—they claim—that the rich must have done something wrong to someone else in order to have seized a disproportionate share.

For Objectivists, wealth is not a fixed pool but a dynamic inventory achieved by producers in proportion to the creative value they deliver into the economy. The producers who contribute value should have a right to the value of their own production. How can that be unfair when, after all, any value is assigned in a free market only by the voluntary choice of customers who deal—or not—with a producer?

For the collectivist, there is no thought given to the *source* of economic value or the means of its creation. In the collectivists' stated view, the world consists of two groups, the victims and the oppressors. Their belief system cannot accommodate an alternative relationship between humans—that of self-reliant equals.

In Rand's ideal world, no one is a slave and no one is a master. All transactions between parties are based on voluntary exchange and open dealings under a limited government that enforces simple rules to protect basic rights, but doesn't interfere in the voluntary affairs of individuals. Risks are borne by those who take them; players don't gamble with other people's chips and expect someone else to pay for their losses, nor do they take someone else's winnings. Benefits accrue to those who practice clean dealings and meet true market needs with value-added products or services.

Who Is Ayn Rand?

Ayn Rand had firsthand experience with the perils of collectivism early in life, which carried through her unwavering body of work.

She was born Alisa Rosenbaum in St. Petersburg, Russia, in 1905. Young Alisa had a front-row view of the Bolshevik revolution of 1917. When the communists confiscated her father's thriving business, the once prominent, solidly middle-class, and well-educated family was consigned to a hardscrabble existence living off minimal state wages. During her college years at the University of Leningrad, free inquiry was replaced by communist doctrine. One by one, her favorite professors were shipped into exile and any of her classmates who dared to protest were sent to Siberia.[15]

Shortly after Alisa immigrated to the United States in the late 1920s, the country fell into the grips of the Great Depression. Communist rhetoric and party membership were on a steady rise, and President Franklin Delano Roosevelt was putting in place the New Deal, vastly expanding the role of government in the economy and in individuals' lives.

During this time, Alisa learned English and resolved to be a writer. She changed her name to Ayn Rand, and began to evolve the philosophical framework and literary talents that would make her newly taken name immortal. She published her first novel, *We the Living*, in 1936 as a semiautobiographical story of the individual's struggles against the state in communist Russia. Two years later, she released *Anthem*, a novella set in a dystopian future and again focused on the triumph of an individual mind over a collectivist state, where even the word *I* had been lost and replaced with *we*.

The Fountainhead was Rand's first major commercial and literary success, published in 1943. Its central character is an innovative and iconoclastic architect named Howard Roark. He is a nearly unique creation in literature—the hero of a story presented from the beginning as a fully realized ideal man. He encounters and overcomes challenges, but goes through no personal growth or transformation in the process, because he is already perfect; indeed, the whole point of the story is to demonstrate how a perfect person handles challenges in a highly imperfect world. Rand's definition of the perfect that Roark embodies is utter individualism, leading to a life of uncompromising creative work and unshakable personal integrity.

Roark is surrounded by four other main characters, every one of them a "second-hander," to use Rand's expression. Roark, the individualist, lives his life firsthand. To live life secondhand is to be less than an individual—it is to put the purpose of your life outside yourself. Two of the second-handers are villains. One is a thief who steals Roark's ideas; the other is an egalitarian collectivist who tries to thwart Roark's career. The other two second-handers are heroes—one a great businessman who mistakenly uses his wealth to achieve power over others, the other a beautiful woman in love with Roark but unable to bear the thought that the world might hurt him. Of the four, three are destroyed by their failure to live life firsthand. The fourth, the woman, overcomes her fear and joins Roark as a first-hander.

After *The Fountainhead* was published, the Cold War began in earnest and it seemed the tide of socialist collectivism could turn into a tsunami that would inexorably soak the West and drown out individual liberty once and for all. Presidential candidate Henry Wallace called for "public ownership of a large segment of American industry, business dependency on government funds, government ownership of banks, and federal control through rationing."[16] By the early 1950s, United Nations forces had been fought to a stalemate by Chinese-backed Communists on the Korean peninsula.

Rand wrote her masterwork *Atlas Shrugged* in reaction to these developments. On its publication date, October 10, 1957, the Soviet Union's Sputnik satellite was on its fifth day of earth orbit. *Atlas Shrugged* became a best seller, and grew in popularity even as Cuba fell to the Communists at America's back door.

Atlas Shrugged is set in an America that Rand extrapolated from the creeping threat of collectivism all around her. Its plot tracks the growth of a counterrevolutionary movement designed to restore individualism and freedom. The unique twist is that the counterrevolutionaries—a growing cabal of industrialists, artists, and professionals disgusted by the devolving world around them—do nothing at all to turn the tide of events. They literally *do nothing*, which is to say that they go on strike and withdraw their minds from the corrupt world, refusing to contribute to it in any way. Rand's key insight here is that evil is powerless in the same way that any parasite is—collectivists require productive individuals whose work they can expropriate, just as a flea requires a dog.

John Galt is the ideal man of *Atlas Shrugged*, the "perfect" one around whom a cast of imperfect heroes and villains orbit. The heroes are industrialists who love their work so much they can't bring themselves to go on strike, and so continue to inadvertently serve the collectivist villains. Those villains are corrupt businessmen and bureaucrats who seek collectivism for a variety of reasons, all having to do with their personal impotence.

Over the course of the novel, Galt recruits more and more able men to his strike, and as their talents are withdrawn from the world, the economy falls into severe decline. The collectivists get increasingly desperate, and expropriate the remaining productive individuals all the more—until finally they, too, join Galt in his strike. Ultimately the economy utterly collapses, and Galt leads his strikers back to the world to rebuild it from the ruins.

Surely part of the twenty-first-century readership revival in Rand's work is a Newtonian reaction to the chain of events that began with the terrorist attacks and global economic collapse of the past decade. That collapse was triggered by decades of an unholy alliance between corrupt businesspeople and corrupt bureaucrats. In the wake of these events there has been a resurgence of government intervention in our personal lives and in the economy, reaching in the United States all the way to government takeovers of major private banks, financial firms, and manufacturing companies—many of which had corruptly inter-twined themselves with government to begin with—and most recently the health care industry. Collectivism is most assuredly not a dated relic of the Cold War era. It's here and now. It's not just the world of *Atlas Shrugged*. It's the world we live in.

Living the Life of an Ayn Rand Hero

Ayn Rand's heroes are larger-than-life projections of her ideals. They lead lives of virtue based on consistent personal convictions with a coherent philosophical system to guide them. Today's real-life heroes universally did the hard work, tedious at times, to achieve their suc-cess based on their own effort and mental acuity. Steve Jobs created the revolutionary Apple II through what one observer called "moxie and energy," and then engrossed himself in mind-numbing details for every nuance of the Macintosh user interface to deliver a tangible product that was often called "insanely great." T. J. Rodgers studied the molecular structure of silicon to make subatomic improvements and create ultra-fast memory chips. Bill Gates spent tens of thousands of hours immersed in the inner workings of computers, writing millions of lines of code.

These heroes are not typically motivated by money per se, but they see money as a tool with which to create and build. Steve Jobs returned to Apple Computer at a symbolic salary of $1. Bill Gates flies commercial without an entourage. He agonized over a $12,000 boat purchase even though he had the means to buy a dozen luxury yachts.

The Randian innovator's life purpose is not some do-gooder vision of altruism or charity, but a core drive to work hard, produce value, and follow an inner vision with supreme self-reliance. Steve Wozniak once said about his Apple co-founder, Steve Jobs, "He's not concerned with what contribution he's making. He wants to astound himself, for himself."[17]

Heroes work from fact. Milton Friedman came to his conclusions about free-market economics through empirical analysis, discovering for himself that the New Deal promises of his early career were patently false in the face of hard evidence. Bill Gates was known as a nimble businessman able to quickly change direction if the facts didn't support his initial ideas. For them, truth is objective and concrete. "Silicon doesn't lie," says T. J. Rodgers.

Heroes stand for principles, not expediency. BB&T CEO John Allison denied his bank millions in fat fees because he believed that exotic mortgages were bad for his customers. T. J. Rodgers resigned from the board of a company he helped found rather than be pressured into lobbying the government for subsidies.

By contrast, modern-day villains are just like Rand's literary ones—expedient, scheming, and leaching value from others rather than doing the hard work of creating. Barney Frank is a lifelong politician who never spent a day working in a bank, brokerage, or financial institution—yet he weaseled his way to the chairmanship of the House Financial Services Committee, where he presided over governmental interventions in housing that catalyzed a historic mortgage bubble. Angelo Mozilo at Countrywide Financial overlooked blatant fraud in his company to make a quick buck off of the government subsidies created by Frank. Together, in the name of the noble-sounding altruistic goal of universal home ownership, the two of them very nearly destroyed the world economy. And they also wrecked the financial and emotional lives of countless individuals they purported to be helping. So much for altruism.

Villains ignore the facts of reality in favor of their own irrational opinions. Their idea of truth is whatever the collective believes, regardless of empirical evidence. Mozilo told investors that his company was sound, as he secretly sold his own shares ahead of the collapse he saw coming. "Fannie and Freddie had nothing to do with the explosion of high-risk lending . . . they didn't do any subprime,"[18] said collectivist apologist Paul Krugman, while Fannie Mae itself published facts admitting to buying up subprime debt. Jesse Jackson's camp called T. J. Rodgers's company (with a 35 percent minority employee base) a "white supremacist hate group,"[19] as punishment for Rodgers publicly challenging Jackson's own hate-based tirades about race.

Why It Matters Today

We could conclude by arguing that living by Rand's philosophy is important today because the threat of collectivism is as salient as ever. Indeed it is as salient as ever, with the United States having just effectively nationalized health care, 14 percent of the economy—and the most innovative and vibrant part of it—by claiming that it is "broken." And indeed the threat is as salient as ever, with China, a totalitarian dictatorship over 1.2 billion souls, now leading the world in industrial development.

But we won't say that. The reason to live Rand's philosophy isn't that it's good for the world. That's altruism talking. The reason is that it's in your own interest to live Rand's philosophy. Do you want to have integrity? Do you want to devote yourself to creative, constructive work? Do you want to be happy and wealthy as a result?

Do you want these things for your own sake? Then make it so. We'll help you by showing you how others have done it, by profiling both the heroes who make our world great and the villains out to destroy it.

If it just happens to save the world in the process, then so much the better.

Chapter 1

The Individualist

Steve Jobs as Howard Roark, the man who reinvented four whole industries just because it was so cool

"I don't intend to build in order to serve or help anyone. I don't intend to build in order to have clients. I intend to have clients in order to build."

"How do you propose to force your ideas on them?"

"I don't propose to force or be forced. Those who want me will come to me."

—The Fountainhead

Who is Howard Roark?

In *The Fountainhead*, Howard Roark is a courageous young architect. Ayn Rand presents him from beginning to end as her ideal man, the complete individualist who lives by his own standards and for his own sake, whose work is an end in itself simply because he loves doing it, and who is utterly indifferent to the opinions of anyone else.

Roark's architecture is boldly original, inspired by his own personal vision. To succeed, he must rebel against the conventions

(Continued)

17

of his era. His architecture of individual inspiration must compete against expectations that architecture should borrow from collectively established classical precedents. At the same time, he has to overcome terrible setbacks at the hands of enemies who want to destroy him, because he symbolizes the individual versus the collective.

His worst enemy is Ellsworth Toohey, an architecture critic for the tabloid newspaper the *Daily Banner* with a web of connections in the arts, high society, government, and unions. He is a madman seeking to rule the world through collectivism, starting by corrupting its intellectual and moral standards. He uses his influence to promote the careers of incompetent architects, and he directly thwarts Roark's career with various ruses engineered to discredit him.

In a typical story, the conflict between Roark and Toohey would end in a fistfight atop an unfinished skyscraper designed by Roark, with Toohey plunging to his death, to Roark's great satisfaction. But Roark is such an utter individualist, he has no interest in defeating Toohey. In one of the book's most memorable scenes, at a low point when Toohey has nearly destroyed Roark's career, the two of them meet by chance. Ever the collectivist who can't resist defining himself through others, Toohey asks Roark to tell him honestly what he thinks of him. Roark, the man who lives entirely by his own opinion of himself, simply says, "But I don't think of you."

Roark triumphs over all opposition, and goes on to build the tallest skyscraper in New York. All the struggles are forgotten, mere distractions incapable of impacting a true individualist. At the end, Roark is the end—an end in himself, as each of us is.

When Steve Jobs took the stage in October 2001, he was a man resurrected, returned home from a classic hero's journey, still true to his singular vision, but battle-hardened from 12 years wandering the business wilderness as a castoff from the tribe he founded. He was grayer and leaner, yet still sharp-edged like tempered steel emerging from the fire, himself the sword the journeying hero forges in the great myths.

Or more exactly, here was Howard Roark—Ayn Rand's brilliant and rebellious architect hero from *The Fountainhead*—returning to the city to erect a stunning skyscraper embodying his own epoch-making vision, after being forced to labor in a granite quarry merely to survive.

Here was the intransigent individualist who invented a worldwide culture of personal computing, and was unceremoniously ousted from the seat of his creation by collective forces bent on harnessing and diffusing his disruptive vision through committees and opaque corporate processes. Along the way, he had a brush with financial death and went on to revolutionize a second industry—only to be recalled to rescue his original creation from the brink of collapse. Jobs was back to lead the rebirth of Apple Computer, clear the debris left by the collective that had ousted him, and rebuild his masterwork on the solid foundations of his individual vision, as he first had 17 years before.

He was close-cropped, scruffy, and dressed in his now-signature black mock turtleneck and jeans; gone were the suit coat, button-down shirt, bow tie, and boyish mop of hair from his 1984 inaugural Macintosh presentation. Gone, too, were the thematic *Chariots of Fire* music and talking computer gimmicks amid a cheering auditorium packed with thousands of devotees. Instead, Jobs cast a deep resonating spell of low-key personal charisma—the kind that captures and holds an audience rapt with a mere whisper.

The new uniform was deliberate. On one level, Jobs was subordinating his corporeal body to his visionary creations by shedding props and presentational artifice to allow a clearer focus on the product of his mind. The question was not "What would Steve wear?" but "What revolutionary new idea will he present today?" It was also symbolic of his simplified approach to Apple upon his return as interim CEO in 1997, when he quickly pared the growing number of foundering product groups from 15 down to a focused three[1] while slashing inefficient overhead, laying off employees, and repopulating his board of directors with handpicked replacements, including Larry Ellison of Oracle and former Apple sales head Bill Campbell, then CEO of Intuit.[2]

In his signature presentation style, Jobs began his homecoming pitch to a small assembly of attendees at an Apple Music event. With a relaxed and unhurried ease he spoke of the market, competition, underlying technology, and the recipe for success in leveraging the

Apple brand. In a seamless and nearly undetectable transition to aesthetics, he then began describing the design and usability of an entirely new-breed model of music accessibility. As he built to a crescendo, the audience was salivating in suspense. "Durable. Beautiful. And this is what the front looks like. Boom!" he exclaimed. "That's iPod. And I happen to have one in my pocket."

Yet the moment had even deeper meaning than the introduction of a cool new product. It was evidence of how Jobs's entire existence symbolized right and left brains harmonized—analytics and creativity coexisting in a symbiotic blend of productive energy focused on the output of human creation instead of the cumbersome tools used to hammer those ideas into reality. He had spent a lifetime transcending the chasm between silicon-based technology and carbon-based humans. The world called that the "user interface." To Jobs, it was a barrier, a gap, and his vision was to make that gap seem nonexistent. And now he was doing it again, with a revolutionary product of his unique mind that would transform the popular culture of the world.

He once called the personal computer (PC) "the equivalent of a bicycle to our minds" as a metaphor for human ingenuity's ability to leverage our physical capabilities beyond anything in the natural world.[3] A person on foot is quickly outpaced by most of the animal kingdom, he would explain. When that same person conceives and designs a set of wheels connected by gears and pedals, he or she becomes the most efficiently self-mobile creature on earth. But just as a bicycle without a rider is a mere hunk of metal, a computer can amplify the intellect only when a human mind is powering it. This interface between mind and machine is where Steve Jobs lives.

According to Apple co-founder Steve Wozniak, "He was never driven by a vision of a better world; he was driven by a vision of himself as a person whose decisions guide the world. He wanted to build a device that moved the world forward, that would take people further. He wanted to build a reality that wasn't there. He wanted to be one of the important ones. He either likes what he's looking at or he doesn't. He's not concerned with what contribution he's making. He wants to astound himself, for himself."[4]

Ayn Rand's first great novel, *The Fountainhead*, was built around such a man, a supreme individualist—or "egoist" in Rand's terms—Howard Roark. In the words of Roark, "I can find the joy only if I do my work in the best way possible to me. But the best is a matter of standards—and I set my own standards. I inherit nothing. I stand at the end of no tradition. I may, perhaps, stand at the beginning of one."

He's been referred to as a charismatic boy wonder, the Alpha Adolescent, a cultural phenomenon, a consumer technology impresario, an adroit chief executive, a cultural revolutionary, a man with three faces, a zealot, the enfant terrible, an arbiter of popular culture, a temperamental micromanager. Yet he is simply an individual—an individual who dares to shape the world in accord with what Roark would call his "unborrowed vision" and his "independent judgment."

Like Rand herself, Jobs dares to judge the world in binary terms, in what Rand would call the Aristotelian mode of determining either-or. Products, in his view, are either "insanely great" or "shit." One is either dying from cancer or "cured." Subordinates are either geniuses or "bozos," either indispensable or irrelevant.[5] And like Rand's iconic individualist Roark, Jobs works for his own reward and satisfaction in his own unbending terms. He returned to lead Apple, accepting a salary of only $1, saying, "The only purpose for me in building a company is so that it can make products."[6] And like Roark, Jobs doesn't rely on the opinions of others to define his own views. He has the self-confidence to know that all great ideas throughout history have sprung from the intellect of a single individual. "The mind is an attribute of the individual. There is no such thing as a collective brain," said Howard Roark.

Jobs doesn't see himself creating something new as much as he is discovering what others can't see. Like the myth of Prometheus and his discovery of fire, Steve is constantly surprising the world by meeting the needs and desires that people never knew they had. Comparing Jobs with Polaroid inventor Dr. Edwin Land, former Apple CEO John Sculley said, "Both of them had this ability not to invent products but to discover products. Both of them said these products have always existed—it's just that no one has ever seen them before. We were the ones who discovered them. The Polaroid camera always existed, and the Macintosh always existed—it's a matter of discovery."[7]

Yet for Jobs such discoveries are, of necessity, the discovery of himself. "If I asked someone who had only used a personal calculator what a Macintosh should be like, they couldn't have told me," Jobs once explained. "There was no way to do consumer research on it, so I had to go and create it, and then show it to people, and say now what do you think?"[8] Apple marketing chief Mike Murray observed, "Steve did his market research by looking into the mirror every morning."[9]

Anyone who has ever been curious enough to disassemble an iPod quickly realizes it looks the way it does on the outside because of what's inside. The economy of space, the use of materials both durable and stylish, the most leading-edge components of the day, the physical layout, and the user interface are all unique to the end function—making software manifest in the physical world while simultaneously making it invisible to the user. In short, Apple products look a certain way because they have to.

According to Sculley, "Steve's brilliance is his ability to see something and then understand it and then figure out how to put it into the context of his design methodology—everything is design. He's a minimalist and constantly reducing things to their simplest level. It's not simplistic. It's simplified. Steve is a systems designer. He simplifies complexity."[10]

Or in describing Howard Roark's architectural design mentor Henry Cameron, "He said only that the form of a building must follow its function; that the structure of a building is the key to its beauty; that new methods of construction demand new forms; that he wished to build as he wished and for that reason only."

Jobs has spent a lifetime living by Roark's own singular rulebook not as the designer of buildings, but as the architect of a new approach to technology. Or in Roark's words, "The purpose, the site, the material determine the shape. Nothing can be reasonable or beautiful unless it's made by one central idea, and the idea sets every detail. . . . Its integrity is to follow its own truth, its one single theme, and to serve its own single purpose. A man doesn't borrow pieces of his body. A building doesn't borrow hunks of its soul. Its maker gives it the soul."

Yes, It All Began in a Garage

Steve Jobs was born on February 24, 1955, in San Francisco, California. His mother was an unmarried graduate student who gave him up for adoption to Paul and Clara Jobs, the couple Steve would always consider his true parents even after reconnecting with his genetic lineage later in life. The adoption almost fell through. Steve's biological mother initially refused to sign the adoption papers, insisting that her son be adopted by college graduates. Clara had never graduated from college. Paul wasn't even a high school graduate. Steve's mother eventually relented when the Jobses promised her they'd send Steve to college.[11]

Paul, the no-nonsense son of a Midwestern farmer, had dropped out of high school and enlisted in the U.S. Coast Guard during World War II, where he mastered the trade of engine mechanics. With his crew cut and tattoos, Paul exuded a hearty and productive blue-collar pride. Possessing an innate mechanical aptitude, Paul loved to tinker with cars. He would buy old junkers and then spend weeks fixing them up to resell at a profit. He was known as a tough negotiator.[12]

It was an ironically concrete beginning for an abstract intellect like Steve's, but that solid family foundation rooted him in an ethic of hard work and personal responsibility. His father's pursuit of profit through hard-nosed entrepreneurship and productive value-added clearly rubbed off on young Steve, who would grow to become an astute and tough-minded deal maker himself. Despite little formal education of his own, Paul also encouraged his son's curiosity and interest in the new field of electronics.

Like many gifted kids, Steve was a rambunctious child who quickly became bored with tedious schoolwork geared toward the middle of the student bell curve. Under the wing of an insightful teacher who recognized Steve's talent, he skipped fifth grade altogether but soon found himself a young brainiac at a rough-and-tumble middle school in lower-middle-class Mountain View, California, with a greater focus on preventing fistfights than cultivating the mind. At age 11, Steve patently refused to go to school and held his ground with his parents.[13] As a result of what would become his trademark persistence in eliminating obstacles in the way of his vision, his family finally relented and relocated in order to enroll Steve in the more upscale, academically focused Cupertino Middle School.

Steve was growing up in the heart of what would become known as Silicon Valley, already in the late 1960s a vibrant epicenter of electronics companies springing up to service NASA's Apollo space program. It was a fresh field fertilized by new silicon transistor and integrated circuit technology that fostered entrepreneurial zeal and new business rules. The Jobses' new neighborhood was populated with engineers who filled their garages with workbenches and spare electronics parts. Age and appearance didn't matter to these technological tinkerers, and they welcomed the opportunity to share information and hardware with an eager and inquisitive kid like Steve when he came around to check out their latest projects.

Conversely, Steve never seemed intimidated by adults despite his youth and inexperience. Once, while working on an electronics project, he realized he was short on parts. Undeterred, he picked up the Palo Alto phone book and cold-called Bill Hewlett, one of the founders of Hewlett-Packard (HP). Bill answered the phone and chatted with Steve affably for a while, then ended up supplying the parts needed to complete Steve's project. It was a determination and gumption that would become a Steve Jobs hallmark. Once he set his sights on an objective, he would wade right in, go for the top decision maker, and persist relentlessly until he succeeded.

It was in the garage of Steve's school buddy and fellow "wirehead" Bill Fernandez where he met Steve Wozniak, the son of an engineer at Lockheed's Missiles and Space Division in Sunnyvale. Five years Jobs's senior, "Woz," as he had been known since grade school, was a brilliant technician and avid prankster who had been kicked out of the University of Colorado after hacking the university's computer system. By the time he and Jobs met, Woz and Fernandez had already built their own personal computer from surplus parts in Woz's garage. It was rudimentary at best—a raw circuit board flashing lights in response to user-thrown switches and hardwired logic circuits—but it was a device Woz created on his own a full five years before comparable home hobby computer kits became commercially available. Woz had the technical genius, and Jobs had the vision and hustle. It was an auspicious meeting that would eventually transform their lives, and the world.

With the end of high school fast approaching, Jobs set his sights on the liberal arts mecca of Reed College in Portland, Oregon. He seemed to embrace the counterculture of the early 1970s—a belief in individuality and a refusal to accept established convention or be intimidated by it. "Steve had a very inquiring mind that was enormously attractive," remembers Jack Dudman, Reed College's dean of students at the time. "You wouldn't get away with bland statements. He refused to accept automatically received truths. He wanted to examine everything himself."[14]

Jobs's drive applied only to subjects he cared about, however. After only one semester at Reed, he found himself failing out of his core freshman classes. Like Howard Roark, who got himself expelled from architecture school, he found that traditional academics offered no value to his internal vision. So in characteristic Jobs style, he dropped out of school and got a refund of his tuition. Instead of returning home, however, he stayed on campus attending classes of his own choosing for free while living in vacant dorm rooms. One of his most notable classes he audited during this time was calligraphy. It was a fascinating window into functional art that Jobs credits with inspiring the first typefaces for the iconic Macintosh computer he would later invent.

Back home as a college dropout in the summer of 1974, Steve saw an employment advertisement for video game maker Atari. According to Atari's chief engineer, Al Alcorn, a human resources rep came to him one day to tell him that some rumpled-looking hippie wouldn't leave the building until they hired him. Jobs's sheer force of will and determination brings to mind Howard Roark's meeting with architect Henry Cameron for his first job. Cameron was known as a mean son of a bitch, but Roark was as fearless with him as Jobs was with Alcorn:

> "I should like to work for you," Roark said quietly. The voice said "I should like to work for you." The tone of the voice said "I'm going to work for you."

"I don't know why I hired him," remembers Alcorn, "except that he was determined to have the job and there was some spark. I really saw the spark in that man, some inner energy, and attitude that he was going to get it done. And he had a vision, too. You know, the definition of a visionary is 'someone with an inner vision not supported by external facts.' He had those great ideas without much to back them up. Except that he believed in them."[15]

At Atari, Jobs would work nights on a variety of projects and was a quick study. When a problem came up in Germany, Alcorn gave Jobs a quick primer and sent him there. Jobs solved the problem in

Germany in two hours and then made his way to India for a prenego-
tiated spiritual sabbatical of sorts.

Jobs was still exploring, trying to find some hidden truth or
resolve some inner conflict born of his adopted heritage or unique
brand of intellect. After tramping around the subcontinent, con-
tracting scabies, lice, and dysentery, he found the experience more
raw and disturbing than enlightening. "It was one of the first times
that I started to realize that maybe Thomas Edison did a lot more
to improve the world than Karl Marx and Neem Kairolie Baba put
together," Jobs recalls.[16]

Back at Atari, Jobs returned to the business of computer electronics with renewed vigor. Even now, it was apparent that he was technically astute, but no engineering genius. His value lay in his creative
vision and his persistence. Around Steve, it seemed anything was possible. It was a trait some employees would refer to as the Jobs "reality
distortion field."[17] When asked to estimate the time required for him
to complete a project, Jobs would quote a schedule of days and weeks
instead of months and years. It was an intensity of work focus he would
carry for the rest of his career.

He also renewed his friendship with Woz, who was then working at Hewlett-Packard. Jobs would sneak Woz in at night to work on
projects for him in return for free playtime on the latest Atari video
games. In one 48-hour stretch, Woz designed the game Break-Out
with unprecedented economy, using a surprisingly small number of
chips. Jobs paid Woz a fraction of the commission for doing essentially
all of the work. Some critics would later claim this as typical of his
approach to business: taking credit for others' creations. Yet it's a bit
like confusing the architect with the bricklayer. One creates the vision,
while the other solves problems to fit the vision. Without the driving force of the uncompromising visionary—imagining the project to
begin with, then harnessing the resources and securing the deals—no
nascent idea would see the commercial light of day.

Howard Roark explains it perfectly: "An architect uses steel, glass,
concrete, produced by others. But the materials remain just so much
steel, glass and concrete until he touches them. What he does with
them is his individual product and his individual property. This is the
only pattern for proper co-operation among men."

Stevie Appleseed

At the time, powerful mainframe computers were still the exclusive domain of governments, universities, and large corporations. Usage time was so precious it had to be purchased by the hour. But with the increasing availability of electronic components and know-how, hobbyists began tinkering like early ham radio operators. In 1975 a group of local enthusiasts formed the Homebrew Club to split the cost of pricey computer kits, share information, and collaborate on ideas. With his acumen in acquiring components, his father's lessons in deal making, and Wozniak's brilliant engineering talent, Jobs was eager to play the next business angle and profit from the emerging field.

Woz had just developed a prototype computer board with the ability to drive a color television display. Inspired, Jobs saw the commercial potential for an inexpensive home computer that did far more than the rudimentary Altair featured on the cover of *Popular Electronics* as the first "personal" computer, which did little more than light up a string of bulbs in response to binary arithmetic hand coded into the machine through a series of throw switches. Recognizing the need for a marketing angle, Steve dubbed Woz's machine the "Apple" in honor of a hippie apple farm retreat he had visited in Oregon.

Sensing commercial potential, on April Fools' Day in 1976 he and Woz incorporated Apple Computer. To buy their first batch of parts, they scraped together $1,500 in part by hawking Woz's expensive HP calculator and Job's VW bus.[18] Then it was time to hustle, which was what Jobs did best.

Paul Terrell had recently started the Byte Shop, which would become the first chain of retail computer stores. A frequent attendee at Homebrew Club meetings, Terrell was in search of new products to stock his fledgling store shelves. Impressed with Woz's creation during a Homebrew demo, he arranged for Jobs to supply 50 fully assembled computer boards at $500 a pop. Despite his young age and apparent lack of credentials, Jobs managed to cajole a local parts supplier into extending him a 30-day line of credit after the supplier confirmed the order with Terrell. Scruffy youth was no concern in the Valley in those days. Business was business.

Terrell commissioned a local cabinetmaker to build a wooden case to house the board for display purposes. An early print ad touts the Apple-I as "The First Low Cost Microcomputer System with a Video Terminal and 8k Bytes of Ram on a Single PC Card." Selling at a retail price of $666.66, the headline benefits read, "You Don't Need an Expensive Teletype" and "No More Switches, No More Lights."[19] By the end of the year, the two Steves had delivered 150 Apple-I's for $75,000 in revenue. They were on their way.

Over Labor Day weekend Jobs and Woz were offered booth space at the very first national microcomputer show, called Personal Computing 76, in Atlantic City. At the time, it was still anyone's guess whether the embryonic personal computer could survive in a world dominated by industrial-strength mainframes and hungry corporate giants—and if it did survive, which firms would take the lead. Big names in electronics like Commodore, Texas Instruments, and RadioShack's parent Tandy were all on the prowl for ways to enter this new market. Among the personal computers displayed were the Altair (running a version of the BASIC computer language coded by Bill Gates at Microsoft—himself an embryonic Randian hero, as we document in Chapter 5, "The Persecuted Titan") alongside Processor Technology's Sol, a self-contained unit in a sleek metal case with integrated keyboard. The Apple-I looked like a crude and amateurish cigar box by comparison.

The show lit a fire in Jobs's brain as he started to understand the marketing and competitive value of an integrated finished product targeted to a mainstream consumer, versus a collection of components and boards geared toward basement hobbyists. He returned to the workshop with a vision that would leapfrog the competition in function and sizzle. Literally working from their garage, the tiny Apple team created the launching pad for a technological revolution—the Apple II, the first personal computer worthy of the name.

While Woz completed the functional prototype, Jobs focused on design, marketing, and financing. Jobs demanded that the Apple II's exterior case look like an integrated KLH stereo—a popular offering at the time among young adults. No detail was too trivial. To reduce ambient noise, he decided to kill the standard cooling fan and "conned"[20]

Rod Holt from Atari into designing a brand-new kind of power supply by promising him $200 a day, an amount the cash-strapped Jobs was in no position to pay at the time.

His relentless quest for the perfect new product even penetrated into the innards of his creation that no user would ever see—almost a metaphor for his own personal internal ethic of minimalist utility. In one instance he decreed that every solder connection be done in a precise, attractive straight line that gave the Apple II's circuit board a surprisingly sharp aesthetic. It's an extraordinary perspective given the nascent state of the industry born from raw silicon components and homemade kits.

Such singular focus and intelligence would cause him problems later in his career. Like Howard Roark, Jobs's uncompromising demands—while right and true to his own individualist vision—made him seem arrogant and inflexible to the more collectively minded around him. According to biographer Pilar Quezzaire, "Jobs' fiery personality and extreme self-confidence tends to leave employees and colleagues fearful as well as awe-struck."[21]

On the business side, he persuaded Frank Burge from ad agency giant Regis McKenna to take Apple's account by badgering him three or four times a day after repeated rejections—until the major executive bent to the will of the 20-something entrepreneur. Then Jobs recruited retired Intel executive Mike Markkula as chairman to provide additional financing and business experience, after convincing him they could change the world by putting computers into homes and small businesses. In turn, Markkula brought in Mike "Scotty" Scott, an executive at National Semiconductor, as Apple's president.

To introduce the Apple II, Markkula spent $5,000 for a flashy booth and front-door position at the West Coast Computer Faire in 1977. Jobs's custom plastic cases arrived at the last minute with cosmetic flaws and no time to reship, so he put together a crew to sand, scrape, and paint them the night before. On opening day, people crowded the booth unable to believe these small, sleek boxes could be responsible for the color images displayed on the big TV monitor. Jobs had to routinely throw back the booth draping to prove there was no secret mainframe hidden from view. Curious engineers asked to pop the hood and were amazed by Woz's cutting-edge design that fit an unprecedented 62 chips on a compact motherboard that looked as sleek as its function. Soon they had 300 orders.

Poisoned Apple

The next few years were tough on Jobs. The business grew under the professional leadership he himself had recruited, but despite his founder's status, Markkula and Scott marginalized the youthful Jobs, leaving him with little true authority and the belittling title of vice president of research and development. Longing for a project he could put his imprint on, he envisioned a brand-new computing paradigm, having been inspired by a trip to the secretive Xerox Palo Alto Research Center (PARC).

In exchange for allowing Xerox to buy 100,000 shares of pre–initial public offering (IPO) Apple, Xerox agreed to open the kimono on some advanced computer research it was conducting. What Jobs saw at PARC changed the face and culture of computing forever. Among the developments were a fully functional prototype computer called the Xerox Star sporting a graphical user interface (GUI), with overlapping "windows," pictorial icons representing programs or commands, a pointing device for user input—now known as the familiar "mouse"—and a fast, silent laser printer that beautifully rendered on paper what you could see on the screen. While these innovations are commonplace today, in the late 1970s era of command-line prompts, green-screen monitors, complicated keyboard-based hexadecimal machine code inputs, and rattling impact printers, PARC's technology was breathtaking. Yet within the bureaucracy of Xerox, precisely nothing was being done to develop its commercial potential. Jobs immediately grasped the possibilities and set to work revolutionizing the personal computer he himself had just invented a few scant years earlier.

The idea was to include every advanced technology and feature he could think of in a compact form that would be so revolutionary it "would put a dent in the universe."[22] Jobs's brainchild would be known as Lisa, named after the daughter he fathered with a past girlfriend. But the professional computer scientists now filling the ranks at Apple balked at his hubris. Markkula and Scott would soon reorganize the company, pulling Jobs from the Lisa project and handing it over to a cabal of uninspired engineers under even less inspiring leadership. As consolation, Jobs would be given the strictly symbolic title of chairman of the board. Eventually, the Lisa would become an overpriced disaster—the product of design by a mediocre collective, not Jobs's individual vision. It would leave Jobs with an even greater appreciation of what he did best: inspiring—and infuriating—small groups of extraordinarily talented individuals to create astoundingly original products under seemingly impossible and uncompromising terms.

Despite Lisa's false start, by 1980 Apple Computer was on a tear. The biggest kid on the PC block, Apple had sold over 250,000 personal computers since 1977. With over 1,000 employees and facilities across the globe, it continued moving nearly 20,000 computers per month and would rack up $300 million in annual sales that fiscal year alone. At a typical hardware cost of $2,500 (or over $6,000 in today's dollars) Apple computers cost twice as much as competitive offerings from Commodore and Tandy, yet eclipsed their sales volume handily (IBM hadn't even entered the PC market yet). It is a testament to Jobs's insistence on usability and sleek design that Apple had tens of thousands of users willingly paying for a premium brand.[23] It was a precursor to the business model Apple would employ with the iPod, iPhone, and iPad.

Apple Computer Corporation went public on December 12, 1980, selling 5 million shares at $22 each, raising $110 million for the company. The offering was oversubscribed even though it wasn't available in 20 states, including the normally IPO-friendly Massachusetts, because the stock was deemed "too risky" by government regulators.[24] At the end of the first trading day, Apple had a market capitalization of over $1.5 billion. The 25-year-old Jobs held over $200 million.

In early 1981, still sidelined, Steve was casting about for a new idea when he remembered an experimental project envisioned by a computer scientist named Jef Raskin who was working on the fringes of Apple. His concept was to make an all-in-one self-contained computer that presented itself to the customer as an appliance, like a toaster. No add-on components would be required, and the machine would instantly boot up without any arcane commands or cumbersome software to load. He dubbed it the Macintosh.

Jobs had originally blackballed Raskin's idea back when Jobs was still leading the Lisa team, viewing it as a conflict with his own project. Now, a project to call his own that would compete with and beat the Lisa was just what he was looking for. According to biographers Jeffrey Young and William Simon,

> Steve no longer had to subjugate his outlaw spirit to the corporate process, rewarded with little but his unceremonious booting off the Lisa project; here was the kind of dedication he understood, the kind he loved. These were crusaders like himself who thrived on the impossible. Steve would inspire this little-noticed team in a corner of a forgotten building. He would show them all—Scotty, Markkula, the whole company, the entire world—that he could lead them to produce a remarkable computer. . . . He set off with guns blazing to make the Macintosh the world's next groundbreaking computer.[25]

It was an internal struggle to reassert himself at Apple, but Jobs also saw it as a race to beat IBM and preserve a place for creative innovation in PCs in the face of an oncoming corporate behemoth. He drove his team with high demands, but also with whimsy and irreverence, carving out their own separate office space for the best talent, instilling a desire for hard work and long hours that would establish each member as part of an elite club that he often referred to as his "pirates."

By this time, Scott—whom Jobs had recruited as Apple's president—had worn out his welcome and then some. His abrasive personality did him no favors among the creative technical teams, and after ordering a brutal series of layoffs in an event known as "Black Wednesday," his days at Apple were numbered. Markkula returned from vacation and asked for Scott's resignation. The board spent months searching for a replacement.

It was not to be Jobs. He felt he was capable of running the company, but he was the only one who thought so. If the board wouldn't let him run the company, at least he could find someone he could work with. John Sculley of PepsiCo seemed like an inspired choice. While considered a technological lightweight, he knew about running a consumer products company and could help support Apple

Computer's efforts to position itself as a name-brand product instead of a hobbyist's box of components. Jobs met with Sculley in New York in March 1983 and posed the now legendary query: "Are you going to sell sugar water the rest of your life when you could be doing something really important?" Sculley joined Apple as CEO shortly thereafter.

While Jobs and his pirates were feverishly working to make their Macintosh user-friendly and aesthetically pleasing, Bill Gates and his brilliant but pedantic programmers at Microsoft, working on IBM's competing operating system, concentrated on power and technical fine points. According to Sculley, "The legendary statement about Microsoft, which is mostly true, is that they get it right the third time. Microsoft's philosophy is to get it out there and fix it later. Steve would never do that. He doesn't get anything out there until it is perfected."[26] And perfected it was, or as near as Jobs could make it, after a series of delays from the initial time line.

To promote the Macintosh launch, Jobs commissioned film director Ridley Scott of *Alien* and *Blade Runner* fame to create an ad to run during the 1984 Super Bowl. It would be a million-dollar bet, significant if not unprecedented in the early 1980s—and it would prove to be one of the most famous and enduring TV ads in history. It depicted a stark Orwellian future filled with drab marching clones brainwashed by a black-and-white projection on a vast screen of "Big Brother" espousing a collectivist ideology. A blonde female athlete bursts through the crowd in vibrant color chased by a jackbooted Gestapo squad, only to hurl a flying hammer into the screen, shattering the collectivist image in a burst of individualist light. The tagline: "On January 24th, Apple Computer will introduce Macintosh. And you'll see why 1984 won't be like '1984.'"

The ad was brilliant. It was unlike anything anyone had seen before. And the Apple board hated it. It was as if Jobs had become Howard Roark himself in the scene from *The Fountainhead* in which he sits in front of the architectural committee of a bank discussing his design for its new headquarters building. It was just too "stark," too "radical." It wouldn't "please the public." In Jobs's case, perhaps the board objected to the commercial precisely for what Ayn Rand would have loved about it: its portrayal of the victory of the individual versus the collective. Indeed, for Jobs this is what the personal computer was all about: the empowerment of the individual user.

The board ordered Jobs to sell back the advertising time, but it was too late. The ad ran only once, on January 22, 1984, but it was so unique, so stunningly original—just so cool—that stations across the country replayed it on the evening news, generating the first instance of the "viral" buzz, as well as the Super Bowl ad frenzy now commonly sought by advertisers. It was a fundamental innovation in the way mass marketing was done—not just for computers, but for everything—and it was Jobs who did it.

Macintosh sales were brisk in early 1984, but slowed down later in the year. By the time of its first anniversary in 1985, 275,000 Macs had been purchased—an impressive number, but still short of Jobs's 500,000 forecast, and not enough to meet critical revenue goals. Part of the problem was that there were few third-party software programs available for the machine, and the ones that did exist had difficulty running on the Mac's scant 128K of memory. Jobs's vision, it seems, was ahead of the technological capabilities of the day.

Internal friction erupted within the company as financial stresses increased. Jobs was chairman of the board above CEO Sculley, while simultaneously working under him as head of the Macintosh division. It was a dysfunctional structure that a weak-kneed, conformist board would ignore until it was too late.

For his part, Jobs felt he could run the company himself and, as its co-founder, railed against his powerful vision being overruled and stymied by a stodgy collectivist bureaucracy. In turn, Sculley came to liken Jobs to Russian revolutionary Leon Trotsky. In *Odyssey*, his memoir of this period, he called Jobs "a zealot, his vision so pure that he couldn't accommodate that vision to the imperfections of the world."[27]

"Apple was supposed to become a wonderful consumer products company," Sculley wrote. "This was a lunatic plan. High tech could not be designed and sold as a consumer product."[28] As it would turn out, Sculley was dead wrong.

Soon an outright power struggle emerged, with various camps simultaneously trying to shift blame and secure their position. Marketing chief Mike Murray circulated a memo to the executive team under the heading "DO NOT CIRCULATE, COPY, OR

SHARE," lambasting Steve for "espousing vision . . . at the clear expense of corporate survival." Then in April, early investor and taciturn board member Arthur Rock sensed weakness and instigated a boardroom coup. Citing poor financial performance, Rock, who was more interested in funding social causes than Jobs's brand of youthful dreams, challenged CEO Sculley to take decisive action. Feeling the noose around his own neck, Sculley sacrificed Jobs, removing him as head of the Macintosh division. The ensuing reorganization consolidated operations and left Jobs conspicuously absent from the organization chart. Sculley refused to acknowledge Jobs or even mention his name at the company-wide meeting to announce the new structure.

In September 1985, relieved of his daily responsibilities at Apple, Jobs tendered his resignation from the board. "The company's recent reorganization left me with no work to do and no access even to regular management reports," he wrote. "I am but 30 and want still to contribute and achieve."[29] In the same spirit as Rand's greatest hero, John Galt, Jobs led a strike of the mind against Apple, hiring away some of its top talent to join him in a new independent venture. The board was furious and contemplated legal action in a petty attempt at restricting Jobs from competing with them at their own game. But Jobs's mind would not be enslaved.

The press at the time presaged the coming decade of Apple's struggles without Jobs and the brains that Jobs took with him when he left. A *New York Times* article in September 1985 predicted, "Apple, while having a solid management, still might miss Mr. Jobs. The company is weak in top engineering talent to guide product development. Moreover, more traditional managers like Mr. Sculley have often proved no more adept at running technology companies than the original entrepreneurs. Some analysts and former employees are worried that Apple is losing its spark and becoming stodgy, a process some refer to as 'Scullification.'" They would prove to be dead right.

The Granite Quarry

The ensuing years for Jobs turned out to be like Roark's time designing mere gas stations instead of great skyscrapers, and ultimately working as a day laborer in a granite quarry. Kept by the world from the work he loved, Jobs would live true to his own integrity, designing and building in areas where he saw value for his own sake. When they were ready to call him back on his own terms, he would be ready.

Jobs formed a company called NeXT to create the next-generation personal computer packed with all of the latest ideas that he felt restricted from pursuing within Apple's corporate confines. The device would use a powerful new Motorola chip, optical magnetic drives, a new breed of operating system called NeXTSTEP, and brilliant anti-aliased graphics, all housed in a 1 × 1 × 1-foot magnesium cube. He would target the higher education market with a computer powerful enough to run complex genetic research simulations while being simple enough for students to use in their dorm rooms.

With investments from Ross Perot and Japan's Canon, Jobs built out a lavish corporate headquarters, spending $1 million on a floating staircase designed by I. M. Pei and $100,000 for a logo from legendary graphic designer Paul Rand. He created a futuristic manufacturing facility filled with laser-guided robotics that outnumbered humans two to one.[30] But ultimately, the amazing design and operating system for the cube failed to overcome its hefty $10,000 price tag. While the computer did sell an estimated 50,000 units over four years,[31] it was a disappointing showing in an industry moving tens of millions of computers per year. Without the deep pockets of a public company and brand reputation in an increasingly mature market, NeXT had an uphill battle.

Meanwhile, always on the lookout for new ideas, he made a trip north to see George Lucas and his Lucasfilm-ILM operation in San Rafael, California. What he saw there stunned him. Here was a group of the most talented graphic artists in the world quietly creating groundbreaking digital images and film sequences on some of the most sophisticated computer systems he'd ever seen. "It was a Xerox PARC moment," according to biographers.[32]

Even more stunning was that Lucas, in need of immediate liquidity in the aftermath of his recent divorce, was eager to sell the entire operation lock, stock, and barrel for $30 million. Jobs was salivating, but his shrewd negotiating sense detected blood in the water, so he decided to wait Lucas out in hopes of a better deal. With such a unique asset, finding a willing suitor on short notice would be next to impossible.

Jobs ended up buying the company for $10 million in 1986 and christened it Pixar.

Hearkening back to the early days of Apple, the company initially focused on selling hardware dubbed the Pixar Image Computer. The device was powerful, but found limited application mostly for complex image analysis in government intelligence services and medical markets. Disney Studios was also a customer. Though Uncle Walt's team still prided itself on traditional hand-drawn animation, it was slowly adopting computers to automate certain tedious coloring processes. It was the beginning of a relationship that would prove fortuitous for both companies in the coming years.

With Pixar in financial trouble from slack hardware sales, former Disney animator and then Pixar executive producer John Lasseter began creating computer-animated commercials for outside companies, generating a trickle of much-needed revenue. In 1988, Pixar also began licensing a software product it had developed earlier, called RenderMan, which allowed animators to quickly and easily refine complex 3-D scenes with appropriate shading and lighting. It remains the most widely used rendering standard in the industry today.

Advertising animation and software generated critical cash flow to keep Pixar on life support, but the company was still hemorrhaging $1 million per month. NeXT wasn't faring any better, and between the two Jobs spent tens of millions from his own pocket just to keep the companies alive. A man who was once one of the wealthiest people in the country now saw his fortune dwindling to perilously low levels.

Despite heart-wrenching cutbacks at Pixar and a bottom-line temptation to close down the animation group altogether, Jobs personally funded the cash outlay to develop a short film to be shown at the SIGGRAPH computer graphics conference in 1988. It was a critical decision that would change the face of moviemaking forever. It was also the kind of move that a play-it-safe bureaucratic CEO would never have made. But an individualist like Jobs could make it, just because he thought the animated short called *Tin Toy* was so cool. It was indeed cool. It would go on to win an Oscar and eventually become the basis for the blockbuster Disney collaboration *Toy Story*.

The late 1980s and early 1990s would spark an epiphany of sorts for Jobs, with curious parallels between NeXT and Pixar. Jobs began to realize that the hardware he had focused so much effort on since the early days at Apple would eventually become a "sedimentary layer"[33] in the evolution of technology upon which others would build. His metamorphosis was to grasp a paradigm that transcended hardware and software. He began to see how technology unlocked a unique experience even more lasting than the computers or software used to create them. Chips and programs lived short lives in the relentless march of technological progress. Music and stories endured for generations.

In his transition toward this experiential model, Jobs sold the Pixar Image Computer hardware division to Vicom systems in 1990[34] and retained fewer than 100 employees to focus on animation. Then in 1993, he withdrew NeXT from the hardware businesses and renamed the company NeXT Software to continue meeting a growing demand for their innovative object-oriented NeXTSTEP operating system.

NeXT hardware was never a commercial success, but it was a notable influence in the history and lore of computing. Tim Berners-Lee created the first Web browser in 1990 on a NeXT machine, claiming, "I could do in a couple of months what would take more like a year on other platforms, because on the NeXT, a lot of it was done for me already. There was an application builder to make all the menus as quickly as you could dream them up."[35] John Carmack of id Software used a NeXT machine to develop the video game Doom—the landmark "first-person shooter."[36] It was the object-oriented NeXTSTEP operating system that would prove to be the crown jewel in Jobs's kingdom, and his passport back to Apple.

Meanwhile, Pixar was struggling to stay afloat, but saw a potential lifeline through an increasing dialogue with Disney. In an attempt to break its string of mediocre films, for the first time ever Disney was thinking about using an outside company to produce a computer-animated feature, but was meeting internal resistance. In their fight against obsolescence, Disney's old-school pen-and-inksters claimed computer animation couldn't possibly live up to Disney's standard of quality. But some early—and secret—computer animation collaboration with Pixar on such classics as *Beauty and the Beast* built a level of trust among the Disney executives that it could indeed be done.

Although in 1991 his company was running out of oxygen, Jobs negotiated with Disney a deal for not one, but *three* feature movies. Disney would pay for production and give a slice of the net from the films back to Pixar. In turn, Pixar would retain all rights to technology and its secret creative sauce. And in a negotiating flourish that was pure Jobs—and must have been very difficult for Disney to swallow—the agreement permitted Pixar's animated logo to be displayed with equal prominence alongside Disney's famous image of Cinderella's castle at the beginning of each film.

Based on the *Tin Toy* short, Disney approved the script for *Toy Story* in mid-1993, clearing the way for production. But months later, Disney's head of feature films, Jeffrey Katzenberg, wasn't satisfied with the character development. On November 17, Pixar received formal notice that Disney was shutting down production.

The dawn of 1994 brought dark days for Jobs. Exactly a decade after the glittering launch of the Macintosh, he was at his personal and professional nadir. He had fallen from grace at Apple and been trounced in the press over problems at NeXT, and now his personal investment in Pixar was sinking beneath the waves while Disney sailed off on the horizon. Jobs was depressed and withdrawn. It seemed to him that his previous success as a boy wonder might just have been a fluke.

But he refused to give up or give in. Learning the ways of fickle Hollywood executives, he shrugged off Disney's blow and picked himself off the mat to fight again. After challenging his writers to recraft the script, he repitched it to Disney. Katzenberg liked the approach and unfroze the project. Then came a moment when Jobs wondered if he was a victor or a fool. With all the resources poured into the film, he figured it would need to gross $100 million at the box office just for Pixar to break even—more than any other Disney feature in recent history. At one point during the ordeal he confided, "If I knew in 1986 how much it was going to cost to keep Pixar going, I doubt if I would have bought the company."

Toy Story opened in November 1995 to rave reviews and a weekend box office take of $29 million—nearly equal to the full cost of production. The movie would eventually gross over $350 million worldwide with an additional $100 million in video sales. Sensing good advance buzz, Jobs had timed Pixar's IPO to coincide with the movie's release, going public on November 29, 1995, at $22. Shares quickly shot up to $44.50 during the first hour in trading. Jobs had invested a total of $60 million in the company and nurtured it for nine years. He was suddenly worth over $1 billion.[37]

Unbelievably, some employees took him to task for being greedy and not allocating more of his 80 percent share in the firm to his workers. At least one former executive, cut from the cloth of Ayn Rand herself, disagreed. "We live in a world where everyone says, 'It's unfair—somebody got more than me.'"[38] Employees negotiated their stock options up front and were fortunate that the company even survived through lean years on the strength of Jobs's checkbook. "Can you really blame Steve if he didn't feel like giving them more stock than they had agreed on when they were hired?"[39] Like Roark, Jobs neither gives nor asks for charity. As Roark puts it, "I am not an altruist. I do not contribute gifts of this nature."

With future films *A Bug's Life*, *Toy Story 2* and *3*, *Monsters Inc.*, and many others, Pixar would rack up billions in earnings and earn the title of the most successful movie studio of all time. More important, Jobs had transformed an entire industry through his audacity and stalwart belief—both in the technologies he thought were cool and in himself. Computers would enter the mainstream of visual entertainment as a vehicle to tell enduring stories. And Jobs wasn't done yet.

Back on Top

By 1995, Apple was on the ropes and struggling to stay standing. Customers were flocking to the latest generation of improved Microsoft Windows software and it looked like Apple might become a footnote in the annals of computer history. Sculley had been forced out in 1993 after Apple's market share shriveled from 20 percent to a measly 8 percent under his watch. Turnaround expert Gil Amelio was installed to right the ship. He recognized that cost cutting would go only so far and began to push for a new operating system to first defend and then rebuild Apple's market share. Increasingly convinced that the foundering in-house team was incapable of developing a solution in time, he cast about for a third-party alternative.

After analyzing the field of players, including several conversations with Bill Gates at Microsoft, Amelio decided that NeXTSTEP might be his salvation and began negotiating with a surprised but amenable Jobs on buying his company outright. Apple eventually paid $325 million in cash to the investors and 1.5 million shares of Apple stock, which went to Steve Jobs.[40] Steve was also retained as a strategic adviser to Apple. NeXTSTEP would become the basis for the Mac OS X operating system and the company's path back to profitability. But it was too little, too late for Amelio.

In mid-1997, Apple's market share had fallen to 3 percent and the company reported a quarterly loss of $708 million. Amelio was ousted and Jobs was installed as interim president and CEO. He would work for the princely salary of $1. According to long-gone CEO Sculley, "I'm actually convinced that if Steve hadn't come back when he did— if they had waited another six months—Apple would have been history. It would have been gone, absolutely gone."[41]

Apple's stock price would seem to agree with Sculley—as we show in Figure 1.1.

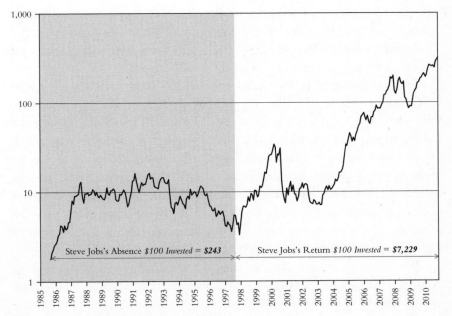

Figure 1.1　　Apple (AAPL) Stock Price

Back at Apple, Jobs quickly focused on revitalizing the business. He killed the foundering Apple Newton, a clunky handheld device that was widely lampooned, including a hilarious sequence in the popular comic Doonesbury.

In August 1998, Jobs introduced the iMac, an all-in-one unit encased in a translucent turquoise plastic shell harkening back to the days of the original Macintosh. Critics called it technically unimpressive and predicted it would be hampered by its overreliance on the universal serial bus (USB) for connectivity to peripherals. Once again, the traditionalist critics were wrong. While a nascent technology at the time, USB would become truly universal, allowing standardized connectivity of keyboards, mouses, printers, and portable memory across PCs and Macs alike. The look of the iMac itself would become a design icon of the late 1990s.

At $1,299 a pop, the iMac received over 150,000 preorders and went on to sell 278,000 units in the following six weeks.[42] Strong sales were reported for both first-time computer buyers and those switching from a Windows-based PC. In October, Jobs reported the first profitable fiscal year since 1995. As one Wall Street analyst remarked, "Steve pulled the rabbit out of the hat over the past year. Apple was in disarray. It was at the gate of extinction. Now we have a company turnaround." The results would catapult Apple back into the mainstream computer market from nearly perishing roadside as an also-ran.

With the company stabilized and on the road to recovery, some CEOs might rest on their laurels and collect a fat bonus. But not Steve Jobs. He doesn't see himself so much as a business executive as an artist always taking new creative risks. In a *Fortune* interview he explained, "If you look at the artists, if they get really good, it always occurs to them at some point that they can do this one thing for the rest of their lives, and they can be really successful to the outside world but not really be successful to themselves. That's the moment that an artist really decides who he or she is. If they keep on risking failure, they're still artists. Dylan and Picasso were always risking failure."[43]

By the end of the decade, music companies were struggling to confront a changing technological landscape. Clinging to old-school models of physical distribution channels, they were helpless in the face of a burgeoning network of Internet connectivity. In the past, music buyers might dub a copy or two of their favorite songs to give to friends. Now the same music buyers could "rip" a CD into a digital file and share it with a worldwide network of millions with the click of a mouse. Why buy a CD when you could get the music for free through file-sharing services like Napster?

For Jobs, music held a special place in his heart, along with respect for intellectual property. He could see the problems emerging in the music industry and was appalled at the spastic response by the record companies. On one hand, they attempted to crack down on criminal pirates—often a kid in a dorm room who was just enthusiastic about music and was listening to emerging artists. On the other hand, they offered restrictive subscription services on a pay-by-the-month model. Jobs saw a middle path and set out to change the landscape.

As he explained to *Rolling Stone*, he set up meetings with record executives. First, he made it clear that he respected the primacy of intellectual property rights—what individualist wouldn't? "If copyright dies, if patents die, if the protection of intellectual property is eroded, then people will stop investing. That hurts everyone. People need to have the incentive so that if they invest and succeed, they can make a fair profit. But on another level entirely, it's just wrong to steal. Or let's put it this way: It is corrosive to one's character to steal. We want to provide a legal alternative."[44]

Next, he demolished their digital business model. "We told them the music subscription services they were pushing were going to fail. Music Net was gonna fail, Pressplay was gonna fail," Jobs would say. "Here's why: People don't want to buy their music as a subscription. They bought 45s, then they bought LPs, they bought cassettes, they bought 8-tracks, then they bought CDs. They're going to want to buy downloads. The subscription model of buying music is bankrupt. I think you could make available the Second Coming in a subscription model, and it might not be successful."[45]

Finally, Jobs described the middle path. He would offer an Apple music store. It would be safe from viruses; it would be fast; and it would be high-quality, inexpensive, flexible, and, best of all, legal. In a way only Jobs's mind could synthesize, he struck an elegant balance between artists' rights and customer usability. Once you bought a song, you owned it. You could burn it onto a CD; you could play it directly from your computer or portable device. You could even share it with a few friends. But the embedded technology would prevent mass distribution and wide-scale pirating. At $0.99 per song, it was affordable—an impulse item—yet artists were compensated for their work. It was brilliant.

And in some ways it took a figure as big and trusted as Jobs to move the industry seized in paralysis as it faced the technological future. Only he had the clout, the appreciation, and the respect to pull an entire industry toward a visionary future. By the end of the decade, Apple iTunes would be selling over a quarter of all music in the United States. Jobs again had rescued and transformed a moribund industry— just because it was cool.

To Infinity and Beyond

What does the future hold for Steve Jobs? His problems with his health are well-known, but as of this writing he's been able to cheat death as brilliantly as he's been able to overcome technology and business challenges throughout his life.

Someday death will come to him, as it must to all of us. What he's built for the world will make him an immortal figure in the history of technology and business. But he's immortal in another sense, in the way that all self-motivated and self-consistent people are—that they don't die a little bit every day by compromising themselves, that during their lifetimes they truly live.

What a fellow artist said of Howard Roark in *The Fountainhead* might have been said of Steve Jobs: "I often think he's the only one of us to achieve immortality. I don't mean in the sense of fame, and I don't mean he won't die someday. But he's living it. I think he is what the conception really means."

Chapter 2

The Mad Collectivist

*Paul Krugman as Ellsworth Toohey, the man
who preaches socialism from the pages of
America's newspaper of record*

*"We've fixed the coin. Heads—collectivism, and tails—collectivism. . . .
Give up your soul to a council—or give it up to a leader. But give
it up, give it up, give it up. My technique . . . don't forget the only
purpose you have to accomplish. Kill the individual. Kill man's soul.
The rest will happen automatically. Observe the state of the world
at the present moment. Do you still think I'm crazy . . . ?"*

—The Fountainhead

Who is Ellsworth Toohey?
In *The Fountainhead*, villain Ellsworth Toohey symbolizes the
collectivist, in contrast to the hero, Howard Roark, who symbolizes the individualist.

Toohey was a brilliant and articulate—but sickly and
puny—child, raised in an impoverished household by a weak
father and an overprotective mother. He was envious of his
wealthier and stronger classmates, and he used his sharp mind
and even sharper tongue to undermine them.

(Continued)

After going through a brief religious phase as a teenager, Toohey becomes an avowed socialist. In adulthood, he drops any overt association with socialist politics, but dedicates his life to promoting collectivism gradually, through his growing influence as a public intellectual.

He writes a book on architecture throughout history, and improbably it becomes a best seller. Toohey parlays that into a regular column in New York's leading newspaper, the *New York Banner*—ostensibly for architectural criticism, but quickly evolving into a personal soapbox from which he promotes all manner of collectivist causes.

Beyond obvious advocacy, Toohey's strategy with the column is to promote architects and other artists—authors, composers, playwrights—of no ability, to enshrine mediocrities as super-stars. His goal is to corrupt the culture—to advance collectivism by default, by eliminating from the culture any great individuals who could have offered an alternative.

Toohey singles out the brilliant architect Howard Roark as his most dangerous opponent—an exemplar of the greatness of the individual, not the collective. To defeat Roark, he master-minds a series of complicated plots aimed at discrediting Roark and economically ruining him, at one point causing him to aban-don architecture and work as a laborer in a quarry to survive.

Throughout, Roark never lifts a finger to either fight Toohey or defend himself against him. Toohey is simply beneath Roark's notice, demonstrating Rand's belief that evil is small and impotent, and best simply ignored.

Christiane Amanpour's eyes darted back and forth in fear and her mouth twisted in disgust, because she could see where this was going. A guest on her Sunday morning political talk show, ABC's *This Week*, was getting dangerously overexcited, and something very regrettable was about to happen.

She could see that he was winding himself up as he talked about how a recent deficit-reduction panel hadn't been "brave enough"—because it failed to endorse the idea of expert panels who would determine what medical services government-funded care wouldn't pay for.[1] When ObamaCare was still being debated in Congress, conservative spokeswoman Sarah Palin had created a media sensation by calling them "death panels," causing most liberals who supported ObamaCare to quickly distance themselves from any idea of rationing care as being tantamount to murder.

Cut to Amanpour's horrified face. Cut back to the guest. Then it happened.

The guest said, "Some years down the pike, we're going to get the real solution, which is going to be a combination of death panels and sales taxes."

It was all the more horrifying because the guest was not a conservative, not an opponent of ObamaCare. This guest was an avid liberal, a partisan Democrat, and an enthusiastic supporter of government-run health care. He was *endorsing* death panels, not warning about them. He was saying *death panels are a good thing*.

Apparently it didn't bother him that his choice of words, "real solution," had historical parallels that are very disturbing in any conversation about government control over who will live and who will die.

And it was even more horrifying because of who this guest was. This was no fringe lefty wearing a tinfoil hat churning out underground newspapers in his parents' basement. This was an economics professor at Princeton, one of the country's most prestigious universities. This was the winner of the Nobel Prize in economics, the highest honor the profession can bestow. This was a columnist for the *New York Times*, the most influential newspaper in the world.

This was Paul Krugman, live, on national television, endorsing government control over life and death. And while we're at it, let's raise taxes on those who are permitted to live.

The Abysmal Pseudo-Scientist

Who does Paul Krugman think he is to think such things, never mind say them on television?

He'd like to think he's John Maynard Keynes, the venerated British economist who created the intellectual framework for modern government intervention in the economy. Keynes is something of a cult figure for modern liberal economists like Krugman, who read his texts with all the exegetical fervor with which Scientologists read the pulp fiction of L. Ron Hubbard. But Krugman will never live up to Keynes. However politicized his economic theories, Keynes's predictions were so astute that he made himself wealthy as a speculator. Economics is called "the dismal science," but as we'll see, Krugman's predictions are so laughably bad *his* economics should be called the abysmal pseudo-science.

If Krugman is not Keynes, maybe he's John Nash, the mathematician portrayed in the film *A Beautiful Mind*. They're both Princeton economists. They've both won the Nobel Prize in economics. And they're both bonkers. In Krugman's own words, "My economic theories have no doubt been influenced by my relationship with my cats."[2] But so far there's been no movie about Krugman, just a cameo appearance as himself in the lowbrow comedy *Get Him to the Greek* in which his lines consist of "Yeah," "Thank you," and "Oh boy."

As a boy, Krugman says his "secret fantasy" was to be Hari Seldon, the "psychohistorian" from science fiction author Isaac Asimov's *Foundation* trilogy, who used what we would now call econometrics to secretly control the progress of human civilization.[3] This inspiration is what drew Krugman to study economics, as he has revealed more than once, as though he were proud of it.[4]

Maybe in practice he's more like Dr. Strangelove, the dark Hari Seldon, the cold war madman of Stanley Kubrick's film masterpiece. They both have near-genocidal notions of how government should determine who lives and who dies—especially what kind of experts they should consult in the decision. Krugman is nostalgic for the cold war era when "the U.S. government employed experts in game theory to analyze strategies of nuclear deterrence. Men with Ph.D.s in economics, like Daniel Ellsberg."[5] Maybe you thought *real* men don't have PhDs in economics. But Krugman does.

But Paul Krugman isn't Keynes, Nash, Seldon, or Strangelove—as much as he'd like to be. The indisputable truth is he is the living embodiment of Ellsworth Toohey, the villain from Ayn Rand's first great novel, *The Fountainhead*.

Krugman mocks people who have been inspired by Rand,[6] but he himself is living Rand with every breath he takes. Truly, the parallels between Krugman and Toohey are downright eerie.

- Both are acclaimed scholars who have written books for the masses on complex topics—architecture for Toohey, and economics for Krugman.
- For both, their erudite texts were the springboard for becoming public intellectuals with high-profile opinion columns in a major New York newspaper—the *New York Banner* for Toohey and the *New York Times* for Krugman.
- Both are bleeding-heart socialists. Krugman confesses he is "an unabashed defender of the welfare state, which I regard as the most decent social arrangement yet devised."[7] He advocates "a state that offers everyone who's underpaid an additional income."[8]
- Both Toohey and Krugman hate the rich. Krugman questions their very right to live, pronouncing that they must be "defenders of the downtrodden" to have any hope of "justifying their existence."[9]
- Both exalt the incompetent at the expense of the competent. Krugman sniffs, "The official ideology of America's elite remains one of meritocracy. . . . But that won't last. Soon enough, our society will rediscover . . . the vulgarity of talented upstarts."[10]
- Both tell lies. Toohey warns, "I shall be forced to state a few things which are not quite true" in the service of his collectivist mission. Daniel Okrent, the Public Editor of the *New York Times*, rendered the judgment in the pages of the *Times* itself that "Paul Krugman has the disturbing habit of shaping, slicing and selectively citing numbers in a fashion that pleases his acolytes but leaves him open to substantive assaults."[11] But we shall see subsequently that when it comes to lies, damn lies, and statistics, Krugman chooses all of the above—including going on national television and falsely accusing his most trenchant critic of stalking him.
- Both have inferiority complexes driven by their physical inadequacy. Rand describes Toohey as "sickly," "puny," and "substandard." Krugman admits, "I am just not imposing enough in person to be inspiring (if I were only a few inches taller . . .)."[12] *Newsweek* once described Krugman (generously) as "gnomishly handsome."[13] Was this what Krugman had in mind when he complained that the Bush administration's tax cuts were a "step on the way to a system in which only the little people pay taxes"?[14]
- As Freud said, "Anatomy is destiny."[15] So the physiologically inadequate but intellectually powerful Toohey and Krugman are driven

to rule the world. Toohey's self-admitted goal is to "rule . . . You. The world." He seeks a future in which power is concentrated in "the hands of a few, a very few other men like me." For Krugman, merely ruling the world would seem to be quite a comedown. His childhood hero, the "psychohistorian" Hari Seldon, ruled the whole galaxy.

- For both Toohey and Krugman, the means of world rule is collectivism. Toohey says, "We've taught men to unite. This makes one neck ready for one leash. We've found the magic word. Collectivism." It turns out that Krugman's beloved "psychohistory" is just another magic word with the same meaning. A *New Yorker* profile of Krugman explains that his idol Hari Seldon "couldn't predict individual behavior—that was too hard—but it didn't matter, because history was determined not by individuals but by . . . hidden forces."[16]

- Such ends justify any means, so both Toohey and Krugman are willing to use their positions as public intellectuals to ruin reputations and lives as they see fit. Toohey's target is Howard Roark, the individualist architect hero of *The Fountainhead*. And here we must shift for a moment to the first person. Because as we will see later, I have been among Krugman's many targets for character assassination. Thankfully, like Roark, I survived the experience.

The Economist Who Couldn't Shoot Straight

Before we proceed, let's get something important out on the table. Most critiques of Krugman as a public intellectual begin with what is apparently an obligatory disclaimer, usually in the very first sentence— something to the effect that Krugman is a very accomplished and well-respected economist. After all, he won the Nobel Prize. Then comes the "But . . ." and the critique proceeds in earnest, often scathingly.

Why concede any honor at all to Krugman?

So what if he won the Nobel Prize? There are plenty of left-leaning political icons (Jimmy Carter, Al Gore, Barack Obama); witch doctors (Egas Moniz, the doctor who pioneered the frontal lobotomy); and even the odd terrorist (Yasser Arafat) who've been kissed on the forehead by the king of Sweden.

Of what real value or distinction is Krugman's work as an academic economist? There was a time a decade or more ago when his work on international trade and currencies was frequently cited in the economics literature, but far less so now, and some in the profession have come to regard it as rather trivial. Nowadays Krugman's work on trade and currencies is limited to rants in his *Times* column directed at China, advocating protectionism that most serious economists regard as retrograde and naive if not downright dangerous.[17]

The real test of Krugman's mettle as an economist is the accuracy of his economic forecasting. The fact is that, with about two decades of evidence now in, Krugman's track record, to use a technical term favored by economists, sucks.

As we'll see, he's not always candid about this. But once, under the pressure of a televised debate with conservative talk-show host Bill O'Reilly, Krugman blurted out an understated if truthful self-evaluation: "Compare me . . . compare me, uh, with anyone else, and I think you'll see that my forecasting record is not great."[18]

The most egregious example of "not great" is Krugman's 1982 utterly incorrect prediction that inflation would soar. He made this prediction from no less lofty a perch than the White House, as staff member of the Council of Economic Advisers (CEA) in the first Reagan administration. Here's how Krugman remembers that time:

> [T]he summer of 1982 was a moment of near-panic among the Reaganauts, as the recession and the debt crisis seemed to threaten catastrophe. They not only hired [Martin] Feldstein, they gave him the freedom to bring in a politically incorrect team of whiz-kids (which included Larry Summers . . .) in the hope that he could turn things around. By 1983, with a recovery well under way, the political types were back in charge.[19]

In other words, according to him, the world was in crisis—but Krugman parachuted in and cleaned everything up. But according to the archives of the Reagan Presidential Library, the truth is that Krugman's only substantive contribution at CEA was a September 9, 1982, memo co-authored with Lawrence Summers called "Inflation During the 1983 Recovery." Krugman and Summers wrote,

The Inflation Time Bomb?
We believe that it is reasonable to expect a significant reacceleration of inflation in the near future. Much of the apparent progress against inflation has resulted from the temporary side effects of tight money and high real interest rates. These side effects must be expected to reverse themselves as real interest rates decline and the economy expands. . . . Our very rough guess is that correction of . . . distorted relative prices will add at least 5 percentage points to future increases in consumer prices. . . . This estimate is conservative.[20]

When Krugman wrote this, the U.S. consumer price index inflation rate was 4.9 percent—high by recent standards, but down significantly from its catastrophic peak at 14.59 percent 18 months before. In that environment, for the self-described "whiz-kid" who found himself in the White House, this was a *very* bold prediction.

It also turned out to be hilariously, side-splittingly, knee-slappingly, rolling-on-the-floor wrong. Except for a tiny uptick the very next month, inflation didn't rise; it *fell*. Four years later, it had fallen to 1.18 percent, a rate so low as to border on *de*flation. It didn't even get back up to the same level at which Krugman had originally warned of a "time bomb" for about seven years. The highest inflation ever got from then through this writing was 6.37 percent, less than a percentage point and a half higher than when Krugman wrote his memo.

In other words, the *entire* inflation rate wasn't much more than Krugman predicted the *increase* in the inflation rate would be.

What does Krugman himself say of this prediction? He simply lies about it. In a June 2004 *Times* column revealingly titled "An Economic Legend," he had the temerity to write, "Inflation did come down sharply on Mr. Reagan's watch . . . it all played out just as 'left-wing Keynesian economics' predicted."[21] Considering that Krugman is a left-wing Keynesian economist, and considering that it all played out exactly the opposite of what he had predicted, this claim would appear to be a lie—unless he's talking about all the *other* left-wing Keynesian economists (admittedly, there are lots of them).

And then there was the time in late February 2000, two weeks before the peak of the dot-com stock bubble at Nasdaq 5,000.

Krugman wrote in his *Times* column that the Dow Jones Industrial Average was overvalued, saying, "let the blue chips fall where they may."[22] As for the Nasdaq—which at that point had almost doubled over the prior year, and more than tripled over the prior three years—Krugman said soothingly, "I'm not sure that the current value of the Nasdaq is justified, but I'm not sure that it isn't."

We all know what happened. As of this writing, the Dow is about 20 percent higher than when Krugman wrote those words—and that's not including a decade of dividends. The Nasdaq is about 42 percent lower. It hit bottom in October 2002 a 75.7 percent loss from where Krugman said not to worry about it. After something of a recovery, stocks fell again. They put in a real bottom—from which the Nasdaq would ultimately more than double—in March 2003. That is, about a week after Krugman wrote a *Times* column asking the rhetorical question, "Is there any relief in sight?" His tragically wrong answer: "No."[23]

Perfect bookends—he missed the top, and then exactly three years later, he missed the bottom. But then he outdid himself. In June 2003, with the Nasdaq up 20 percent since Krugman's "No," did he recognize his error and reverse course? Again: "No." Krugman wrote that "the current surge in stocks looks like another bubble."[24] From there the Nasdaq was to rally another 75 percent.

At around the same time, afraid of what he called a "fiscal train wreck" that would lead to disastrously high interest rates, he announced in the lead paragraph of a March 2003 *Times* column: "So last week I switched to a fixed-rate mortgage. It means higher monthly payments, but I'm terrified about what will happen to interest rates once financial markets wake up to the implications of skyrocketing budget deficits."[25]

Rates didn't rise, even when budget deficits skyrocketed beyond anything he could have imagined then, driven by government "stimulus" spending that he himself urged. He has acknowledged that error, confessing, "I wrongly believed that markets would look at it the same way."[26]

The Little Man Lives Large

For Krugman, "wrongly believed" may just be a fancy way of saying, "I lost money on that one." Perhaps lots of money, because Krugman probably has a great deal of mortgage debt. That's because he's being hypocritical when decries what he calls the "lifestyles of the rich and tasteless" and the mansions of "plutocrats."[27] His own home in Princeton is a custom-built 6,000-square-foot compound, which according to records of the Township[28] sports a four-car garage, music room, library, and greenhouse, and a fire-pit where he and his faculty friends burn effigies of prominent conservative politicians.[29] He also has a vacation home in St. Croix and a $1.7 million co-op in New York City.[30]

In this one way, Krugman is very unlike Ellsworth Toohey. Toohey is an honest socialist, if such a thing is possible. At least he's an ascetic, living in a "monk's cell" of an apartment, "scornful of material display." But Krugman lives large. How does he afford it? Clearly, he's not making the big bucks as a speculator as Keynes did (unless in his personal trading account he's deliberately doing the opposite of what he advises his readers to do). There are speaking fees, no doubt. All public intellectuals feed from that trough. And they get to meet the most interesting people there.

For instance, there's the time in 1999 when Krugman was in Kuala Lumpur, Malaysia, speaking at a business conference.[31] While he just happened to be in town, he just happened to spend a day with Malaysia's prime minister, Mahathir Mohamad, including, according to Krugman, a "staged 'dialogue'—which was played out in semi-public, in front of a disturbingly obsequious audience of a hundred or so businessmen."[32]

Mahathir is a rabid anti-Semite, who has demonized Jews for causing Malaysia's economic problems. Krugman shrugged that off, sighing that he knew Mahathir "would try to use me politically—to provide a veneer of respectability. . . . But sometimes an economist has to do what an economist has to do."[33] Like what, exactly, in this case? What duty was discharged by Krugman's appearance with the loathsome anti-Semite Mahathir, other than enjoying a day as the center of attention "at the Palace of the Golden Horses, a vaguely Las Vegas–style resort outside Kuala Lumpur"?

In a *Times* column in late 2003, he defended Mahathir's anti-Semitism, rationalizing it as a realpolitik response to the U.S. invasion of Iraq.[34] Apparently in Krugman's mind, however bad anti-Semitism is, George W. Bush's policies are worse. The *Times* column ran with the subhead, "Anti-Semitism with a purpose." The Anti-Defamation League was not amused, slamming Krugman for being tolerant of anti-Semitism because of "his obsession with criticizing U.S. policy."[35]

In the ensuing controversy, Krugman claimed, "I have never received any money from Mahathir."[36] But that's not a claim he can make with respect to some of the other bad actors he's gotten himself involved with.

Adding Consult to Injury

One of Krugman's worst predictions—and quite an honor it is to earn that designation, considering how much competition there is for it—was not an economic one, but a sociological one. No doubt thinking of some of Keynes's farsighted observations, Krugman prophesied in a January 2002 *Times* column, when the ashes were still warm at Ground Zero in lower Manhattan, "I predict that in the years ahead Enron, not Sept. 11, will come to be seen as the greater turning point in U.S. society."[37]

Lunacy, to be sure. U.S. history books a century from now will feature pictures of the World Trade Center aflame. Who, even now, remembers much about Enron? Oh yeah—it was that company that cooked the books. A couple of its executives went to jail, didn't they?

Yep, that's the one. But Krugman will never forget Enron, even if the rest of us already have. That's because at the time it was quite *le scandale*, and it turned out that Krugman was caught right in the middle of it, with his hand in Enron's cookie jar.

In 1999 Krugman wrote an article for *Fortune* magazine.[38] It was unexceptional for that heady time, basically a puff piece about the wonders of the so-called new economy driven by technological and managerial breakthroughs. What was exceptional about it was that the company that served as the centerpiece of the article, the paradigm of "The Ascent of E-Man," was Enron.

Krugman was totally taken in. He even rhapsodically described the company's "pride and joy"—its trading room—which later was exposed as a fake set up to fool Wall Street analysts.[39] You'd think he would have known better, because by the time he'd written that article he'd become an Enron insider.

He mentioned in the text of the article that he had "recently joined the advisory board at Enron"—and then went on to praise the company, and to aid and abet its projection of a fraudulent facade. But he didn't mention the fact that the pay for a year on the advisory board was $50,000.[40] Maybe that's what kept him from seeing the truth about Enron, even though from his position he was able to look at the company up close and personal.

Once Enron was exposed as a fraud—by others, by people who were *not* on the take from the company—Krugman wrote about it frequently in his *Times* columns. The specific idea was to link the Texas-based company to Texan George W. Bush, and the more general idea was to attack private business and use Enron as an excuse for more government regulation. For all the thunderbolts Krugman hurled at Enron from the Olympus of the *New York Times*, he disclosed his involvement with the company only once, at the very beginning.

In a January 2001 column, Krugman said he'd "signed on" to the advisory board—bracketing this confession fore ("this newspaper's conflict-of-interest rules required me to resign") and aft (calling the board "a hatchery for future Bush administration officials").[41] But that was it as far as disclosure was concerned—though he was to write about Enron many, many times, accusing the Bush administration of "crony capitalism" without mentioning that he himself was one of the cronies.[42]

The low point in Krugman's Enron hypocrisy was surely reached with a *Times* column in December 2001, where he heaped scorn on its "vision thing: it would create markets in everything, and make money by trading in those markets."[43] He blasted "business gurus" and "consultants" who acted as though Enron's critics "just didn't get it."

Not one word about the fact that he himself was one of those business gurus who, just two years before, had praised Enron's "vision thing"—right down to the (fake) trading room where they would "create markets in everything." And not one word about the fact that he was a consultant to Enron itself, and at the same time as he'd helped *Fortune* magazine's readers to "get it."

Let's see if we "get it" now. How did Krugman use the consulting fees he was paid from Enron—and, for that matter, the payment we assume he got from *Fortune* for helping its readers lose 100 cents on the dollar invested in Enron? Was that the down payment on the vacation home in the Caribbean? Or did it pay for that fire-pit for effigy-burning?

The Krugman Truth Squad

The plot of *The Fountainhead* revolves around the conflict between Ellsworth Toohey, the villainous collectivist, and Howard Roark, the heroic individualist. Toohey is an active antagonist in the conflict, constantly scheming to thwart Roark's brilliant career. But Roark is passive; he defeats Toohey by eventually outlasting him, and in the meantime not wasting his time on him.

In one of the book's most memorable scenes, Roark and Toohey encounter each other by chance, at a point where Toohey has very nearly ruined Roark's career. Ever the second-hander, needing to define himself through others, Toohey asks Roark to tell him honestly what he thinks of him. Roark, the man who lives entirely by his own opinion of himself, simply says, "But I don't think of you."

Maybe I should have followed Roark's example, but I didn't. I spent years thinking about Paul Krugman. That makes this an anomalous chapter in a book created to help people emulate the success of Ayn Rand's heroes. But my story with Paul Krugman shows that real-life Rand villains can be defeated. If it serves your values to oppose them, it can be done.

I don't remember now exactly how it started. But in 2002, I decided to write a book. It was going to be called *The Conspiracy to Keep You Poor and Stupid*. The idea was to explain how big government, big business, big media, and big academia block your road to financial freedom—and tell you it's for your own good. In October of that year I started a blog by the same name to help me write the book. The blog took on a life of its own, thanks to Krugman, and ended up consuming so much of my time that I never wrote the book.

From the beginning, I had Krugman in mind as a prime mover in the conspiracy, standing at the intersection of big media and big academia. Early on I became aware of the connection between Krugman and Ellsworth Toohey. It was Krugman himself who tipped me to it, in a *Times* column in February 2003 in which he taunted

Federal Reserve chairman Alan Greenspan for betraying his longtime friendship with Ayn Rand. He went so far as to quote Rand quoting Aristotle: "A is A: non-contradiction."[44] In a blog posting I said, "Rand's intense advocacy of *laissez faire* capitalism and her heroic sense of life couldn't be more antithetical to Krugman's welfare-state politics and his apocalyptic vision."[45] And that's when I realized that Krugman was Toohey, "the little but brilliant man with an inferiority complex who wants to take over the world."

My first post about Krugman was on the eighth day of the blog's life, and several days after the 2002 midterm elections in which the Republicans consolidated their control of Congress.[46] I was commenting on a Krugman *Times* column in which he blames the GOP's victory on "the real conservative bias of the media." Yes, believe it or not, that's what he said—and in a blatant display of his own partisan bias, he went on in the course of the column to gradually morph the editorial we from "us" to "some of my friends" to "Democrats" and finally, simply "the party."[47]

I started blogging more and more about Krugman because I was fascinated by his deepening descent into a very public paranoia about the Bush administration and the Republican party—and as an economist myself, I resented the way he was using the imprimatur of the profession to enhance his credibility. He was also using the imprimatur of the *New York Times*, pushing the envelope of how aggressive one could be on its editorial pages. His attacks on the Bush administration became increasingly aggressive, strident, and bizarre: comparing him to the emperor Caligula, gratuitously evoking his youthful alcohol abuse, accusing him of outright corruption, and—in a book of collected *Times* columns—likening the Bush administration to the Third Reich.[48] These utterances were unseemly, nasty, vindictive, personal, and hate-filled—the stuff of tabloids or ranting blogs, not journalism's "Gray Lady."

Maybe Krugman's hateful attitude was just a way of getting rich and famous. As N. Gregory Mankiw, the respected Harvard economist, said of Krugman, "I guess if you're a columnist, you want to be widely talked about and be the most e-mailed. It's the same thing that drives talk show hosts to become Jerry Springer."[49]

Whatever his motive, I was intrigued by the vicious cycle he was stoking. The *Times* let Krugman get away with his spew of hate, and in doing so, this standard setter for American journalism redefined what is considered acceptable within mainstream political commentary. As the boundaries of discourse loosened and coarsened, Krugman would just keep throwing dirt at them; they'd then loosen and coarsen some more. The same thing happened in *The Fountainhead* with Ellsworth Toohey and the *Banner*—and it ended up destroying the *Banner* as it may yet destroy the *Times*.

At issue was not just the tone that the *Times* permitted Krugman to take. At the same time, Krugman's columns became increasingly filled with distortions, exaggerations, contradictions, out-of-context quotations, and misquotations. On the pages of what is widely regarded as America's "newspaper of record," these distortions had the power of truth and entered the history books as facts.

I set out to expose those distortions, and to force the *New York Times* to correct them. If the *Times* would correct them, then we could excuse them as mere rhetoric, or perhaps errors. But if no corrections were made, then the very failure to correct would make them willful lies.

I started first on my blog, and soon afterward in a series of columns for *National Review Online*—the web site of the venerable conservative magazine—called "The Krugman Truth Squad" (KTS).

The inaugural KTS column appeared on March 20, 2003.[50] The series of columns was structured as what is now called "crowdsourcing" —within several hours of a Krugman column appearing on the *Times* web site, I and a network of fellow bloggers would put it under a microscope and discover all the filthy microbes hiding in every crack. We'd fact-check every claim, confirm every quotation, run down every source, and compare every statement for consistency with statements made in the past. The KTS called Krugman "America's most dangerous liberal pundit," and our promise to readers was: "We'll read Paul Krugman so you don't have to."

I won't cite here very many of the dozens upon dozens of prevarications that my Krugman Truth Squad exposed in 94 columns over five years. If you are interested, look up my name in the author archives of *National Review Online*, where most of the KTS columns can still be seen.

In most cases, any given one of Krugman's prevarications—if uncorrected, his lies—will seem trivial, as though I were nit-picking to focus on it. But the cumulative effect of them all—every exaggerated statistic designed to bolster some economic argument, every out-of-context quotation designed to make some conservative politician look venal or conservative economist look stupid, every inaccurate historical citation designed to make conservatives into crooks and liberals into heroes—is to shape Krugman's narrative with a persuasive power it would never achieve if it were confined to the truth. In the same sense, the cumulative effect of my persistent blogging, and of the Krugman Truth Squad columns, has been to gradually erode that persuasive power.

My Truth Squad got Krugman's attention right away. After just a month, in an April 2003 KTS column, I took Krugman to task for a whopper he'd told the day before in his *Times* column.[51] Concerning claims by the Bush administration for job creation as a result of its proposed tax cuts, Krugman wrote,

> [L]et's pretend that the Bush administration really thinks that its $726 billion tax-cut plan will create 1.4 million jobs. At what price would those jobs be created? . . . The average American worker earns only about $40,000 per year; why does the administration, even on its own estimates, need to offer $500,000 in tax cuts for each job created?[52]

Sounds sensible if you read it fast—and pretty damning of Bush's plan—especially you assume you don't have to question Krugman's claims, since these words were written by a Princeton economist on the pages of the *New York Times*. But now: stop, think, and question.

That $726 billion number came from a report prepared by Bush's Council of Economic Advisers (yes, the same White House office for whom Krugman had written that foolish report about the "Inflation Time Bomb" two decades earlier). The estimate of 1.4 million jobs created was *just for the first single year* of the tax cuts, 2004. Yet the $726 price tag was for *10 years*. In other words, Krugman was pushing the entire 10-year cost of the tax cut onto a single year of jobs creation.

It was a remarkably arrogant and sloppy thing for Krugman to put in writing. Especially considering that a couple of months earlier he'd made a similar claim in a television interview, and without missing a beat the interviewer had caught the distortion—and forced Krugman to backtrack. PBS's Geoff Colvin asked Krugman, "Well, but it's going to go for longer than just this one year, right?" And all Krugman could say was "Well, yeah. . . ."[53]

But then he repeated the distortion, and having already acknowledged it to Colvin, the second time around it wasn't just a distortion—it was a lie. And it was in writing, in the pages of the *New York Times*. There was no backtracking—and for Krugman, certainly no confession. All Krugman could do was try to justify it retroactively, which he did in a lengthy series of posts and updates on his Princeton web site. Emitting increasingly alarming screeches of desperation, he cited abstruse charts and graphs based on Keynesian macroeconomic theory to justify his erroneous claim—which for all the highfalutin econobabble was self-evidently simply the result of his having failed to divide by 10.[54] Keynes would be rolling in his grave, only he's too busy laughing. Perhaps that's why Krugman's last gasp on the subject was a link on his web site pointing to a scene from Monty Python.[55]

After that my KTS dogged Krugman relentlessly, catching dozens upon dozens of errors, distortions, and misquotations in his columns, which when left uncorrected became lies.

Krugman couldn't help but take notice. In a May 2003 blog posting as part of the divide-by-10 fiasco, he called me "my stalker-in-chief."[56] Four months later, when Tim Russert on his CNBC television show confronted Krugman with one of the embarrassing self-contradictions pointed out in my Krugman Truth Squad columns, Krugman said he'd been "so far just stalked, uh, intellectually."

Okay, it was funny. But then things got very nasty.

Ordeal by Slander

In October 2003 I attended a lecture by Krugman in an auditorium on the campus of the University of California at San Diego.[57] It was part of a tour to promote his new book, a collection of *Times* columns called *The Great Unraveling*.

The experience was very much like living out the scene in *The Fountainhead* in which the character of Ellsworth Toohey is first introduced. Toohey is giving a lecture in a crowded auditorium, exhorting the audience to support a striking union, concluding with a call to collectivism: "Let us organize, my brothers. Let us organize. Let us organize. Let us organize." While Toohey is described by Rand as "puny," when he speaks before an audience his voice "unrolled as a velvet banner. . . . It was the voice of a giant." We witness the scene from the viewpoint of two members of the audience, who for reasons they don't understand are gripped with horror when they hear Toohey, and flee the auditorium.

Krugman was introduced by a University potentate saying, "God bless Paul Krugman,"[58] and the audience erupted in cheering and applause. Krugman gave an intense, commanding speech, and the audience hung on every word. On television, Krugman's voice is high-pitched with a crude New York accent, and he stammers and stutters and pauses and repeats himself—but that night it was Toohey's velvet banner.

I was gripped with horror. I'd spent months debunking and defanging Krugman; but until I saw that cheering audience, I'd never really grasped the vastness of the force I was dealing with. It wasn't just Krugman; it was the millions of people who adore him, who already believe the kinds of things to which he merely gives voice, and who made him possible in the first place. I just wanted to get out and go back to my hotel and take a shower.

But I was with a friend, and we'd agreed that when it was over we'd get him to sign copies of his book for us. I waited in line for a few minutes while he banged out scrawled signatures by the dozen, and when he was done with mine, I asked, "Would you inscribe it to me personally?" He said, "Yeah, all right—what's your name?" I said, "Don . . ." and he wrote Don. Then I said, "Luskin: L-U-S-K-I-N," and by the time he got halfway through, he realized. His eyes started shifting, like Richard Nixon, but he said nothing. I said, "Now you keep up the good work, Paul." He muttered, "Yeah, yeah, fine."[59]

I went back to my hotel and wrote a blog post about the experience.[60] Within hours, a link to my post had been put up on the blog called Eschaton, posted by the pseudonymous Atrios (who turned out later to be the leftist economist Duncan Black). The entire text of Atrios's post consisted of the words: "Diary of a Stalker By Donald Luskin."[61]

Ten days later, on October 17, Krugman went on national television, on the Fox News show *Hannity & Colmes*, and said of me, "That's a guy, that's a guy who actually stalks me on the Web, and once stalked me personally."[62]

Let me be clear about what happened here. Krugman wasn't speaking metaphorically or jocularly, as he had been months earlier when he called me his "stalker-in-chief." This was an accusation of actual stalking—"personally," as Krugman put it. Stalking is a felony, one with a connotation of particular malice, if not perversion, and I had just been accused of it.

And let me say to anyone who thinks I am exaggerating when I refer to Krugman as a liar, *this proves that he is*. I did not stalk Paul Krugman. Meeting him at a public book-signing is not stalking. For him to say that I stalked him is an attack, a character assassination, and a bald-faced lie.

What did it feel like? Everyone wants their 15 minutes of fame. You tell yourself that any publicity is good publicity in our celebrity-driven culture. But no one wants what my family and I went through: week after week in which I was accused, over and over again on the Internet by the hate-filled leftist blogging community, of having committed the kind of felony associated with psychopaths. By November, the affair had become such a cause célèbre it had even been chronicled in the *New Yorker*.[63] The worst parts were the death threats aimed at my wife and daughter.

Here again I felt I was living out scenes from *The Fountainhead*. Ellsworth Toohey deliberately used his position in the media to ruin the reputation of Howard Roark, who represented in Toohey's mind the primal spirit of individualism to which his own philosophy of collectivism was fundamentally opposed. I wish I could say anything so cosmic was at work in Krugman's attempt to destroy me. Sure, a clash of philosophies was involved. But for Krugman I doubt that had much to do with it; I was marked for destruction simply because I'd gotten in his way, and from his narcissistic point of view as a wannabe "psychohistorian" whose "secret fantasy" was to control the galaxy, that was enough.

However, unlike what happened to Howard Roark after one of Toohey's smear campaigns, I didn't have to go work in a granite quarry. My career survived Krugman's attack. And my Krugman Truth Squad stayed on the job, and moved on to achieve several decisive victories against Krugman.

The Errors of His Ways

In addition to exposing Krugman's lies on my blog and in the Krugman Truth Squad column, I pelted the *New York Times* with requests for formal corrections—and was consistently rebuffed or ignored. That was to change dramatically. But at first I was surprised, since the *Times* has a reputation for absurd punctiliousness when it comes to corrections—setting the record straight concerning the slightest details, sometimes months or years after the error was originally run.

But I learned that the *Times* editorial page is managed entirely separately from the rest of the paper. It reports to the publisher, not to the executive editor. At that time it had no formal corrections policy whatsoever, except that corrections were at the discretion of the opinion writer; so human nature being what it is, there were hardly ever any corrections at all. I set about to change that—and I did.

Again, this isn't the way Ayn Rand's heroes dealt with her villains; they mostly ignored them. But if it's a value to you to take on the villains in the real world, and you're willing to pay the price, then this story proves you can do it.

I got my break when the Jayson Blair scandal erupted. Blair was a young *Times* reporter who resigned after he was caught fabricating stories and plagiarizing from other newspapers. To help rehabilitate its damaged reputation, the *Times* created the post of "Public Editor"—what other newspapers call an ombudsman—to act as an independent watchdog to assure the paper's integrity and serve as a disinterested conduit for reader concerns. The man they hired was Daniel Okrent, and I made it my mission to recruit him to the Krugman Truth Squad.

We struck up an ongoing e-mail correspondence. When I met with him personally, his first words to me were: "You're much better looking than Paul Krugman." He told me that the *Times* didn't deserve to be called the "newspaper of record" and vowed, "When I'm done with this assignment, I want everyone to know that."[64]

I raised with him how strange it was that the editorial page had no corrections policy. I shared with him various errors and misquotations in Krugman columns that I felt were simple and objective enough to merit formal correction. Over time, in a number of cases he agreed with me about the errors, and went to Krugman and to Krugman's editor, Gail Collins, to get corrections with or without a formal policy.

But Okrent got stonewalled, just as I had. He wrote,

> I learned early on in this job that Prof. Krugman would likely be more willing to contribute to the [GOP Senator] Frist for President campaign than to acknowledge the possibility of error. When he says he agreed "reluctantly" to one correction, he gives new meaning to the word "reluctantly"; I can't come up with an adverb sufficient to encompass his general attitude toward substantive criticism.[65]

Frustrated that working behind the scenes was not producing results, Okrent threatened to use his Public Editor's column to expose Krugman's and Collins's intransigence. As a result, in March 2004 the *Times* put in place for the first time a columnist corrections policy. Okrent described the policy this way, quoting in part a memo from Collins:

> [C]olumnists must be allowed the freedom of their opinions, but . . . they "are obviously required to be factually accurate. If one of them makes an error, he or she is expected to promptly correct it in the column." Corrections, under this new rule, are to be placed at the end of a subsequent column, "to maximize the chance that they will be seen by all their readers, everywhere."[66]

It was a victory, but a partial one to be sure. The corrections are to be worked into subsequent columns, not flagged in the paper's separate corrections department, nor are the columns in which the errors were originally made to be flagged in the archives as having been subsequently corrected. With all those loopholes remaining, Krugman must have breathed a sigh of relief. But how his blood must have boiled when he read Okrent saying in the same column,

> Paul Krugman, writes Donald Luskin of Palo Alto, Calif., has committed "dozens of substantive factual errors, distortions, misquotations and false quotations—all pronounced in a voice of authoritativeness that most columnists would not presume to permit themselves."

For a wider audience, Luskin serves as Javert to Krugman's Jean Valjean. From a perch on *National Review Online*, he regularly assaults Krugman's logic, his politics, his economic theories, his character and his accuracy.[67]

A year and a half later, Okrent moved on. In his final column as Public Editor, he took a parting shot at Krugman, listing among the things he regrets he didn't write more about that "Op-Ed columnist Paul Krugman has the disturbing habit of shaping, slicing and selectively citing numbers in a fashion that pleases his acolytes but leaves him open to substantive assaults."[68]

A new Public Editor, Byron Calame, took Okrent's place. And my Krugman Truth Squad was ready to take our battle for columnist corrections to the next level.

Putting Krugman in the Correctional Facility — for Life

In August 2005, Krugman claimed in a *Times* column concerning the disputed 2000 Florida presidential election:

> Two different news media consortiums reviewed Florida's ballots; both found that a full manual recount would have given the election to Mr. Gore.[69]

On the same day, on my blog I called him out on what was an egregious lie.[70] The *Times* itself was a member of one of the consortiums, and said in 2002 that "Mr. Bush would have retained a slender margin over Mr. Gore if the Florida court's order to recount more than 43,000 ballots had not been reversed by the United States Supreme Court."[71] I immediately started a dialogue with new Public Editor Byron Calame to force Krugman to correct it. It should have been a slam dunk, but it took many weeks, and many e-mails and phone calls to Calame.

Over the ensuing weeks, Krugman pulled every possible trick to avoid making a correction. In his next *Times* column three days later on August 22, he wrote about the "outraged reaction" about his original claim.[72] He used this column, as new Public Editor Calame would later complain on his blog, only "to explain the misstatement without admitting any errors. . . . absent a formal correction, the information didn't get appended to his flawed Aug. 19 column."[73]

Then, four days later in his August 26 column, Krugman added a new correction that was itself erroneous.[74] Calame exploded, "It was wrong on the results of the *Miami Herald* statewide manual recounts. And it didn't deal with the fact that the original Aug. 19 generalization, the Aug. 22 column and the formal correction all erred in describing the findings of the other news media consortium (in which *The Times* was a participant)."[75]

What was so tricky about it was that Krugman's error had come, in part, from reliance on an erroneous story in the *Miami Herald* (which had performed the recount for the media consortium) in which one of the scenarios where Bush won was omitted. I ran this down personally by locating and contacting a former *Herald* editor who had since moved to Washington, D.C., and who at my insistence went up to his attic to obtain the records necessary to establish the facts—which I passed on to Calame.

Calame's complaints were posted on his blog on September 2, which drove Krugman to post later the same day a statement on the *Times* web site—but not in print—acknowledging his original error, but blaming it on the *Miami Herald*, and asserting that it didn't matter anyway.[76]

There it remained for two weeks, with no formal and complete in-print correction. I kept hectoring Calame. Then on September 16, Calame wrote a blog post protesting,

> Mr. Krugman still hasn't been required to comply with the policy by publishing a formal correction. Ms. Collins hasn't offered any explanation. . . .
>
> All Mr. Krugman has offered so far is a faux correction. . . . Mr. Krugman has been allowed to post a note on his page that acknowledges his initial error, but doesn't explain that his initial correction of that error was also wrong.[77]

Finally, two weeks later, Calame announced on his blog that a new columnist corrections policy would be forthcoming from Collins.[78]

No longer would corrections be appended only to future columns. Instead, they would be appended in the archives to the original columns in which the errors appeared, so that readers doing Web-based searches, or using services like LexusNexus or Factiva, would be informed that the articles they were viewing had been subsequently corrected.

Several days later, on October 2, Collins revealed the policy, saying that Krugman "asked if he could refrain from revisiting the subject yet again in print." We can just imagine that conversation—the word "asked" is probably not entirely accurate. Whined? Pleaded? Begged? Whatever—Collins's column concluded with a full and formal correction of Krugman's multiple errors, misrepresentations, and evasions about the Florida election, and the same text is now appended to all the Krugman columns involved.[79]

The same day's editorial page carried another correction under the new policy—a particularly telling and funny one.[80] Three (count 'em: *three!*) of the *Times*'s columnists had to recant a single falsehood that *all* of them had made in the attempt to portray cronyism in the Bush administration—with Krugman having made it *twice!*

Op-Ed columns by Paul Krugman (Sept. 5 and 9), Maureen Dowd (Sept. 10) and Frank Rich (Sept. 18) said Michael Brown, the former FEMA director, was a college friend or college roommate of Joe Allbaugh, his predecessor. They went to different colleges and later became friends.

Cut Down to Size

Several years have passed since then. I've stopped posting to my blog, The Conspiracy to Keep You Poor and Stupid, and I haven't written a Krugman Truth Squad column for many months. I decided that it was time to declare victory. And what do you know—that book of mine finally got written. Or at least a version of it, which you are reading right now.

With all I and my fellow Krugman Truth Squad members did to expose Krugman's lies, and with a new columnist corrections policy that imposes a formal reputational cost on Krugman if he keeps on lying, it seems that Krugman has nothing to say—at least nothing that has the power to influence the national debate, as his columns once did. It turns out that it's a lot harder to convince people when you have to stick to the truth.

Need proof? Just think how Krugman must have felt in late 2010, when the 2003 Bush tax cuts he did so much to oppose—including embroiling himself in the humiliating divide-by-10 contretemps—were extended by a Democratic president and a Democratic Congress. Impotence just doesn't get any more humiliating than that.

At the same time, Krugman has become a victim of his own success. His vicious cycle of ever looser and ever coarser discourse has reached a dead end, and left him facing a new generation of competitors as loose and as coarse as he is. He just doesn't stand out anymore.

There are other victims. It may be that Krugman's vicious cycle has reached a dead end in a tragically literal sense, with the January 2010 shootings in Tucson of a congresswoman and several bystanders. There's never been any evidence that the shooting was politically motivated, but before the blood was dry Krugman had published a post on his *Times* blog instantly leaping to the conclusion that "odds are that it was," and asserting that she had been targeted because "she's a Democrat who survived what was otherwise a GOP sweep in Arizona." He went on to blame "the rhetoric of Beck, Limbaugh, etc." for creating a "climate of hate."[81]

Barack Obama disagrees. When he spoke in Tucson the following week, Krugman no doubt felt personally dressed down when the president said, emphatically, regarding whether the "lack of civility caused this tragedy," that "It did not."[82]

But if it *did*, then by Krugman's own theory of a "climate of hate," this assassination attempt could be seen as the deadly fruit of seeds he himself had sown years before when he began to use the *Times*—America's "newspaper of record"—as a platform for personal destruction of his enemies.

Chapter 3

The Leader

John Allison as John Galt, the man who walked away after building America's strongest bank

"He turned and answered, 'I will stop the motor of the world.' Then he walked out. We never saw him again. We never heard what became of him. But years later, when we saw the lights going out one after another, in the great factories that had stood solid like mountains for generations . . . and the world was crumbling quietly, like a body when its spirit is gone—then we began to wonder and to ask questions about him. . . . You see, his name was John Galt."

—Atlas Shrugged

Who is John Galt?

Ayn Rand's magnum opus *Atlas Shrugged* is set in a time of a growing economic, cultural, and political crisis. We hear over and over a slang expression adopted by people from all walks of life to capture their despair and resignation: "Who is John Galt?"

It turns out that John Galt is an actual person, and that he has deliberately fomented the crisis. He is a brilliant young scientist who conceived a breakthrough invention—a motor that

(Continued)

could be driven without fuel, something of incalculable economic value that today would be called green technology. Yet he walks away from his invention, and his career.

Galt's abdication—his "mind on strike"—is triggered when the factory that employs him adopts a managerial model based on the Marxist maxim "From each according to his ability, to each according to his need." He believes that this collectivist philosophy, which would punish the competent and reward the incompetent, is both immoral and a recipe for economic collapse. The only moral response is to refuse to participate in such immorality—which would have the side effect of hastening the collapse.

But Galt takes his strike one big step further. He sets about persuading other men of ability to go on strike, too, giving up their work as industrialists, businessmen, financiers, teachers, artists, and doctors. He recruits them to his strike by explaining to them the fundamental moral basis of capitalism, and the inherent immorality of a culture that expropriates their talents, turning their own virtues against them.

At the climax of the book, Galt takes to the radio, revealing himself to the world and explaining his strike and the philosophy behind it. Galt's speech is the key reference documenting Rand's philosophy of "Objectivism."

In November 2008, 30 days before his scheduled retirement, John Allison sat atop a black office tower in Winston-Salem, North Carolina, preparing to sign away his life's work.

He'd spent 37 years, his entire career, at BB&T (or, more formally, Branch Banking and Trust Company). When he arrived in 1971, it was an obscure farm bank with 250 employees and $250 million in assets. Allison became president in 1987 and chief executive in 1989, and by 2008 he was the longest-serving bank CEO in the United States. Under his leadership BB&T had grown into a bank holding company with 1,800 branches sprawling over 12 Southern states and

Washington, D.C., among the top 10 banks in all but one of those markets. BB&T has 30,000 employees and over $150 billion in assets, making it the 12th largest U.S. bank.

Now he was being forced to give substantial control of it to the U.S. government.

And not because BB&T had failed, as so many other banks had in the terrifying banking crisis of 2008. No, BB&T was being punished because it had succeeded.

BB&T had made no subprime mortgage loans. While other banks blew themselves up with high-fee negative amortization and "pick-a-payment" loans that supported a cancerous housing bubble, BB&T resisted temptation and wrote only conventional mortgages.

Yet after Congress enacted the Troubled Asset Relief Program (TARP), banking regulators forced even healthy banks to take government money, that is, to accept the government as a shareholder. That meant committing to pay the government hundreds of millions in preferred dividends, and giving up valuable warrants so that the government could later purchase common stock at fire-sale prices. Adding insult to injury, Allison had to sign a waiver that allowed the government to unilaterally change the terms of his compensation from the company he'd served for 38 years.

But he had no choice. BB&T was a strong bank, with more than enough capital and more than enough liquidity to see it through the crisis, and a strong loan portfolio. Yet his banking examiner from the federal government told him that the rules had suddenly changed.

According to Allison, "They called us and said, 'Okay, we've had these capital rules forever, and you guys got a lot more capital based on those rules. But we've decided we're going to have some new capital rules. And based on these new capital rules, we don't think you have enough capital. Now, we don't know what the rules are, but we're confident that if you don't take the TARP money, you won't have enough capital.'"[1]

Allison knew that the bank examiner was just a messenger boy for his bosses in Washington, D.C., where the Federal Reserve under chairman Ben Bernanke was desperate to save a few insolvent mega-banks, even if the entire banking system had to pay the bill do it.

Allison says, "There were three large financial institutions in serious trouble in the capital markets." Presumably he means Citigroup, Bank of America, and General Electric Credit. But Bernanke didn't want to reveal to the public how weak these three really were—so *all* banks would be forced to take TARP money. "He felt like if he forced all the large banks, all the $100 billion banks and over, to participate, the market couldn't figure it out. . . . It was a huge rip-off for healthy banks."

Allison signed. He had to. He had adamantly opposed TARP when it was being debated. He thought it was wrong. He thought it was unfair. He thought it was unnecessary. But he had to sign. A Southerner who often expresses himself in gracious understatement, Allison says, "To be forced to do that with 30 days left in your career, on something you were adamantly opposed to in the first place, was not much fun."

For Allison, it all had a certain sense of déjà vu. Specifically, as he puts it, "It is right out of *Atlas Shrugged*. I mean, it's eerie. It is eerie. It is eerie."

And Allison should know. All his life he has been inspired by *Atlas Shrugged* and the other works of Ayn Rand. He explicitly created BB&T's management philosophy on Randian principles of Objectivism, and for decades he has required all BB&T executives to read *Atlas Shrugged*.

BB&T is the bank that *Atlas* built. Its success, and its durability in a crisis that destroyed so many other banks, is testimony to the real-world, real-money impact of Rand's value system: purpose, reason, and self-esteem. The crisis itself is testimony to the real-world consequences of the philosophy of Rand's villains—the looters, the power seekers, and the altruists.

Like Rand's greatest hero, John Galt, Allison chose to walk away from the looters' world at the height of his powers. He started eyeing the exit after the 2002 passage of the Sarbanes-Oxley Act. He says, "That was kind of a precipitating event, where you were considered to be a criminal if you were in business, and that things were considered fraud that were just honest business mistakes. I mean just the whole tone changed—criminalization of honest business activity."

Retiring at a young and vigorous 58 years old amid a crumbling banking system, Allison has left behind the bank that *Atlas* built. Like Galt, he's devoting himself no longer to business, but instead to evangelism for the morality of capitalism.

Discovering Rand

No one would have predicted that John Allison, born in Charlotte, North Carolina, and raised in a deeply religious family, would turn out to be an Ayn Rand devotee, and certainly not the real-world embodiment of Rand's great hero. As with so many Rand-heads, the conversion happened in college.

Allison was at the University of North Carolina, Chapel Hill, majoring in business administration. In his economics classes, he says, "even though my professors were largely left-wing, they actually pushed me to the right because I didn't agree. Their ideas just didn't make any sense. They weren't my experience in life. So it's funny: I think they intended to indoctrinate me to the left, and they ended up pushing me right."

Then, between his junior and senior year, he discovered Ayn Rand.

Most people start with the fiction, *The Fountainhead* or *Atlas Shrugged*, seduced into Rand's philosophy as they are swept away in the heady romanticism of these compelling stories and their mythic heroes. Not Allison. He started with Rand's nonfiction masterpiece, *Capitalism: The Unknown Ideal* (published in 1966), stumbling upon it by chance in a bookstore.

Allison says, "I was really impressed with particularly the first part of the book where she talks about the principles underlying capitalism." Though Rand's philosophy was aggressively secular, it appealed to Allison's religious instincts. "I was raised in a very religious background which put a premium on values, and derived in a religious way, so I guess in a certain sense I've always been interested in the issue of principles—how you really should live your life."

He was hooked. He says, "Then from that I read *Atlas Shrugged*, read *The Fountainhead*, and then basically read everything I could get of her materials and every book she recommended."

After getting his master's degree in management from Duke University, in 1971 Allison went to work for BB&T in the small farm bank's loan administration group. Amid a group of stodgy older executives, Allison's boss was a bright young go-getter who put Allison into the bank's management development program. But that consisted pretty much of just slumming on the teller line for a while to see how

the other half lived. After 10 months, Allison's bright young boss figured out that Allison himself was a bright young man, and challenged
him to create a real management development program.

It turned out that Allison and his boss were both Rand fans. So the
first thing they did in the new program was give everyone a copy of
Atlas Shrugged. Allison remembers, "We got a lot of the future leadership to read *Atlas*. . . . It wasn't officially required, but it was officially
encouraged. . . . A lot of the best people did read it."

By 1973 four other bright young men had showed up at BB&T,
and joined Allison in what would turn out to be the leadership nucleus
of a Rand-based build-out of the sleepy farm bank into a colos-
sus. They all read *Atlas* and they all were transformed. Allison says,
"Anybody that reads *Atlas Shrugged*—that comes with a general business background in particular—it does change their worldview. They
may say, 'Well, I reject this aspect of Rand,' or 'I reject that aspect,'
but . . . the particular thing I think almost everybody gets out of it is
the destructive role of government."

For Allison himself, Rand resonated with his personal quest for
meaning in life. He recalls, "Before Rand, first I had a hodgepodge
of philosophical beliefs. I was trying to be religious, but I wasn't really
active in a way that was consistent with the religion that I was taught,
so I was torn in a certain sense. I made pretty good grades, but I was
just doing my schoolwork to make good grades. It didn't have any bigger meaning to me. When I saw her characters, spiritually what I got
was, man, they're purposeful and they're doing it in ways that I could
enjoy—building a business."

Like Allison, the new leadership nucleus of BB&T were Southern-
born and deeply religious. For some, Rand's aggressive atheism didn't
sit well, and still doesn't.

Kelly King, who has succeeded Allison as CEO, recalls that he
reacted favorably to *Atlas Shrugged* when he first read it at Allison's
request: "I kinda liked the book. I hate big government. I like capitalism. I like productivity." But later, on learning more, he found, "I
disagree with her need to take reason to its ultimate extreme, which of
course defeats all forms of mysticism and faith. I don't find that to be
productive or necessary in business."

But Allison says, "Our agreement was to try to take religion out of the bank. This was a secular organization. People were entitled to their religious beliefs, but the bank had to be run by some secular principles. That's the agreement with the shareholders of how you run the bank. . . . And they respected that."

The Man with a Purpose

Allison became president of BB&T in 1987, and chief executive in 1989. He continued to spread the word about Rand and get everyone to read *Atlas Shrugged*. But the Randification of BB&T kicked into high gear in 1994. That's when Allison discovered *Objectivism: The Philosophy of Ayn Rand*, written three years earlier by Rand's longtime associate and designated intellectual heir, Leonard Peikoff.

"Though I'd read all of Rand and agree with it," Allison says, "I really, in retrospect, didn't truly understand it. I understood its politics, and I understood parts of it, but I never was able to totally integrate it until 1994, when I read *Objectivism: The Philosophy of Ayn Rand*. And that was a huge integrating event for me, because I was able to really get it from A to Z."

For Allison "the timing was great," because the next year came the seminal event in BB&T's rise to dominance in the Southern banking market: the merger of equals with competitor Southern National Bank, handing CEO Allison the challenge of integrating two $10 billion giants.

It was a classic integration problem: How do two proud business cultures come together as one? And the most pointed question: Faced with the inevitable functional overlaps between two similar businesses, who lose their jobs and who keep their jobs?

The answer was Rand. After years of promoting Rand's ideas in a general way within the bank, Allison turned them into a formal system. Most big businesses have a mission statement. But Allison took it much further. For BB&T, he used Rand's ideas to create a corporate *philosophy*. It became embodied in a lengthy booklet that Allison wrote himself, and that still serves BB&T substantially unaltered after all these years.

Allison got buy-in on the philosophy from his senior leadership team. Again, Rand's reputation as an atheist was a sore spot for some. But Allison recalls, "They all agreed with the philosophy. And this is an interesting thing: Everything in that is, by the way, in the Bible. . . . So that's how I think the group reconciled it—they were already living it."

As the Southern National merger proceeded, and then for all the years since, the Rand-based BB&T philosophy has been what Allison calls "a filter." Not everyone accepts it, but the ones he wants in his bank do. "What I've found is that better people like the ideas."

Allison is especially good at getting people to like the ideas. Rand herself was good at it, too, couching the ideas in novels so compelling that they are still best sellers more than half a century since they were written. Yet as much as Rand and her ideas are admired by her readers, at the same time they are reviled by critics on both the political left and the political right who accuse her of advocating "greed" and "selfishness."

Those objections don't seem to come up when Allison talks about Rand's ideas in the BB&T philosophy. Maybe it's his unpretentious North Carolina accent, his boyish wavy hair, the ever-present smile on his face, or his tendency to laugh as he speaks (he resembles a more slender David Letterman).

Or maybe it's that Allison exudes leadership. Meet this man, and you'll wish he'd offer you a job—because you know instantly that he's someone you'd love working for. It's because he believes so utterly in his philosophy, because there is no internal doubt—because, like John Galt, his is a "face without pain or fear or guilt."

What is it like to have a philosopher for a CEO? Edward D. Vest, who rose up through the ranks to become BB&T's chief financial officer, speaks of Allison more as a life coach than a boss. "He teaches you how to think. He teaches you the importance of purpose. Once you find that purpose, you almost get this magnificent obsession of going for something with everything you've got, and never letting a second go by, wasting it through evasion, through laziness, through avoiding what you know to be true. So it's been liberating."

At first the BB&T philosophy doesn't look all that different than the usual corporate pabulum. The stated vision is "To Create the Best Financial Institution Possible."[2] The mission is "To make the world a better place to live."

But then we get to the bank's purpose, and that's when things start to get interesting. It was "purpose" that first attracted Allison to Rand—what he finds living is all about.

> Our ultimate purpose is to create superior long-term economic rewards for our shareholders.
>
> This purpose is defined by the free market and is as it should be. Our shareholders provide the capital that is necessary to make our business possible. They take the risk if the business is unsuccessful. They have the right to receive economic rewards for the risk which they have undertaken.

A Randian creed, indeed—it brings to mind some of the more flamboyant statements by Francisco d'Anconia, the noble and eloquent defender of capitalism in *Atlas Shrugged*. He said that "the most depraved type of human being" is the "man without a purpose." And he said that "I want to be prepared to claim the greatest virtue of all—that I was a man who made money."

For critics of Rand, such statements supposedly argue for greed and selfishness. For her admirers like Allison, they are the enshrinement of the honorable matter of earning one's living with one's own productive work.

For Allison, *all* companies exist to make money for their shareholders, though most pretend there's some other more altruistic purpose. That's a fundamental hypocrisy that undermines a business's relationships with its employees. Allison says, "If you throw in a value system that has some kind of altruism, which most businesses do, then people know you're not serious, because . . . you're not treated that way, and you can't be treated that way."

A typical altruistic purpose is to claim, necessarily falsely, that the business is all about serving clients—as though shareholder profits were to be sacrificed to make customers happy. BB&T turns this on its head in the statement of purpose, saying that client satisfaction is an essential means to the end of shareholder wealth creation.

> . . . our purpose, to create superior long-term economic rewards for our shareholders, can only be accomplished by providing excellent service to our clients, as our Clients are our source of revenues.

If this sounds familiar to Rand fans, it should. Howard Roark, the rebellious architect hero of *The Fountainhead*, said, "I don't intend to build in order to have clients. I intend to have clients in order to build."

But does this focus on clients and shareholders mean that employees of BB&T are to altruistically sacrifice themselves? Hardly. The next point in the statement of purpose states:

> To have excellent client relations, we must have outstanding Employees to serve our clients. To attract and retain outstanding employees, we must reward them financially and create an environment where they can learn and grow.

Shareholders, clients, and employees, all working to mutual benefit. Nobody sacrifices; everybody gains. Does this sound familiar, too? The great industrialist Henry Rearden explained it in *Atlas Shrugged*: "I do not sacrifice my interests to them nor do they sacrifice their interests to me; we deal as equals by mutual consent to mutual advantage— and I am proud of every penny I have earned in this manner." Allison calls it the "trader principle."

He explains, "We talk about the trader principle over and over again. . . . You never should ever take advantage of other people, nor should you self-sacrifice. What life is about is creating win–win relationships, figuring out how to get better together, and you ought to do that consciously. What's in it for you is a fair question, but what's in it for them? . . . And you do that internally and externally. You treat your clients the same way. You never take advantage of clients, but if somebody's trying to take advantage of you, I've told our employees many times, they are people you don't want to do business with."

Finally, the statement of purpose brings it all together in one big integration of the trader principle:

> Our economic results are significantly impacted by the success of our Communities. The community's "quality of life" impacts its ability to attract industry for growth.

Therefore, we manage our business in a long-term context, as an integrated whole, with the ultimate objective of rewarding the Shareholders for their investment, while realizing that the cause of this result is quality client service. Excellent service will be delivered by motivated employees working as an integrated team. These results will be impacted by our capacity to contribute to the growth and well-being of the communities we serve.

For BB&T, imbuing employees with a coherent purpose isn't just a human resources exercise. It's a high-powered competitive weapon.

That's because BB&T is organized as a network of 33 community banks, designed to operate in a highly decentralized way, aimed at meeting the unique needs of every individual market they serve. So typical centralized, one-size-fits-all command-and-control management techniques won't work. Every employee has to be a self-guided missile, which means every employee has to be superlatively trained.

It's not cheap to superlatively train 30,000 employees. To afford it, BB&T spends less on advertising than its competitors do. BB&T sees a well-trained and empowered workforce as the best advertising in a business inevitably based on service, trust, and word of mouth.

That's why there's BB&T University, where every year thousands of management-level employees are not only trained in the technical skills required to do their jobs, and not only trained to be more effective leaders, but also put through rigorous psychological workshops designed to eliminate unconscious barriers to excellence. For example, Allison believes that for many natural leaders, intelligence can get in their way. For some, it becomes a weapon that unintentionally drives colleagues away. For others, it becomes a wall that prevents them from hearing the feedback they need. Allison says, "If you really want to change people's behavior, you've got to take them through a process where they can honestly look at their negatives."

For every single employee, from tellers to executive vice presidents, every single day, the Ayn Rand–inspired BB&T philosophy is the cultural glue the holds the far-flung organization together—and has kept it from getting into trouble while other banks have spectacularly blown themselves apart.

Every employee is encouraged to read *Atlas Shrugged*. Every employee is given a printed copy of the BB&T philosophy embodying Allison's Randian value system. Every year Allison, and now CEO Kelly King (a longtime Allison intimate), gives a one-hour presentation before all employees renewing the bank's commitment to the philosophy.

Where the rubber really meets the road is through semiannual performance appraisals, in which every employee from top to bottom is evaluated in terms of whether he or she successfully lived the BB&T philosophy.

The bank's purpose—to create value for shareholders—is only the jewel in the crown of the philosophy. Supporting it are 10 values that every employee is expected to bring to life every day on the job.

Value #1: Reality

Huh?

Isn't *every* business based on reality? In fact, isn't *everything* based on reality?

Actually, no. Lehman Brothers, Bear Stearns, AIG (American International Group), IndyMac, Washington Mutual, Countrywide, and all the other banks that blew themselves to smithereens in 2008 weren't basing their businesses on reality. They were basing their businesses on sheer fantasy, wish, and whim—and an unhealthy dose of greed, the most unrealistic thing of all. They believed the housing market would always go up. Credit markets would never be illiquid. People with no jobs could pay back their mortgages.

As the mortgage credit bubble was inflating in the mid-2000s, Allison could see that it was all underpinned by a single key denial of reality. According to Allison, at the peak, by any normal metric of affordability, housing prices were 30 percent above any historical experience. Housing prices were simply too high, and at a certain point they just couldn't go any higher—so they had no place to go but down.[3]

That was reality. And it was denied at almost every bank but BB&T. Every subprime mortgage, every exotic mortgage, every mortgage derivative—they were all based on the same denial.

It seems obvious in retrospect, but while it was happening the denial of it was a subtle and complicated thing. In Allison's view, politicians have for years overpromoted housing in the United States, distorting economic incentives with subsidies and tax breaks to favor home building and home ownership over other forms of investment. And in the early 2000s, these distortions were amplified by the Federal Reserve's keeping interest rates artificially low.[4]

Allison tells the story[5] of a meeting with Barney Frank, the powerful chairman of the House Financial Services Committee and leading defender of the overleveraged government-sponsored housing lenders Fannie Mae and Freddie Mac, which did so much to put Americans into homes they couldn't really afford (we'll meet Frank again in Chapter 6, "The Central Planner"). For Allison, Fannie and Freddie were "a disaster you could see happening."

He told Frank, "I know housing's a good thing, but . . . getting them into a home they can't afford isn't necessarily a good thing. If that were so, then next time somebody commits a crime, instead of putting them in jail, why don't we give them a house?" How did Frank react to Allison's sarcasm? Allison recalls the moment, rocking with laughter: "He looked at me like it was a serious proposal."

For the private sector, like it or not, all the government-induced distortions were reality. So in an important sense, the orgy of subprime lending that nearly destroyed the U.S. banking system was rational—it was an adaptation to reality. But that reality was, ultimately, an unreality. We'll see shortly how the BB&T philosophy kept Allison's bank from succumbing to it.

Value #2: Reason

Reason is a key value because it is the means by which we capture and hold the first value, reality.

What Allison demands from his employees is what he calls an "active mind"[6]—a mind committed to learning from experience, profiting from mistakes, and being free from evasion. That's the kind of mind that can discover reality and profit from it.

Allison says, "The ultimate psychological sin we talk about is evasion. . . . I think everybody evades some; some people evade a lot more than others, and evasion is very dangerous. And the smarter somebody is, I think, the more dangerous an evasion is." As Allison surveys the graveyard of once-great banks now laid low by their foolish and risky investments at the height of the mortgage bubble, he says, "I guarantee you people were evading like crazy."

In the bubble, a key means of evasion for the seemingly smartest bankers was mathematical modeling of the economy, the markets, and the riskiness of their investment positions. Models seem on the surface to be the height of reason—they are based on numbers and run on computers, and their outputs are beautiful graphs and deep decimal precision. But in the mortgage crash, they pretty much all failed—and in some cases took down the banks that used them.

Allison says, "We were told over and over again if we just had mathematical models like Wachovia and like Bank of America . . . we would be wonderful from a best practices perspective."[7] Thanks to the utter failure of their models to capture the true risks they were taking in the mortgage portfolios, Wachovia failed in mid-2008 (it was sold by the Federal Deposit Insurance Corporation [FDIC] to Wells Fargo), and Bank of America had to be rescued by extraordinary interventions by the Treasury and the Federal Reserve in early 2009.

Has anything changed, now as we stand in the rubble of a model-driven banking blowout? Nope. "This is bizarre," says Allison. "They still believe it. We're still being told we need mathematical models like Wachovia's. . . . There's still a religious belief in mathematical models."[8]

Allison thinks the models are doomed from the get-go because they are based on fundamentally incorrect notions. "They always assume normal curves, and they try to manage things to a 99 percent probability. That means there's only a 1 percent probability that certain bad things can happen. Well, there's an interesting thing with a 1 percent probability: Give it long enough, and it becomes certain."[9]

Value #3: Independent Thinking

Allison calls independent thinking "the most important psychological decision you can make, to be responsible for yourself."[10] It's the root of all creative achievement, and creative achievement is the root of all human progress—practically by definition.

Have you ever worked for a bank? If you have, and if it wasn't BB&T, chances are you weren't encouraged to think independently. Quite the contrary. Indeed, banks are known for their hidebound conformist cultures. That's why most banks haven't grown like BB&T has, at least not without taking absurd levels of trading risk that came back to bite them in the mortgage collapse.

At the same time as they were taking those absurd risks, most banks failed to think independently. It was a lethal combination— crazy risk taking and herd mentality—and it was imposed by fiat by banking regulators.

Allison points a finger at so-called fair-value accounting—newfangled accounting rules imposed on banks for the first time several years ago, requiring them to appraise their investment positions based on transitory mark-to-market prices rather than independent analysis of value.

"That sounds good," Allison admits, "but there are times when you can't mark to market because you can't figure out what it is. And fair-value accounting violates the basic laws of supply and demand. For there to be a market price there has to be a willing seller and a willing buyer."[11] In the mortgage crisis of 2008, there were no willing buyers or sellers of so-called toxic assets—and the fire-sale prices that resulted from what few trades were done gave an unrealistically low appraisal of these assets' worth.

Fair-value accounting violates the principle of "going concern," Allison says, "because it assumes that everyone has to sell assets when they don't have to sell assets."[12]

Allison thinks this was "a major cause of the liquidation we had"[13] because banks like BB&T weren't willing to take the accounting risk artificially imposed on them by fair-value accounting. If they'd stepped forward and bought the toxic assets that were being sold by distressed banks, they'd have to show on their books large losses if those assets subsequently traded at unrealistic fire-sale prices, even though they knew to a moral certainty that they were worth much more. Without fair-value accounting, it would have been just the opposite. They could have booked immediate profits by buying assets on the cheap— and in doing so, they would have supported a market that was desperately looking for buyers.

There was another failure of independent thinking that contributed to the mortgage crash: the overreliance on the three rating agencies, Standard & Poor's (S&P), Moody's, and Fitch. Allison calls them "a government monopoly,"[14] and blames their too-optimistic ratings of mortgage-backed securities for helping to transform problems in the small market for subprime lending into a large-scale systemic banking crisis.

When mortgage-backed securities that had been rated investment grade suddenly became toxic assets, the market "totally lost confidence in the ratings system." In other words, a market that had not done any independent thinking (it had just relied on S&P, Moody's, and Fitch) suddenly had nothing to go on. "So we had a real lockup in liquidity," Allison says, even in "instruments that really were performing . . . because nobody trusted the ratings system."[15]

Value #4: Productivity

Rand's character Francisco d'Anconia expressed it this way: ". . . there's nothing of any importance in life—except for how you do your work. Nothing. Only that. Whatever else you are will come from that."

Okay, maybe that's a bit much. For Allison, BB&T is looking for high performers who have "a gut level commitment to getting the job done."[16] BB&T wants to filter out low performers who "seek reasons to fail." High performers "face the same obstacles" as low performers, according to Allison, but they get over them and succeed.

If the bank's purpose is to produce shareholder wealth, then it has to produce profits. What are profits? Allison says they're just the difference between the value BB&T creates for customers and BB&T's cost of creating that value—"the bigger the difference the better."[17]

The way you make that difference bigger is through efficiency and productivity. It's really just that simple.

Value #5: Honesty

Honesty doesn't mean just keeping your fingers out of the till. Any bank insists on *that*. With BB&T it's an obsession with ethical conduct

24/7, complete transparency—not even a white lie, and no exceptions for the bosses at the top of the pyramid.

Allison says, "No fudging. . . . We acquired companies that had a couple leaders that really weren't totally honest. They weren't totally *dis*honest. . . . But particularly they wouldn't disclose. They may not lie to you, but they would effectively lie because they wouldn't disclose when something was going wrong. Well, in our organization, that's not tolerable. So we drove that kind of leader out."

Rank-and-file employees are glad to see less than honest leaders shown the door. Allison says, "The employees know something is going on. And once we dealt with some of these issues . . . people would say, 'Man, I'm glad you got rid of Joe! Joe wasn't telling you the truth about this, and he was kind of keeping me from telling you the truth about this.'"

There's no exception for employees just because they're making a lot of money for the bank. Allison recalls, "Our number-one mortgage producer—this was before the mortgage market busted—number one in production, number one in revenue. . . . We found out he was fudging on his reports, and we fired him. And we fired him immediately, without hesitation or reservation, even though he was our number-one producer." It didn't matter one bit that "most of our mortgage production is sold in the secondary market, so in a way you can argue there was no 'risk' in what he was doing."

But there was risk. This sleazy "number-one producer" went to BB&T's competitor Countrywide Financial after he was fired. Allison says, "I think he got fired there. . . . He got fired as they all went broke." It's no coincidence that Countrywide was run by Angelo Mozilo, whom we'll soon meet in Chapter 4, "The Parasite." If Allison is *Atlas Shrugged* hero John Galt, then Mozilo is villain James Taggart, the corrupt businessman who'd stop at nothing, even the destruction of his own company.

Value #6: Integrity

Integrity is different from honesty. It means always doing the right thing, always acting consistently with one's philosophy, no matter what. Sometimes it can mean doing the right thing even when clients seem to be clamoring for you to help them do the wrong thing.

In the housing bubble, plenty of home buyers wanted pick-a-payment mortgages. These allowed the borrower to choose to defer payments of interest and principal each month, effectively making the amount owed to the bank larger and larger. That's fine if the value of the underlying real estate rises, keeping up with the rising amount owed. But if the value goes down, or even stays flat, home buyers can find themselves under water— owing the bank more than the house is worth.

While just about every other bank was making a fortune with pick-a-payment mortgages because they commanded much higher fees, BB&T refused to make such loans. Allison says it wasn't "because we had a brilliant insight on the real estate markets, but we knew real estate wasn't going to appreciate 10 percent per year forever. That was just mathematically impossible."

It's not about the money; it's about integrity. Allison insists that "one of the fundamental commitments in our mission is to help our clients achieve economic success and financial security. I would expect to make a profit doing it, but one thing I say to our employees over and over: never consciously do anything that's bad for your client. Even if you can make a profit in the short term, it'll always come back to haunt you. Even if he seems to want it. . . . It was really an ethical decision to do that, and it saved us a fortune."

You might think that Allison took some career risk in making the tough call to not do pick-a-payment mortgages, turning his back on a red-hot product that was earning billions in profits for competitors. Actually, Allison didn't make the call at all. "There's a guy that runs our mortgages here that's been with us a long time, that is very aligned with our culture. He made the decision on his own, without ever talking to me. Now, when I heard about it, I told him I thought it was a wonderful decision."

Another example of integrity in action at BB&T is the way the bank reacted to the U.S. Supreme Court's decision in *Kelo v. City of New London*. In that landmark case, the court upheld a city's right to take private property under eminent domain and then transfer that property to private parties. The logic was that if the city believes that the property will generate higher tax revenues or otherwise further the city's goals when placed in new private hands, then that satisfies the

U.S. Constitution's requirement for "public use" to justify a taking of that property.

From Allison's perspective, the *Kelo* decision "threatens property rights, which is the foundation for being in our whole business." So he decided to protest by announcing that BB&T wouldn't make loans to real estate developers to buy or improve property acquire through eminent domain.

What happened next was a surprise. Allison remembers, "First thing, honestly, I didn't think people would pay much attention to it." But then, "We had thousands of people move their accounts to BB&T. And you know what a lot of them said? It was partly about eminent domain but it was partly about businesses acting on principle. People believe that businesses have no principles—they'll do anything for a buck. And I got tons of letters saying, 'Yeah, eminent domain is awful, and gosh, it's nice to hear a business might do something over principle.'"

Value #7: Justice

This is where BB&T makes a key commitment to every employee. Justice, as Allison puts it, "means you're going to award superior performance and deal with nonperformance."

BB&T obsessively measures performance, quantitatively and qualitatively. And every single employee, right down to the teller line, is eligible for incentive compensation based on good performance.

And the reverse is true. Poor performance means no incentive compensation, though the bank will always invest in its people through training to help poor performers learn to be excellent ones. But break the bank's values, especially in the domains of honesty or integrity, and it's time to leave.

It wouldn't be justice if Allison himself didn't have to eat his own cooking. His compensation as CEO has always been mostly on an at-risk basis, determined objectively by the reality of whether BB&T hit agreed targets for earnings-per-share growth, return on assets, and return on equity.

Justice has another critical meaning for BB&T employees, who have seen their bank grow over the years by a series of acquisitions and mergers, every one of which potentially poses a threat to job security. Remembering the merger of equals with Southern National Bank that started it all, Allison says, "The justice was, if we clearly had a better person to do the job, we would get the person to do the job. Easy. But a lot of times, that ain't so clear. Because you've got different inputs, you've got different people. . . .We were going to try to create balance between the two organizations, because part of the justice was being fair to both teams."

This has been absolutely key to BB&T's growth, which has been to a large extent driven by a series of acquisitions, made at the right price and then executed perfectly. Chief operating officer Christopher Henson recalls, "Prior to Southern National, we had built up over the years a preferred acquisition status because we had a no-layoff policy." But all that had to change when BB&T did deals where "we were going to have to have 35 percent to 40 percent cost saves."

Yes, in those situations jobs would be lost. But, according to Henson, "I think the market understood, the acquired understood, that we would take a wholesome approach, as wholesome an approach as one could with the employee base. . . . Social issues get in the way if you don't have a culture that focuses on doing the right thing." And when social issues *don't* get in the way, everybody wins. According to Henson, because BB&T was a trusted acquirer, there were many acquisitions when other banks without a well-trusted value system were willing to pay more money, but BB&T was the one that got the deal.

Finally, there is one more meaning of justice for BB&T, perhaps a somewhat special meaning considering that it operates entirely in the Southern United States. The BB&T philosophy's section on justice states unequivocally, "At BB&T, we do not discriminate based on nonessentials such as race, sex, nationality, etc."

In today's politically correct business climate, how refreshing to see BB&T characterize race, sex, and nationality—which have become obsessions in the workplace and everywhere else—as "nonessentials."

So what's "essential" at BB&T? No politically correct compromise here: "We do discriminate based on competency, performance, and character. We consciously reject egalitarianism and collectivism."

Value #8: Pride

Ayn Rand's most admired philosopher was Aristotle, and Aristotle's most admired virtue was pride:

> Pride, then, seems to be a sort of crown of the virtues; for it makes them more powerful, and it is not found without them. Therefore it is hard to be truly proud; for it is impossible without nobility and goodness of character.[18]

Note well that the bank's value of pride is not talking about arrogance. Aristotle would have called that "hubris," about which he said:

> As for the pleasure in hubris, its cause is this: men think that by ill-treating others they make their own superiority the greater.[19]

Or as Allison puts it, pride is "the greatest of all virtues, because to have it you had to have all the others."[20] He wants BB&T to be proud of its employees, and every employee to be proud of BB&T. "This requires that the company and its employees live the values consistently. "

Value #9: Self-Esteem

At first blush, self-esteem may seem to be the same thing as pride. But it's not quite the same. In the BB&T philosophy, pride is what you earn by living your values, and self-esteem is what you earn by doing excellent work.

So the BB&T philosophy is clear that employees are expected to work hard for the company. Again, there is nothing politically correct about it: "If you do not want to work hard, work somewhere else."

Value #10: Teamwork

After celebrating the intensely individual values of pride and self-esteem, it may seem strange—even a bit of a compromise—for BB&T to talk about teamwork. But there's nothing in the Randian worldview of intense individualism that says that individuals can't work together.

Quite the contrary. The best teams are made up of proud individuals brimming with self-esteem. Think about it: Who would you rather have on *your* team? Winners who have earned their pride and self-esteem, and who can help you become a winner, too? Or would you prefer losers with no pride and no self-esteem?

The answer to that question may say a lot about whether *you* have pride and self-esteem.

The false paradox of individualism on the one hand and teamwork on the other ties into Ayn Rand's concept of "the virtue of selfishness." In her celebrated and reviled essay of the same name, she answers the question most often hurled at her by her critics:

> "Why do you use the word 'selfishness' to denote virtuous qualities of character, when that word antagonizes so many people to whom it does not mean the things you mean?"
>
> To those who ask it, my answer is: "For the same reason that makes you afraid of it."[21]

Allison, being a businessman first and a philosopher second—unlike Rand, who was a philosopher only—uses less provocative language, more eager to persuade than to rebuke. He talks about pride, self-esteem, and teamwork, but these are all tied together by the idea of self-interest, or "selfishness" if you insist.

In the language of Rand's hero John Galt, the idea is that "By the grace of reality and the nature of life, man—every man—is an end in himself and lives for his own sake, and the achievement of his own happiness is his highest moral purpose."

This means that BB&T's employees don't exist to serve its shareholders, and its shareholders don't exist to provide a living for its employees. Together, the shareholders and the employees don't exist for Barney Frank to provide housing to people who can't afford it. The shareholders and the employees, each individual among them, exists for his or her own sake.

So when they come together as a team—the shareholders committing their capital and their risk, the employees committing their time—it is a voluntary arrangement to mutual gain. It's Allison's "trader principle."

When Galt says "by the grace of reality," what he means is that no other arrangement is really possible. Any other arrangement, one in which people did not exist for their own sakes, would mean that someone was being made to do something against his or her will. Such arrangements are no better than (indeed no different than) "might makes right." And in reality they are inescapably a formula for savagery.

Arrangements *not* based on "selfishness"—that is, not based on pride and self-esteem—can only be based on some degree or form of slavery. "Selfishness" in Rand's sense is a synonym for "self-determination," for "freedom."

Applied to a business like BB&T, a business dedicated to attracting people who are unashamedly proud of themselves and possessed of great self-esteem, and interested in trading their skills with others like them, it's a synonym for "success."

Do pride, self-esteem, and teamwork—people coming together for their own sakes—mean that it would be wrong to be charitable?

Hardly. Allison and BB&T are big boosters of the United Way. Allison says it's in his own self-interest: "I wouldn't want to live in the kind of community that would exist if there weren't a United Way."[22] And he doesn't think his own admitted self-interest makes his charity any less charitable. He says, "Because I believe it's in my own self-interest, I give more, and I give more consistently."

At the same time, Allison is very clear that "charity is secondary." He says, "Producing is more important than giving away, because you have to produce before you can give away."[23]

He sees what extremely wealthy men like Microsoft founder Bill Gates (whom we meet in Chapter 5, "The Persecuted Titan") and mega-investor Warren Buffett have done, giving away much of their great fortunes to charity—and in the case of Gates, devoting his considerable intellect to the administration of that charity. Allison says, "Gates's great contribution was creating Microsoft, and the world is worse off that he's not focusing on making Microsoft better. What if Thomas Edison had quit when he was Bill Gates's age? What would we have lost?"[24]

We'll see. Maybe Gates's genius—and his money—really will solve some of the world's problems. Allison is skeptical. "Because of comparative advantage, what he was special at was computers, not solving poverty in Africa, but maybe he'll get lucky."[25]

In Defense of Capitalism

After John Allison signed the document surrendering substantial control of BB&T to the whims of the federal government, after he put down the pen, after he rode down the elevator from the top floor of the tall black building in Winston-Salem and walked into the chilly November night—after he walked away from the world—where did he go, and what did he do?

Rand's hero John Galt, the man who walked away from the world, went to Galt's Gulch, hidden in the mountains of Colorado, and recruited other great minds to join him on strike against the looters, the power seekers, and the altruists. Allison hasn't exactly done *that*, but in his own affable Southern way, he's done something almost as subversive.

Instead of Galt's mountain fastness, Allison can be found on Wake Forest University's leafy campus, in a small office crammed with books by and about Ayn Rand, teaching courses in leadership and directing a growing campaign to teach the morality of capitalism in America's colleges. Like Galt, he's spreading the word.

It started when he was still at BB&T. He recalls, "For years, banks have been big contributors to community projects. It's kind of expected in the business, and it's probably a legitimate part of the business, because a lot of our clients are involved in stuff and those kinds of things. . . . Our focus . . . has always been on education. So we were a pretty big contributor to universities."

Which makes BB&T no different than any other bank. But John Allison is very different from other bank CEOs—he's a Randian. So when he asked himself, "What is the issue that maybe we could have a big impact on?" there was just one possible answer: "Capitalism."

Allison wasn't interested in helping universities teach economics. He was interested in helping universities teach *the morality of capitalism*—the philosophy underlying it, and the reasons why it is the only way of arranging economic affairs that is consistent with human freedom.

"There's really no economic argument against capitalism," Allison says. "We're just losing the ethical fight. . . . And ethics always trumps economics." In other words, no matter what heights of wealth and advancement capitalism leads the world to, it seems there's always somebody complaining about the brutality of its innate competitiveness or the unfairness of the inequality it produces. So the system that abolished slavery from the face of the earth and makes it possible for 7 billion souls to live on it is nevertheless always under political attack.

"So we've got to have an ethical fight," decided Allison. "And of course, based on my beliefs, I said, well, we've got to get Rand into the fight."

But that wouldn't be easy. Rand considered herself a serious philosopher, but she's scarcely taught in university philosophy departments. Perhaps it's because she chose to express her philosophy in accessible popular novels rather than in impenetrable textbooks. Or perhaps it's because she has always been seen as a political conservative, something not exactly embraced by today's liberal-dominated college faculties.

"Rand has obviously been consciously not included," Allison claims. "Academics, they don't want her in. They're scared of her, in my opinion. She's threatening."

So Allison decided to build an entirely new academic initiative for the advancement of the morality of capitalism, with Ayn Rand at its heart—just as decades earlier he had set out to build a banking empire the same way. "We started working with a number of universities," he recalls. "Our first program was at Duke and we did something at Carolina. They'd agree to require *Atlas Shrugged*, and we'd say, okay. If they want to teach it and say it's stupid, that's fine. I'll let the students read it and make their own judgments."

Building an education revolution takes time, just like building a bank did. "We're now up to 60 programs," Allison says, beaming. "Almost all of the major universities in our footprint now, and lots of other colleges and universities. . . . And I get really positive feedback about this. I have talked to numerous students who have said, 'Man, this course changed my whole worldview, and I am a better human being for it.'"

John Allison also has a long list of Randian recommendations for repairing the American economy in the aftermath of the mortgage crisis that nearly destroyed it.

He'd like to see the Federal Reserve stripped of its limitless powers to print money, and return to an objective standard of monetary value such as gold. He'd like to see the tax code transformed so that consumption, not investment, is taxed. He'd like to see Social Security, Medicare, and education privatized. He'd like to see immigration liberalized so that the best and the brightest can come to the United States. He'd like to see banks given more stringent capital requirements, and have them return to more traditional forms of mortgage lending.[26]

Most important, he wants to change the culture. He wants the attacks on capitalism to stop, for capitalism to be embraced as the most effective and the most moral system of economic organization. And it's to that most important objective that he's devoting his attention now, through his sponsorship of university programs on the morality of capitalism.

Can he win? Can capitalism win? Can Ayn Rand's ideas win? At least for Allison, they're winning the war on the home front. He says, "My son read a lot of Objectivist stuff, seemed to agree with it, went away to college, and became very down on Objectivism. Then he graduated from college and took a couple months after he graduated, reread all the stuff, and said, 'Wow!' He said, 'You know, Rand's right.'"

So perhaps there's hope. Maybe someday Allison will return from academia to the world and, like John Galt, raise his hand over the desolate earth and trace in space the sign of the dollar.

Chapter 4

The Parasite

Angelo Mozilo as James Taggart, the businessman who corrupted government and nearly wrecked the U.S. economy

The controlling stock of Taggart Transcontinental was left to James Taggart. . . . Dagny had expected the Board of Directors to elect him. . . . They talked about his gift of "making railroads popular," his "good press," his "Washington ability." He seemed unusually skillful at obtaining favors from the Legislature.

—Atlas Shrugged

Who is James Taggart?

James Taggart is one of the key antagonists in *Atlas Shrugged*, a corrupt businessman who, knowing that he lacks the skills required for legitimate success, uses political influence to build his business, the great railroad Taggart Transcontinental. Every corrupt move by Taggart sets in motion unintended consequences that actually damage the railroad and spill over into the rest of the economy.

(Continued)

Taggart's sister Dagny, a businesswoman whose sparkling competence is set in stark contrast to her brother's impotence, is constantly scrambling to undo the damage he causes. Whenever Dagny's efforts succeed, James takes credit for them.

As Taggart's web of corruption becomes increasingly unsustainable, he marries a naive shopgirl who is awed by his apparent business success. She eventually learns the truth about him, and as their marriage deteriorates, she seeks comfort from Dagny. In one of the book's most poignant moments, the heartbroken girl tells Dagny, "But you see, I married Jim because I . . . I thought he was *you*."

James Taggart is Ayn Rand's deepest exploration of the mental state underpinning evil. She argues that her own philosophy of self-interest is rooted in the objective survival requirements of man's life on earth as a thinking being. The opposing philosophy of collectivism and altruism undermines man's ability to live, and those who pursue it implicitly advocate the only egalitarian state possible—death. At the climax of *Atlas Shrugged*, Taggart consciously realizes for the first time that his life has been dedicated to the pursuit of death, and he is driven to madness.

As he sat down at the conference table for Countrywide Financial's quarterly earnings call on July 24, 2007, beads of sweat formed under CEO Angelo Mozilo's starched French collar. It wasn't the 90-degree heat outside the window of Countrywide's Calabasas, California, headquarters that wrung perspiration from his pores, but rather the agonizing prospect of what he was about to do.

He was about to lie to his shareholders and to the world. He knew he was looking at imminent ruin, and he knew that the moment he admitted it, that very admission would make that ruin actually happen. So Mozilo sweated while he prepared himself to say whatever he had to say to keep his multibillion-dollar house of cards from collapsing for at least another couple of weeks.

What he didn't know then was that the collapse of Countrywide was about to trigger a global near-depression, as the subprime credit bubble Mozilo did so much to create—by manipulating for decades the power of government for private gain—was to suddenly burst.

Mozilo is the man Ayn Rand warned us against exactly 50 years before that fateful 2007 earnings call: the corrupt businessman who forges an unholy alliance between capitalism and government. Rand's literary template for Mozilo is James Taggart, the principle villain of *Atlas Shrugged*.

Taggart, the heir to a railroad fortune, is ambitious—hungry for power, hungry for approbation. But he lacks the energy or ability to really run or grow the railroad. So he cultivates connections in government, and uses their power to obtain subsidies for his railroad and to destroy his competitors—all the while spouting high-minded rationales based on public service. By the end of *Atlas Shrugged*, Taggart's corruption and all its unintended consequences have nearly destroyed the entire U.S. economy.

Unlike Taggart, Mozilo didn't look the part of the corporate titan. With his perma-tan face framed by platinum hair, loud pinstriped suit, flashy tie, and gleaming extra-white Guy Smiley grin, Mozilo looked more like a goodfella turned daytime game show host than the head of a publicly traded company. In truth, this son of a Bronx butcher presided over the nation's largest mortgage lender, built from a two-man start-up at his partner's kitchen table decades ago.

Through the years he had positioned himself as the consummate front man of the company, the guy's guy, able to move deftly in the right circles of influence well above his lowly origins. His feelings of inferiority drove him to fight past the old-money club and eventually beat those pretentious old-school mortgage bankers at their own game. "I run into these guys on Wall Street all the time who think they're something special because they went to Ivy League schools," he told the *New York Times*; "it bothered me when I was younger—their snobbery and their looking down on us."[1]

If you didn't look closely, you could admire Mozilo's rags-to-riches story. But the reality is that competing against the well-equipped armies of traditional bankers on the sunlit field of open competition was too daunting a prospect for this squire with dreams of becoming king. Instead of facing them head-on, he'd operate from the dim shadows cast by government-induced market distortions and conduct his business through favoritism and political pull supplemented with a healthy dose of outright deceit.

Driven by a no-holds-barred marketing campaign and governmental lobbying effort, he'd turn a modest-margin business with a consumer mind share on par with a municipal utility into a popular fad with national brand-name recognition. Countrywide's ticker symbol, CFC, would become known at one point as the "23,000% Stock"[2] for a two-decade run of 30 percent average annual gains.

Mozilo was a key architect of the U.S. housing bubble — or maybe more accurately, a key arsonist whose government-subsidized subprime mortgages were the accelerant to what turned out to be a housing and credit conflagration. All along the way he'd rationalize his actions in altruistic terms of social progress. "I gave a lot of people the opportunity to realize the American dream"[3] was his typical refrain. "Our unifying mission is to close the gap in minority homeownership"[4] was another of his do-gooder mantras. All the while, his real aim was to skim as much vigorish as possible from high-risk loans that had little if anything to do with supporting actual home ownership.

The chief co-conspirator in Mozilo's grand scheme was a government-sponsored enterprise (GSE) known as Fannie Mae (it, in turn, was motivated by a government co-conspirator, Barney Frank, whom we'll meet in Chapter 6, "The Central Planner"). By buying Mozilo's risky and sometimes fraudulent mortgages and thus freeing up Countrywide's capital so it could solicit even more business, Fannie supplied the rocket fuel that helped Mozilo blast Countrywide from obscurity past Citigroup and Wells Fargo to the top of the mortgage heap. "If it wasn't for them," Mozilo said of Fannie, "Wells [Fargo] knows they'd have us."[5]

Why did Fannie play along? Simply because Fannie's government bureaucrats funneled tens of millions of these subsidized dollars into their own pockets in the form of outlandish salaries and incentive bonuses.[6] "These are the most successful corporate hermaphrodites in world history," consumer advocate Ralph Nader said of Fannie Mae and the other GSEs. "[They] report massive profits, provide their top executives with huge compensation packages and laugh all the way to the bank with government guarantees. It's a paradigm of how to influence Washington."[7]

Like James Taggart, Mozilo skillfully cultivated his buddies in Washington; *that's* the one thing he was actually good at, if not downright brilliant. To make sure politicians and regulators didn't raise an eyebrow at the deteriorating credit quality of Mozilo's loans purchased by the agencies under their control, he'd buy off senators, congressmen, congressional staffers, lobbyists, local politicians, home builders, and law enforcement officials with sweetheart VIP mortgage deals under a program known as the Friends of Angelo. "Countrywide's VIP loan program was a tool with which the company built its relationships with Members of Congress and Congressional staff," read a Staff Report from the U.S. House of Representatives Committee on Oversight and Government Reform.[8] "It was also a tool it used to protect its relationship with Fannie Mae."

Back in Calabasas, he handpicked his board of directors, just like Taggart did, building what amounted to a personally controlled audience of dutiful admirers. Business qualifications? Don't ask—Countrywide's board included a former basketball star with nary a dribble of banking experience on his stats sheet. It was just a puppet show to provide the appearance of corporate governance and oversight. "When we had to fill a spot, I just took on the responsibility of trying to find someone" is how Mozilo explained his board makeup. "It started from me and therefore it was difficult for the board to say 'We don't like him.'"[9]

When bankers or the press pushed for GSE reform, Mozilo would rise to their defense as an "independent" industry leader operating for the social good of home ownership. "America has the world's highest rate of homeownership because we're the only country that has a Fannie or Freddie," he'd cry out to the *New York Times*. "Nobody wins if they're damaged or impeded. Housing is the only thing driving the economy right now."[10] When Jack Kemp, George H.W. Bush's Department of Housing and Urban Renewal (HUD) secretary, tried to scale back some government assistance for the mortgage market in 1990, Mozilo publicly denounced him as "the worst person who could possibly have been put in that position."[11]

For Mozilo, subprime lending, which began as a competitive enterprise to tap an underserved market for home financing, had devolved into a mere financial scheme. He had become the street dealer of high-risk loans sponsored by a pseudo-government kingpin who packaged and resold them in disguise, complete with a heavy guarantee unwittingly lashed to the backs of the American taxpayer. The entire cabal of players, from the home builders to the Realtors to the industry lobbyists to Mozilo and Countrywide itself, took a cut. As long as the money kept flowing, all was good in the family.

But Mozilo was sweating before that 2007 earnings conference call because the strings of personal favors done and influence purchased through the years had spun into a tangled web that now threatened to strangle him. He must have felt like James Taggart did when his railroad was falling apart, and his sister Dagny—the sparklingly competent businesswoman who actually ran the railroad—warned him, "I have no idea what sort of games you're tangled in, you and your Board of Directors. I don't know how many ends you're playing against the middle, or against one another, or how many pretenses you have to keep up in how many opposite directions."

But there was a key difference. In *Atlas Shrugged*, Dagny's brilliance saved Taggart from himself, over and over. In 2007, no one could save Angelo Mozilo. During the prior year, Mozilo had become acutely aware that his reckless underwriting and market-share-at-any-cost strategy had generated a landfill of decomposing loans. "We have no way, with any reasonable certainty, to assess the real risk of holding these loans on our balance sheet," he wrote behind the shroud of internal corporate e-mail in the middle of 2006.[12] The assets, he said, were "toxic," "poison," and "the most dangerous product in existence." As for the prospects of his company, he privately acknowledged, "The bottom line is that we are flying blind."[13]

Like a rat in a trap, for this man who had held tight to his founder's shares since the very inception of his company decades before, the only priority was to get out. From November 2006 through August 2007, Mozilo exercised over 5.1 million stock options and sold the underlying shares for total proceeds of over $139 million.[14] He had done a monumental job of secreting his gold out of the treasury, but as he sat there sweating in July 2007, ready to face his stakeholders, he wasn't quite free and clear yet.

He knew that any pullback in business or acknowledgment of risk to the markets would expose his house of cards for what it was, and bury his remaining fortune under a crush of rubble. In 2006 Mozilo had written about his concern that a "reputational event," as he euphemistically called it, could destroy Countrywide's ability to offload its poison onto a marketplace tricked into thinking it was good medicine.[15] All he needed was a few more months. He had to hide the truth under a facade of business as usual. Now, on the conference call in front of hundreds of analysts and members of the media, Angelo Mozilo was about to pull off the snow job of his life—a con that would make the slickest grifter blush.

"We remain optimistic at the long-term future growth prospects and profitability of the Company," he began on a high note. "We believe that the Company is well positioned to capitalize on opportunities during this transitional period in the mortgage business, which we believe will enhance the Company's long-term earnings growth prospects,"[16] he assured the audience.

When asked point-blank by an analyst how many shares of stock he currently held, Mozilo acted like a kid caught with his hand in the cookie jar. "I don't know the answer to that question," he stammered. "I own, including options—I think it's around 11 million, 12 million, something like that," all the while knowing he held a dwindling stake of just a few million shares after a blistering selling spree during the prior nine months. (See Figure 4.1.)

What about downside risks to current shareholders? "There is a limit to this in terms of our total," Mozilo stated authoritatively. "The total residual on our balance sheet is about $400 million. If everything collapsed, that would be the extent of our residual exposure."[17] In hindsight, $400 million would have been a gift, a mere rounding error in the eventual collapse of his own creation that Mozilo knew was looming.

Just three weeks later, on August 16, Countrywide announced that it would tap its entire $11.5 billion line of credit just to meet immediate cash demands.[18] Moody's immediately downgraded the company's senior debt to one notch above junk status, warning that further deterioration was imminent.[19] Countrywide shares took their largest drop ever, surpassing even the losses borne during the crash of 1987. The same stock that Mozilo had pumped up to analysts three weeks earlier (while furiously dumping the day before at $34.22 per share) fell to the midteens.

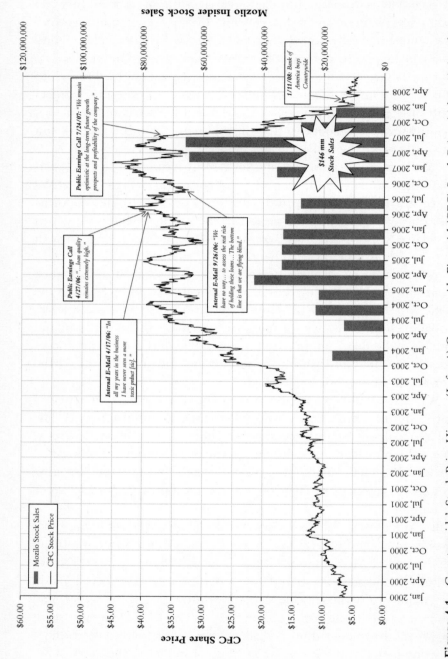

Figure 4.1 Countrywide's Stock Price History. (*Left axis*) Countrywide Financial (CFC) Stock Price; (*right axis*) Angelo Mozilo Insider Stock Sales (Value in $ Millions)

SOURCE: United States Securities and Exchange Commission Form 4 filings

Global stock markets went into a tailspin. Credit markets across the world froze. The Federal Reserve injected $62 billion in reserves into the market that week to boost liquidity.[20] Then, on Thursday, August 17, the day after Countrywide's meltdown, the Fed cut the discount rate by half a percentage point to 5.75 percent from 6.25 percent.[21] Analysts suggested bankruptcy was possible and hinted at the prospect of a worldwide recession.

Little did they know. . . .

The Birth of Countrywide

James Taggart got his inferiority complex from being born rich, and unworthy of his fortune. Angelo Mozilo got his by being born to humble circumstances, but without any humility. He was born to immigrant parents in a Bronx rental flat in 1938. As he was growing up, his father encouraged him to follow his footsteps into the butcher's trade, but Angelo and his mother had bigger plans. At the age of 14, his uncle helped him break into the white-collar world by arranging a job for the scrappy youngster as a messenger for a small Manhattan mortgage company. It was there that he would earn enough to pay his way through college at Fordham University. In the process, he'd rotate through all the company's departments, learning the business from the ground up.[22]

In 1960, the year he graduated from college, his employer merged with the larger United Mortgage Servicing Company, headed by a man named David Loeb. Although 15 years his senior and the conservative antithesis to Mozilo's pitchman style, Loeb would become a mentor and partner to his young protégé.

When United Mortgage was acquired in 1968, Mozilo and Loeb set out to start a business of their own. Like Taggart, Mozilo was spurred on as much by malice as by a desire to build. "I think it was vengeance," Mozilo posited years later as his prime motivation for launching the new company. "We ran into tremendous problems with these people and were essentially forced out," he said about the conglomerate that swallowed up his lifelong employer. "So, naturally, we were out to get them."[23]

Mozilo sank his life savings of $25,000 into the venture and secured a personal bank loan for $75,000 more. Whatever else may be said about him, at least this man who conned so many Americans into going so deeply in debt wasn't afraid to get in hock up to his eyeballs personally. Loeb invested another $300,000, and with a third partner they capitalized themselves as a private company with a total of $500,000. Just nine months later, in 1969, Mozilo and Loeb took the company public. They failed to raise the $3 million in new capital they had hoped for, but at least they got a couple of status symbols: a ticker symbol and a board of directors.[24]

Though they weren't the first nonbank mortgage company, they were the most ambitious. While others in their sector were typically small local shops, Loeb and Mozilo had national aspirations. They would dub their new creation "Countrywide" to remind them daily of the prominence they hoped to achieve.

The going was tough at first. Without a banking charter, Countrywide was prohibited from taking deposits and found itself completely dependent on outside lines of credit to fund its loans. Once these credit lines were fully tapped, Countrywide had to sell the loans off of its balance sheet to generate more lending capacity. But at that early stage in the development of the mortgage market, they could sell only a small number of the mortgages that qualified for government insurance, namely Federal Housing Authority (FHA) or Veterans Administration (VA) loans.

Then, in 1970, Congress unwittingly gave the company a lifesaving jolt by allowing federal Fannie Mae to buy so-called conventional non-FHA or VA loans from private originators, and back them with an implicit government guarantee. The loans had to conform to a strict set of standards, including a borrower's credit score, ability to repay, and loan-to-value (LTV) ratio. Despite these conservative restrictions, this single legislative change unleashed a flood of new capital for mortgage companies like Countrywide desperate to find willing buyers for the loans they originated.

In just a few years, nonbank mortgage companies like Countrywide began to overtake the commercial banks. The market share of mortgage originators like Countrywide went from near zero to 19 percent by the end of the 1980s. By 1993, they accounted for more than half of the mortgage business done in the country. In 1990, Countrywide wrote $3.6 billion of mortgages, reaping revenues of $104 million. It was still a tiny drop in the $3.4 trillion ocean of U.S. mortgage debt outstanding that year, but Countrywide was now definitely on the map.

The Loeb Years

While Mozilo pushed relentlessly for business expansion and drove for market share with entrepreneurial zeal, David Loeb, his partner and Countrywide chairman, remained largely behind the scenes, managing risk and acting as a sober check on Angelo's hyperactive run at market dominance.[25] Instead of making high-risk loans for high fees, Loeb steered the ship with a steady hand, focusing on high credit quality coupled with efficient operations.

For years, mortgage lending at Countrywide was a plain-vanilla affair. Up to 95 percent of the loans originated by the company were basic fixed-rate obligations. The company held its costs of servicing a loan to about one-third below the industry average by rolling out optical scanning equipment and automated systems that slashed manual paperwork. All of its nationwide branches were simple, low-overhead operations consisting of one loan officer and two assistants.

Even more unusual, the loan officers all earned a fixed salary instead of the industry-standard commission. Performance bonuses were based not on sales volume irrespective of the loan's soundness, but on the number of borrower delinquencies. If branch loan officers signed up too many loans that defaulted, they'd be fired. This operating discipline cost Countrywide business at times, but it also helped keep the company's delinquency rate below the national average. From 1985 through 1989, the portion of Countrywide's loans that were over 90 days past due on their payments was only 0.7 percent, compared with national averages prepared by the Mortgage Bankers Association of over 0.9 percent.[26] Yes, as hard as it may be to believe today, Countrywide was once a model of probity—at least under the watchful eye of David Loeb.

Mozilo was unsatisfied. Among the staff, his motto was "We don't execute, we don't eat." He once told a Countrywide executive, "If you ever stop trying to make your division the biggest and the best, that's the day you die."[27] The problem wasn't that he pushed his people hard. The problem was that he pushed the boundaries whenever Loeb didn't stop him.

In the 1980s, tax law changes eliminated the deductibility of interest payments on normal consumer debt like credit cards and auto loans, while mortgage interest remained tax-deductible. With his gift for slick sales angles, Mozilo realized that he could use this new asymmetry in the tax law to get people to favor deductible mortgage borrowing over other nondeductible forms of borrowing.

Thus was born the idea that one's home is not just a residence, not even an investment—but a source of equity to borrow against, a piggy bank, an ATM. With Countrywide's help, homeowners could extract wealth from their homes by borrowing to pay for everything from investing in junior's college education to outright consumption of vacations, cars, boats, large-screen TVs, or anything else. Thanks in large part to Mozilo's marketing and spurred on by declining interest rates, "refi" would enter the popular vernacular.

In 1992, refinancings accounted for 58 percent of Countrywide's business. In 1994 they accounted for a whopping 75 percent. In many ways the refinancing boom was the result of a brilliant innovation that took advantage of a tax asymmetry and arguably created more liquidity in the overall economy. From one perspective, this was simply capitalism at work—adapting to the reality of a government-induced fiscal distortion. In the real world where such distortions exist, rational self-interest calls for the productive innovation required to adapt.

But in *Atlas Shrugged* we see that the heroes are doing something better than this—they are creating value *de novo*. It is the villains like James Taggart and his steel tycoon crony Orren Boyle who profit from adaptation—and who corrupt government specifically to create the distortions that they can adapt to, dressing up their ambitions with altruistic rhetoric. At this point Mozilo's days of corrupting government were still in the future, but he was already limbering up his rhetoric. Relentless pushing of refi loans was cloaked in high-minded collectivist talk about the virtues of home ownership. He was already setting the stage for the next phase of his shady dealings, one that required the active assistance of the government using the banner of home ownership to shroud their corrupt arrangements.

In the meantime, to generate even more deal flow, Mozilo had another big idea. Looking at Countrywide's already low-cost branch structure, he thought he could do even better. Rather than pay fixed salaries and overhead to staff loan officers in company branches, he pushed Countrywide to begin using independent mortgage brokers to originate loans. Usually these were refugees from the defunct savings and loan industry, local operators who already knew the grassroots markets and Realtors. Even better, they worked on 100 percent commission. If they didn't produce, they didn't cost Countrywide a dime.

Loeb was decidedly against his young partner's approach. Brokers had no skin in the game. Once they passed the loan off to Countrywide and collected their fee, there was no further responsibility or recourse back to the originator. "They're crooks," Loeb said about brokers, with a reputation for falsifying documents for the sake of commissions. Mozilo prevailed, however, and the seeds were sown. "I think it's going to be a big mistake"[28] was Loeb's final summation. He would prove to be dead right.

But thanks to Mozilo, the U.S. housing market would turn out to be just plain dead.

Unholy Alliance with Fannie

Longtime Democratic politico James "Jim" Johnson was named chairman and CEO of Fannie Mae in 1991. Sensing an opportunity to use his new position for personal enrichment far in excess of his previous go-around in Washington as Vice President Walter Mondale's executive assistant, he lost no time going on the road to schmooze with potential collaborators.

Fannie's West Coast office was strategically located just across the street from Countrywide's headquarters, where it babysat an already significant volume of conforming loans.[29] Johnson wanted even more volume to catapult his government-wage public utility into financial stardom complete with Wall Street–style bonuses for senior executives like himself.

It didn't take long for Jim Johnson to realize that Mozilo "was the guy," said one of Johnson's aides. "When Jim realized how much volume Countrywide was taking down, especially in California, he made it his mission to get to know Angelo," said the anonymous aide. "Jim knew that he had to do everything he could to make Angelo think, 'I'm his best friend.' If Jim was traveling to the West Coast he'd say, 'We need to call Angelo and set up a golf game.' "[30]

As much as Johnson needed loan volume from Mozilo, Countrywide needed Fannie's flow of cheap, government-subsidized cash to keep its loan machine humming. In *Atlas Shrugged*, James Taggart conspired with government officials and other corrupt businessmen in a dark saloon designed to look like a dank cave. Mozilo and Johnson and their cronies did it a little differently: playing golf together, flying around on Countrywide's corporate jet, and watching plays from box seats at the Kennedy Center. But the result was the same—they concocted the beginnings of a symbiotic relationship based not on value-added business, but on gaming the system through politics and pull.

As if to cement this unholy alliance, in 1999 Fannie Mae reached a "strategic agreement" with Countrywide wherein Mozilo would sell certain Countrywide loans exclusively to Fannie. In exchange, Fannie agreed to lower its guarantee fee on Countrywide loans. The relationship tacitly amounted to a noncompete agreement, designed to lock Fannie's sister company Freddie Mac out of the market for Countrywide's production. But it was so much more. By striking a chummy deal with Countrywide, Johnson had bought himself a pit bull for his front yard. Feeding and sheltering the beast ensured fiercely loyal protection against any who might try to intrude on their conspiratorial collaborations. Put more tartly, Mozilo said that when Fannie catches a cold, "I catch the fucking flu."[31]

To add a sweetener to the already saccharine deal, during the very time Countrywide was negotiating with its governmental benefactor, Mozilo offered and personally approved the first so-called VIP loans to employees of Fannie Mae. All told, Mozilo would make over 150 loans to Fannie employees granting below-market interest rates, reduced fees, or manual overrides to approve loans to buyers who would not have qualified under standard programs. Johnson alone would receive more than $10 million worth.[32] The value to the borrower often represented hundreds of thousands of dollars over the life of the loan.

If that kind of money had been handed to a politician in cash, there'd be just one word for it: bribe.

It's not like Johnson needed the money. Yes, government pay is typically limited at the top, even for officials who run enormous agencies. The postmaster general, for example, running an agency with more than 700,000 employees and more than $65 billion in revenue, was paid a flat $175,000 a year during the time Johnson presided at Fannie.[33] But during 1998, the last full year of Johnson's tenure at Fannie Mae, he would receive $21 million in compensation.

That same year, Johnson also improperly deferred $200 million in corporate expenses to ensure that he and his subordinates received their full annual bonuses. Johnson himself received an additional $2 million in bonus money as a result. His successor, Franklin Raines, collected $1.1 million in undeserved compensation. Without Johnson cooking the books, bonuses that year would have been exactly zero.[34]

According to the *Washington Post*, Fannie Mae had become a place where former government officials and others with good political connections could go to make millions of dollars. Franklin Raines was about to get his share, and then some.[35]

Slide into Subprime

When David Loeb retired from Countrywide in 2000 and died a few years later in 2003, there was nobody left to hold back the scheming Mozilo. "With Countrywide, you could see there was a cultural change when it was David and Angelo to when it was just Angelo," said Josh Rosner, a mortgage securities expert at independent research firm Graham Fisher in New York. "Before David died, he seemed to recognize the company's future was predicated on taking risks he wasn't comfortable with."[36]

In the hypercompetitive mortgage brokerage market of the housing boom era, borrowers with solid credit and plenty of income were already saturated with plain-vanilla, low-interest loans. The only way to gain market share was to lower lending standards and tap the remaining higher-risk population. But once he'd originated them, how could

Countrywide sell these riskier loans off in the vast volumes Mozilo sought? The free market would place a natural cap on the amount of risk investors were willing to take on at any given price, and that price wasn't cheap enough for him to realize the riches he dreamed of.

For businessmen like Mozilo or Taggart, if the free market won't play along, then it's time to get the government involved. The timing was perfect.

Franklin Raines, Johnson's successor at Fannie Mae, was seeking new ways of transforming the GSE from a boring but stable financial institution dedicated to making homes more affordable into a risky venture that exploited its special government status for Raines's personal profit. Improved earnings meant multimillion-dollar bonuses for executives, but Fannie was effectively locked out of the most lucrative loans for the very reason that they were too risky. Or were they? Like Taggart and his fellow parasites in *Atlas Shrugged*, Mozilo and Raines together would concoct a backroom scheme to corrupt the markets and trick the nation into backing the risks they took, all the while blathering about the noble-sounding virtue of social equality.

"Everybody wins if we can increase minority homeownership, so together we're taking on the challenge of getting more people into homes,"[37] Mozilo stated in living color on a full page in Fannie Mae's 2003 annual report, pictured wearing a flamboyant black chalk-striped suit and a garish yellow tie that made him look more like a Prohibition-era rumrunner than a mortgage banker. The report continued,

> Fannie Mae shares this vision, and together we're working harder than ever before to make homeownership accessible to more Americans. . . . Right now only 50 percent of minority families own homes. The task for companies like Countrywide is moving it from 50 percent to 80 percent. . . . As Mozilo notes, "You can't quantify the emotional impact of home ownership in people's lives." So as long as there is a gap in minority and non-minority homeownership rates, Fannie Mae and Countrywide will continue to make sure all Americans have the chance to realize the dream of homeownership.

These are absolutely ludicrous statements. Never mind minorities—achieving Mozilo's goal of 80 percent home ownership meant that a household earning $15,000 per year[38] (that's just $288 a week, regardless of the color of your skin) would own a home with all of the financial responsibilities for mortgage payments, insurance, property taxes, and upkeep. But astonishingly, no one in a position of power called Mozilo or Fannie Mae out. No member of Congress, no shareholder, and no member of the respective boards of directors challenged the premise of this socially noble-sounding rhetoric.

Mozilo had devised a deviously brilliant formula. Under the cultural creep of hypersensitive political correctness, who could possibly question a statement with the word *minority* in it without coming across as racist? Who could question home ownership for all without seeming elitist? But home ownership was not Mozilo's or Raines's real goal; it was a mere smokescreen to shroud the ill-gotten gains of a few perpetrating a grand fraud on the American people. In rich irony, the worst of the fraud would be perpetuated on the most vulnerable: the low-income minorities that Countrywide and Fannie claimed were the beneficiaries of their noble policies and programs.

"Act now to make every month National Homeownership Month,"[39] Mozilo urged in *Mortgage Banking* magazine. Washington politicians, many already in the pocket of Countrywide as part of his VIP lending program, heeded the call.

Under pressure that Mozilo and Raines helped create, the Clinton administration ordered Fannie Mae to increase home ownership rates among low-income borrowers. To comply with the mandate, Raines lowered his company's lending standards to include "individuals whose credit is generally not good enough to qualify for conventional loans."[40]

Fannie Mae starting buying up risky subprime and Alt-A loans at an accelerating pace to meet its ever-increasing government goals. Down payment requirements fell to 3 percent, then to zero. Fannie took risky loans and bundled them together with gilt-edged ones. Wall Street was glad to buy up these mortgage cocktails without even questioning the ingredients, because Fannie Mae was deemed a government-insured behemoth "too big to fail."[41]

Countrywide, for its part, had a field day. With a combination of high interest and big fees on shaky loans funded by cheap money from Fannie, Mozilo was driving a government-subsidized profit machine unwittingly backed by the American taxpayer. Whereas the profitability of a high-quality prime loan was less than one percentage point of the mortgage's value, subprime loans produced nearly quadruple the profit.[42] On some subprime loans that carried high prepayment penalties, Countrywide's profit margins could reach 15 percent of the loan value—$75,000 on a $500,000 mortgage.

To Beg or to Bribe?

Mozilo was also working every political angle he could find to corrupt the markets in his favor and protect his personal cash cow, Fannie Mae. Referrals of VIPs with the potential to influence legislation affecting Countrywide often came from Mozilo's man in Washington, Jimmie Williams, Countrywide's chief lobbyist. According to a former Countrywide managing director, Sydney Lenz, Williams and Countrywide's Washington guys routinely identified potential customers on Capitol Hill to "keep their edge," then actively offered to buy their influence with special Friends of Angelo loan deals.[43]

One beneficiary was Franklin Raines himself. According to a congressional investigation, when Raines refinanced his mortgage in June 2003, his assistant telephoned Countrywide on his behalf. According to the phone message, she stated that "per Angelo, Frank needs to refi." Countrywide gave him a full percentage point off of a million-dollar loan and waived other fees that, according to the *Wall Street Journal*, would have ordinarily cost Raines at least $10,000 at closing.[44] The loan also represented a $215,000 reduction in cost over the life of the loan—an outright kickback not available to regular customers such as, say, a butcher like Mozilo's father.

These weren't just one-off deals, either. Mozilo and his team took a systematic and analytic approach to buying political power, weighing the financial cost of the favor against the potential benefit of influence on legislation or regulation. In one case during 2002, the mayor of Billings, Montana, approached Jimmie Williams about canceling the mortgage insurance he was legally obligated to pay on his home loan. During an ensuing internal e-mail discussion, Lenz blatantly laid out the cost-benefit analysis for Williams.

I'm usually in favor of settling on the side of the borrower with political influence. However, in this case, I think the MI [mortgage insurance] payment for the life of the loan has the potential of being a greater number than the Mayor of Billings Montana['s] influence. Jimmie, since you work with the mayors, what's your opinion?[45]

Williams responded by reciting the mayor's credentials, mentioning his wife's role at the Democratic-leaning *New Republic* magazine and noting he "sits on the Advisory Board of the U.S. Conference of Mayors" and he "is also very likely to hit the speaking circuit." Ultimately the decision was made and issued via another e-mail.

Due to the Mayor's (and his wife's) potential influence and accessibility to media outlets and publications, offer him a refi and either give him a .25 credit toward the discount or a $500.00 credit toward closing costs. Either way, we're showing our good faith.[46]

Mozilo often priced the VIP loans himself and proudly made the specialized treatment known to the recipients through notes or business cards attached to their lending documents. While hundreds of potential benefactors were members of the Friends of Angelo club, particularly troubling were those with primary responsibility to determine how Fannie and Freddie would be administered. In addition to Raines and Johnson, recipients of these buy-offs included:

- **Senator Kent Conrad (D-ND)**, chairman of the Budget Committee and a member of the Finance Committee, arranged a $1.07 million refinance in 2004 for a mortgage on a vacation home in Bethany Beach, Delaware. Mozilo ordered "take off 1 point," noting, "make an exception due to the fact that the borrower is a senator,"[47] saving Conrad $10,700 up front, or $240,096 over 30 years.
- **Senator Christopher Dodd (D-CT)**, member of the Committee on Banking, Housing and Urban Affairs (elevated to Committee chairman in 2007), who saved approximately $75,000 by refinancing his home at a reduced rate.[48]
- **Senator John Edwards (D-NC)**, member of the Judiciary Committee, who was referred to the Friends of Angelo program

when trying to finance the purchase of a $3.8 million home in Georgetown.[49] "Edwards will probably be either the vice pres or pres candidate for the Democrats for 2004," Mozilo informed his VIP loan staff via e-mail. "Do whatever it takes to get it closed by the 23rd and call me for the pricing."[50]

- **Alphonso Jackson**, **secretary of Housing and Urban Development**, who received two loans through the VIP program, and whose daughter was referred to the VIP program by a Countrywide lobbyist. Jackson's second loan was for a $308,000 vacation home on a golf course in Hilton Head Island, South Carolina. Both of Jackson's loans included undisclosed discounts.[51]

- **Clinton Jones III**, **senior counsel of the House Financial Services Subcommittee on Housing and Community Opportunity**, who was referred for "specialized handling" to the Friends of Angelo program by a Countrywide lobbyist, resulting in ".5 off and no garbage fees." Countrywide's normal lending policies were manually overridden for Jones, who would not have ordinarily qualified for the loan he was given.[52]

- **Daniel H. Mudd, Fannie Mae CEO**, who succeeded Raines, received two mortgage loans for about $3 million each, with undisclosed discounts.[53]

At the same time Mozilo was personally granting generous preferential treatment to members of Congress, congressional staff, lobbyists, regulators, and assorted influential bureaucrats, Congress was considering legislation to reform the GSEs. The most notable reform effort died in the Senate Banking Committee, where Senator Christopher Dodd—a Friend of Angelo whose sweetheart deal saved him $75,000—was a member. Reform legislation never passed out of Dodd's committee, let alone get voted on by Congress.[54]

Carnival Barker of Loans

If you had influence, you got a great deal from Countrywide. But if you were just a nobody, you still got a mortgage even if you were a deadbeat—as long as you paid Countrywide's full-fare rates and fees. According to Countrywide's own product list, it would lend $500,000 to a borrower rated C-minus, the second riskiest grade. It would lend to borrowers with credit scores as low as 500 out of 850. It would lend to borrowers who had filed for personal bankruptcy or those who had been delinquent for more than 90 days on a previous mortgage twice in the previous 12 months. One Countrywide manual stated that a loan could be made to a borrower even if he or she had just $550 of income left to live on each month after making the housing payments.[55] If you paid the up-front fees, apparently all that Countrywide required was that the borrower exist—and if the game could have gone on a little longer, we have no doubt it would have relaxed even that last remaining standard by creating exceptions to the definition of existence itself.

Mozilo prided himself on the explosion of new products he created to lure even the most unqualified consumers into his lending trap. At one point during an investor presentation, he sounded like a carnival barker as he listed some of the 180 loan products Countrywide offered. "We have ARMs, one-year ARMs, three-year, five-year, seven- and 10-year," he said, rapid-fire. "We have interest-only loans, pay-option loans, zero-down programs, low-, no-doc programs, fast-and-easy programs, and subprime loans."[56] For the once-staid company that had prided itself on conservative lending practices and below-average defaults, Countrywide might as well have been standing up on a packing crate with a megaphone crying, "Step right up and see the freak show!"

One particularly devious loan structure was called the pay-option adjustable-rate mortgage (ARM). A pay-option ARM allowed a borrower to pay only a fraction of the loan interest due each month and none of the principal. Designed to put the financially strapped into homes they couldn't afford with conventional financing, the product was a disaster in the making. For starters, any payment shortfall was added to the mortgage balance, which would then grow in size and accrue interest. Even if the borrower made a down payment in a steady or rising housing market, over time the loan balance owed could easily exceed the home's value. Then, the A in ARM meant that interest rates could adjust or reset higher—sometimes dramatically—slamming unexpected costs on a homeowner who was already hanging by the fingernails on a reduced mortgage payment.

Heroic banking executives like John Allison at Branch Banking and Trust Company (BB&T), whom we met in Chapter 3, "The Leader," had the courage and discipline to walk away from seemingly easy profits, shunning pay-option ARMs like radioactive sludge from Chernobyl. Countrywide slurped them up with gusto because the profit on them was so huge—at least in the short term. Talking points on one internal sales document called "Pay Option A.R.M.'s Made Simple" asks, "What kinds of customers would be interested in these loans?" The answer: "Anyone who wants the lowest possible payment!" It should have read, "Anyone who wants the highest possible risk of financial ruin!" In 2005, the year of peak home prices in the housing bubble that was about to burst, pay-option ARMs accounted for over one-fifth of Countrywide's mortgages versus just 3 percent the previous year.[57]

Bad loans were starting to collect like raw sewage in Countrywide's basement, but to the outside world the picture couldn't have seemed more glorious. By the end of 2004, Countrywide had leaped in front of Wells Fargo to be the nation's largest mortgage company. It originated a stunning $363 billion in mortgages that year. A year later, Countrywide originated almost $500 billion in mortgages. Senior executives had taken to telling investors that Countrywide expected to originate $1 trillion worth of mortgages by 2010.[58] Mozila was halfway to that goal—though without knowing it, a few steps away from the gates of hell.

Exceptions Are the Rule

Over time, even the risky borrowers of our nation became fully leveraged. So Countrywide began using more aggressive tactics—it started treating even the most creditworthy borrowers as though they were deadbeats. In other words, brokers and sales reps were encouraged to peddle risky high-commission subprime loans to customers even if they could qualify for a safer low-commission loan a notch or two up the quality scale. Mozilo incentivized his brokers with commission rates based on the value of the mortgage, not on the quality of the credit. "The whole commission structure in both prime and subprime was designed to reward salespeople for pushing whatever programs

Countrywide made the most money on in the secondary market," an unnamed Countrywide sales executive said.[59]

Let's say a customer with documented income, a 10 percent down payment, and a 620 credit score could qualify through the FHA for a standard 30-year fixed-rate mortgage at a payment of $1,829 a month. The very same customer priced through Countrywide would have been offered a subprime loan at $2,387 a month—a difference of $6,696 a year.[60] Why would such customers pay more than necessary? Because at those rates, Countrywide would lend them more money, using exotic gimmicks like pay-option ARMs to make it seem practically as though the loan would never have to be paid back.

But ultimately, in the last gasp of the housing bubble, Countrywide wrung the last drops of commission dollars out of the exhausted marketplace by basically lending any amount of money to anybody, on any terms, provided the commissions were large enough. Subprime borrowers could get a loan up to $1 million. The maximum loan-to-value ratio was by then 100 percent. The only qualification for doing a stated-income loan—that is, a loan based on what you state your income is, not what you can actually prove it is—was that you were a "wage earner." Countrywide offered interest-only loans to borrowers with 580 credit scores.[61] According to Dave Zitting, an old-fashioned mortgage banker at Arizona-based Primary Residential, the standard became "Breathe on a mirror, and if there's fog, you got the loan."[62]

Countrywide then adopted a "matching strategy," which committed the company to offering any product or matching any underwriting guideline available from at least one "competitor," which included subprime lenders. If Countrywide's stated minimum credit score for a product was 600, but a competitor's minimum score was 560, Countrywide would reduce its minimum to 560 in order to match its competitor and make the loan. What resulted was a race to the bottom—an amalgamation of the very worst underwriting standards in the industry all under one roof. Countrywide also prohibited its loan officers from the common industry practice of referring risky loan applicants to other brokers or institutions in exchange for a small referral fee.[63] These combined practices all but ensured Countrywide would become like a drain trap for the kitchen sink, catching and retaining the foulest of sludge from the market's garbage disposal.

Despite official lending standards that were, in Countrywide's own words, "among the most aggressive in the industry,"[64] Mozilo would allow loans to be approved on an even more lax, ad hoc basis. Countrywide's automated underwriting system, called "CLUES," didn't even have a "reject" option. Loans were either, (1) approved, (2) approved with caveats, or (3) "referred" to another loan desk for further consideration or manual underwriting. Manual underwriting consisted of overriding Countrywide's own already lenient internal checks and balances on an "exception" basis. The exceptions culture, which started and ended at the top with Mozilo himself, became the rule. So when it came to creditworthiness, Countrywide may have had CLUES, but it didn't have a clue.

After three separate attempts to underwrite failed even on an exception basis, loan applications would be referred to Countrywide's Secondary Markets Structured Lending Desk, where no attempt at all was made to underwrite the loan. The sole criterion for approving the loan was whether the secondary marketing desk could sell it to someone else. This is the dark secret at the core of Mozilo's otherwise seemingly impossible scam factory. How could Countrywide have made such bad loans? Simply because it immediately sold them to someone else. It's history's most egregious example of the "greater fool" theory of investing: it's okay to be a fool, as long as someone else is a greater fool.

That fool was likely to be Fannie Mae. As of 2007, Countrywide alone originated 23 percent of Fannie Mae and Freddie Mac's total volume of mortgages.[65] The greatest fool, then, would ultimately be the American taxpayer. And the problem wasn't just limited to the explicitly labeled subprime category. Countrywide's chief risk officer, John McMurray, later revealed to analysts that Fannie would classify loans as prime to meet its affordable-housing goals even with credit scores that would typically be considered subprime. "There is a belief by many that prime FICOs [credit scores] stop at 620," McMurray said. "That's not the case. There are affordability programs and Fannie Mae expanded approval, as an example, that go far below 620, yet those are still considered prime."[66]

In his capacity as risk officer, McMurray repeatedly lobbied the financial reporting department to disclose more information about

Countrywide's credit risks. He was unsuccessful.[67] In 2007, well before that year's first-half earnings call, he presented Mozilo and other top executives with a summary of where the company was likely to suffer losses and urged them to report it publicly. They didn't.

Mozilo himself often personally approved loans that were in direct contravention of Countrywide's own credit policies and underwriting guidelines. When McMurray attempted to intervene in one instance, Mozilo berated him for becoming involved in loans that Mozilo had "already approved" and asserted that Countrywide's balance sheet was "big enough" to handle his exceptions.[68]

By Force or by Fraud

In the final days, Mozilo, like James Taggart in the climactic final scenes of *Atlas Shrugged*, seems to have suffered a complete break from business reality. No businessman truly interested in success would have done the things either man did. "When I look a homeowner in the eye, I can tell if they'll pay," Mozilo would tell his staff. Never mind that eye contact isn't a proven method for measuring default risk any more than it can ID serial killers in a lineup; Countrywide didn't even conduct personal interviews any longer as part of the loan application process.

In other instances, Mozilo seemed to genuinely believe his own irrational assumptions that the party would continue, propped up by permanently increasing asset values. "Over the entire history of this country, housing prices have never gone down nationally," he told CNBC in early 2005, a few months before a peak in prices preceding a 35 percent drop.[69]

Then, in other cases, he allegedly lied outright to cover knowingly fraudulent activities of his company and their collaborators. According to a lawsuit filed by the Mortgage Guaranty Insurance Corporation (MGIC), Countrywide deliberately disregarded signs of fraud in order to increase its market share.[70] By about 2006 Countrywide's internal risk assessors knew that in a substantial number of its stated-income loans—fully a third—borrowers overstated income by more than 50 percent. Mozilo also knew that many appraisers were overstating property values to drive originations by making loans appear less risky.

"I think the primary issue has been an issue of speculation, rather than fraud," Mozilo would tell investors in 2007. "I mean, I think, it's probably nonexistent today, because everything has tightened up so much, that everybody's antenna has been so sensitized to all the possibilities here that it's pretty hard to get through the system now if you're not telling us the truth."[71] Later evidence would reveal a dramatically different reality, including facilitation of rampant borrower, broker, appraiser, and other fraud stemming from documents riddled with materially false information.

In one case, a part-time Chicago housekeeper applied for a mortgage, truthfully telling a Countrywide loan officer that she earned just $200 per week. Instead of rejecting her application outright, the loan officer prepared a false document stating that the borrower was an employee of Paulen Auto Body Shop earning $6,833 per month. Based on the falsified paper trail, she was given a $339,000 mortgage loan; she then promptly left the United States and returned to her home in Poland without ever making a single payment.[72]

In another case, Countrywide gave a $350,000 loan to an illiterate California dairy worker making just $1,100 per month, by deliberately misstating his income. The loan payment alone represented four times his actual monthly pay. Another Countrywide lender gave a $398,050 loan to a woman in Ceres, California, who had been unemployed since 1988.[73] These were just a few of the many jokers dealt out by Countrywide's originators that were holding up Mozilo's house of cards.

The Rats Flee the Ship

By 2007, the housing engine, pumped full of cheap high-octane government fuel and then run all-out for years well beyond the redline on the tachometer, finally started to sputter and smoke. Some of the latest, most egregiously reckless loans signed by the greatest fools from the dregs of the market began defaulting almost immediately, even before the ink was dry on their contracts. Housing prices in the hottest sunshine states of California, Nevada, Arizona, and Florida began to slow and then decline.

Residential real estate flippers and speculators betting on an ever greater high by chain-smoking an escalating series of unafford-able mortgages quit cold turkey, defaulted on their obligations, and walked away to suffer their own personal financial withdrawal. More than 2.2 million foreclosure filings—default notices, auction sale notices, and bank repossessions—were reported during 2007, up 75 percent from 2006.[74]

Countrywide saw its loan default rates spike alarmingly. As word leaked out, $15 billion of Countrywide shareholder value evaporated during the first eight months of 2007 in a major stock market sell-off. After Countrywide tapped its entire $11.5 billion line of credit, Bank of America stepped forward to inject another $2 billion just to keep Countrywide afloat. Mozilo announced plans to eliminate 10,000 to 12,000 jobs—approximately 20 percent of his workforce—and take a $125 million to $150 million pretax restructuring charge resulting from the downsizing.[75]

For his efforts in catapulting millions of households into home-lessness and financial ruin, Mozilo was awarded a $1.9 million salary in 2007, $20 million in stock and option awards, $44,454 for use of company aircraft, $8,581 for country club fees, and $23,755 for auto-mobile use.[76]

Bank of America finally bought the struggling Countrywide outright in January 2008 for an all-stock deal valued at $4.1 billion. Shareholders who had purchased Countrywide shares during the sum-mer of 2007 after Mozilo's conference call lost more than 80 percent of their investment. All told, Countrywide shareholders saw more than $20 billion in value go up in smoke.

Bank of America CEO Kenneth Lewis probably thought he was quite the lion of Wall Street, picking off a juicy piece of prey by acquiring a red-hot mortgage originator on the cheap in a time of turmoil. He didn't know yet that he was to be Mozilo's next vic-tim, when a year later Countrywide's toxic sludge would bring Bank of America begging to the federal government for a bailout. For now, Lewis basked in the idea of taking the reins of Countrywide from Mozilo: "Angelo has told me that he will do anything that we want him to do. I would guess that he'll want to go have some fun."[77] Fun indeed. After the Bank of America buyout, Mozilo took home another

$44 million on top of the $140 million in Countrywide stock he sold off during 2006 and 2007.[78]

But there was one more victim for Countrywide—the biggest one of all.

Washington, We Have a Problem

On June 30, 2008, Fannie guaranteed $619 billion—approximately 23 percent of Fannie's book of single-family business—in so-called junk loans (i.e., subprime, Alt-A, or other risky loans knowingly misclassified in the prime category). It is likely that up to 40 percent of the mortgage volume Fannie Mae added to its single-family book of business during 2005 to 2007 consisted of these junk loans.[79] Much of that volume was purchased directly from Countrywide.

Just a year earlier, Fannie had reserved less than $1.2 billion—just 0.05 percent of its entire book of business—to cover potential credit losses. In the second quarter of 2008 alone it reported $5.35 billion in credit-related expenses. At least 85 percent of its losses were related to its holdings of both subprime and Alt-A loans. It was a financial Hurricane Katrina that burst Fannie's feeble cash levies. Worse was yet to come.[80]

On July 7, 2008, a Lehman Brothers research report indicated Fannie Mae and Freddie Mac were grossly undercapitalized, suggesting the two might need as much as $75 billion in new capital between them. Knowing what we know now, it's ironic that this report would come from Lehman, which itself was so grossly undercapitalized that it would go bust two months later. Be that as it may, in July panicked stockholders dumped Fannie and Freddie shares, sending them to 16-year lows. Fannie tumbled more than 16 percent.[81]

Former St. Louis Federal Reserve Bank President William Poole said in a *Bloomberg* interview on July 10 that Fannie and Freddie were insolvent and might need a U.S. government bailout.[82] A sell-off of their stocks was furious and spread into their bonds, long perceived as having the implicit backing of the U.S. government. That day Fannie shares ended down by another 14 percent. The next day, shareholder panic reached a crescendo even as both companies insisted they were adequately capitalized. Fannie bottomed out at less than $7, off from the mid-$60s just a year earlier. All told, Fannie and Freddie would deliver a shocking loss of $100 billion in shareholder value over the first eight months of 2008.[83]

Later that month, Treasury Secretary Henry Paulson urged Congress to grant him new authority to seize Fannie and Freddie should further catastrophe strike, arguing, "If you've got a bazooka, and people know you've got it, you may not have to take it out."[84] His words backfired as soon as they escaped his lips.

While Paulson climbed the parapet to defend the GSEs and rally the market troops, investors recoiled in horror and deserted the ranks in droves. What they quickly and correctly realized was that rather than serving to protect private investment capital, Hank's finger on the government takeover trigger guaranteed a sort of unilaterally assured destruction. If Uncle Sam nationalized the GSEs to save them, any remaining private investment interest would be instantly incinerated by the back-blast, rendering it financially worthless. Hank's gambit, then, became a self-fulfilling prophecy. With the threat of government intervention, private investment fled. Yet without private investment, government intervention was inevitable.

As if to prove once and for all that once greater discretionary government powers are granted they will be exercised, just a few weeks later, on September 6, 2008, the U.S. government placed Fannie Mae and Freddie Mac into conservatorship—essentially a full-blown nationalization of the businesses. Together, the two GSEs guaranteed around half of the entire $12 trillion mortgage market. It was an amount equal to the entire U.S. mortgage market just seven years earlier. The very government forces that set them up to fail now deemed them too big to fail. Yet the shareholder losses would be dwarfed by the total wealth that American homeowners saw evaporate since the credit crisis started—an amount in the trillions.

By early 2010, Fannie and Freddie had received more than $126 billion in taxpayer infusions, a number that is likely to grow even greater as mortgage defaults continue to rise. Douglas Holtz-Eakin, a former director of the Congressional Budget Office, said that the collapse of Fannie and Freddie would leave taxpayers with the "single largest bill we will face in this episode."[85]

In the months that followed, inquiries were launched and fingers were pointed. Opinions varied widely about the major culprit in an attempt to pin blame for the collapse on a single source. Few got it right.

Armando Falcon, the former head of Fannie's federal regulator, the Office of Federal Housing Enterprise Oversight (OFHEO), said the collapse of the companies "was clearly a failure of management" and reflected a "deeply rooted . . . culture of arrogance and greed." Mr. Falcon asked how a business "with the most generous government subsidies possible" could be run "into the ground."[86]

Ayn Rand could have explained it. As one of the heroes of *Atlas Shrugged* said, "There's a way to solve every dilemma of that kind. . . . Check your premises." In this case, the implicit premise is that government subsidies ought to help businesses prosper. But just the opposite is true: Subsidies corrupt businesses, virtually guaranteeing that they will be run "into the ground."

Indeed, they corrupt the entire world in which businesses operate. That's why Countrywide was destroyed under Angelo Mozilo, just as in *Atlas Shrugged* Taggart Transcontinental was destroyed under James Taggart. Though Taggart "had obtained a subsidy from Washington for every train that was run, not as a profit-making carrier, but as a service of 'public equality,'" in doing so, he sucked the life out of the economy whose health was ultimately necessary for his railroad to thrive.

BB&T CEO John Allison had this principle in mind when he declared that his bank wouldn't make loans to real estate developers whose property had been acquired by eminent domain. Sure, on paper it sounds great to back projects where otherwise unobtainable land is acquired on the cheap by government fiat. It's the ultimate subsidy. But in the process, the sanctity of property rights is destroyed, because the original owner's property is taken against his or her will and handed over to the developer. If there are no property rights, then of what value is the collateral banks hold against their loans? Without a legal claim on its borrowers, banks cannot exist. Some subsidy.

SEC v. Angelo Mozilo

On June 4, 2009, the Securities and Exchange Commission (SEC) filed civil charges against Angelo Mozilo in U.S. District Court for fraud and insider trading. According to court filings:

> Defendant Mozilo made numerous public statements from 2005 through 2007, praising the quality of Countrywide's underwriting and distinguishing Countrywide from subprime lenders, stating, for example:
>
> - "[w]e don't see any change in our protocol relative to the quality of loans that we're originating";
> - he "was not aware of any change of substance in [Countrywide's] underwriting policies";
> - "Countrywide had not taken any steps to reduce the quality of its underwriting regimen";
> - Countrywide "backed away from the subprime area because of our concern over credit quality";
> - "pay option loan quality remains extremely high";
> - Countrywide's "origination activities [we]re such that the consumer is underwritten at the fully adjusted rate of the mortgage and is capable of making a higher payment, should that be required, when they reach their reset period";
> - "Countrywide views the product as a sound investment for our Bank and a sound financial management tool for customers"; and
> - "Performance profile of [the Pay-Option ARM loan] is well-understood because of its 20-year history, which includes 'stress tests' in difficult environments."
>
> In addition, Countrywide's 2006 Form 10-K stated "[w]e believe we have prudently underwritten" Pay-Option ARM loans.

The paper trail reveals that Mozilo knew full well that his public statements were outright lies. On May 19, 2006, Mozilo wrote an internal e-mail to his lieutenants stating that pay-option loans presented a long-term problem "unless [interest] rates are reduced dramatically from this level and there are no indications, absent another terrorist attack, that this will happen."[87] On June 1, 2006, Mozilo advised in an e-mail that he had become aware that the pay-option ARM portfolio was largely underwritten on a reduced documentation basis and that there was evidence that borrowers were lying about their incomes in the application process.

On September 25, 2006, Mozilo wrote another e-mail, stating, "We have no way with reasonable certainty, to assess the real risk of holding these loans on our balance sheet." In the fall of 2006, Mozilo even recommended selling Countrywide's portfolio of pay-option ARM loans, recognizing the risks of retaining them on Countrywide's balance sheet. Pay-option ARMs represented approximately 14 percent of Countrywide's total loan production and 46 percent of Countrywide's loans held for investment for the 2006 fiscal year.[88]

Caught on record, Mozilo couldn't very well deny his own statements or the rock-solid time line of events. Instead, he tried to weasel his way out of the charges using what the prosecutors called "sleight of hand." For instance, Mozilo would claim that despite his knowingly false statements, the truth about Countrywide's mortgage loans could be found by the public in separately filed documents from four indirect subsidiaries under names like CWALT, LLC and CWHEQ, LLC.[89]

According to court filings, the documents contained aggregated and raw data about hundreds or thousands of loans that Countrywide had securitized while maintaining a residual financial interest. It's a bit like saying a pharmacy rep could sell you a vial of cyanide and arsenic as a safe and effective remedy as long as raw statistics proving this claim to be a lie were buried in a canister somewhere in the state of New Jersey. Besides, even Mozilo's statistics failed to address the bad loans Countrywide had retained in full.

The court rejected Mozilo's spurious and desperate arguments. Rather than face a jury trial with such damning evidence stacked against him, Mozilo agreed to settle the charges of fraud and insider trading by paying $22.5 million in civil penalties in October 2010.

Bank of America made up the balance of his $67.5 million total fine. It surely would have galled that would-be lion of Wall Street, Ken Lewis, to write that check—but at that point he was gone, ousted over controversies swirling around another of his toxic acquisitions, Merrill Lynch.

During his career at Countrywide, Angelo Mozilo reaped over $400 million in compensation. Even after he and his insurers paid his penalties,[90] he took home a net of over a third of a billion dollars in exchange for destroying trillions of dollars of America's wealth.

James Taggart was not so lucky; at the climax of *Atlas Shrugged*, he went mad. But who knows what private hell Mozilo lives in now and for the rest of his days? He knows that, like Taggart, he was never a real creator, but only a parasite. Yes, he justified himself to the world— and to himself, we suspect—with highfalutin talk about the virtues of home ownership. History's worst despoilers have always used the language of altruism and collectivism to disguise the reality of their actions and deflect the forces that might challenge them.

Angelo Mozilo wasn't the only James Taggart at work in the era of corruption that led to the Great Recession. And as long as the world accepts the collectivist lies that disguise parasitism behind a curtain of high-minded social ideals, he won't be the last Taggart—and the Great Recession won't be the last crisis our economy has to face.

Chapter 5

The Persecuted Titan

Bill Gates as Henry Rearden, the businessman who created revolutionary technologies and was criminalized for his success

And yet—he thought—through all the generations of political extortion, it was not the looting bureaucrats who had taken the blame, but the chained industrialists, not the men who peddled legal favors, but the men who were forced to buy them; and through all those generations of crusades against corruption, the remedy had always been, not the liberating of the victims, but the granting of wider powers for extortion to the extortionists. The only guilt of the victims, he thought, had been that they accepted it as guilt.

—Atlas Shrugged

Who is Henry Rearden?

In *Atlas Shrugged*, Henry Rearden is a steel tycoon who refuses to join John Galt's "mind on strike" until his business is utterly destroyed by corrupt politicians, fellow businessmen, and his envious wife.

(Continued)

Rearden came from poverty, assembling an empire over many years of relentless effort, managerial skill, and personal risk. At the peak of his career he invents a new alloy, both lighter and stronger than steel, and christens it "Rearden Metal." The new metal is so revolutionary it threatens to displace the established industrial order, and Rearden finds himself blocked at every turn.

A single visionary industrialist—railroad executive Dagny Taggart, the main protagonist of *Atlas Shrugged*—places an order for the metal to build a high-speed track into Colorado, the only flourishing region of the economy. Rearden's and Taggart's ride together on the first train to use the new track is the most thrilling scene in Rand's fiction, portraying the emotional pinnacle that can be reached by those who achieve business and technology breakthroughs.

The Taggart track proves the metal's value, but this only intensifies Rearden's problems. The government passes a law seizing patents, and at first Rearden refuses to turn over the formula for his metal. He relents when the government blackmails him with evidence of his affair with Dagny Taggart, begun in the exultant moment following their thrilling train ride. The government passes so many new regulations that Rearden's steel mills become virtually state-controlled. Ultimately the government manages to stage a fake labor disturbance resulting in the mills' outright seizure.

An unintended victim of the incident is a young government bureaucrat whom Rearden had befriended. As he dies in Rearden's arms—in the most emotionally touching scene in Rand's fiction—Rearden sees the evil of the collectivist system that destroys even its own adherents, and finally joins Galt's strike.

The news hit him like a punch to the solar plexus on that blustery fall day in Redmond, Washington. Despite his unwavering fight against the forces bent on destroying him, Bill Gates was slipping ever deeper into his own personal hell. "U.S. Judge Declares Microsoft Is a Market-Stifling Monopoly," blared the newspaper headline on November 6, 1999.[1] In a bluntly worded 207-page "Findings of Fact,"

Judge Thomas Penfield Jackson, a career public jurist and demonstrated technophobe—he didn't even use e-mail—concluded that Microsoft had used its "prodigious market power and immense profits to harm any firm that insists on pursuing initiatives that could intensify competition against one of Microsoft's core products." He added, "The ultimate result is that some innovations that would truly benefit consumers never occur for the sole reason that they do not coincide with Microsoft's self-interest."[2]

For Gates, the finding was outrageous. The company he had dropped out of college to build from a ragtag crew of computer geeks into a world force in software development had always competed aggressively but fairly. Of course he had pursued his own self-interest—and vigorously advanced opportunities to create new products and exchange fair value with his customers. That's what a free-market system is all about. "Who grew this market?" he asked himself. "We did. Who survived companies like IBM, ten times our size, taking us on?"[3] In the process, like an early metallurgist at the dawn of human civilization, he created a brand-new substance called software that would power our society into the next level of permanent technological orbit.

On the day Gates was born in 1955, fewer than 500 electronic computers had ever existed in the entire world, their total retail value amounted to less than $200 million, and the term *software* had not yet been coined.[4] By 1999, nearly half of all American households owned a computer,[5] with annual global shipments exceeding 100 million units.[6] Microsoft software ran on nearly all of them. Bill Gates had come close to realizing his youthful dream of a computer on every desk with Microsoft on every computer. But that success, while seemingly destined in retrospect, was in the beginning hardly guaranteed among the primordial soup of competitors in a chaotic personal computing field all vying for prominence—or mere survival.

Along the way Gates had lived the American dream. His own personal effort had made him the wealthiest person on earth with a net worth in excess of $80 billion[7]—the vast majority of it still at work invested in Microsoft stock, but an amount larger than the annual gross domestic product of the Philippines or Singapore.[8] His company was an American success story that ensured the United States' place as a leader in global technology for years to come.

And while it wasn't his primary intent, Bill Gates himself was far from the main beneficiary of his industrial endeavor. By creating a de facto standard in computer operating systems, he unlocked widespread cross-compatibility of applications and files, which boosted global workforce productivity throughout the 1980s and 1990s to historically astronomic levels. The same work output that had previously required a bank of financial analysts poring over hand calculations or a pool of typists hammering away at carbon-copied memos could be accomplished by a single office worker in a fraction of the time, and then disseminated instantly to a worldwide audience using a compatible DOS or Windows-based PC.

A single $21 share from Microsoft's 1986 initial public offering (IPO) would be worth more than $10,000 just 12 years later. A $1,000 investment on the secondary market even after Microsoft's 40 percent first-week IPO pop would have grown to $483,000 by the end of the 1990s. Thousands of employees and investors alike made lifetime fortunes by taking a risk on Bill Gates and his competitive drive. For that matter, thousands of competitors, far from being shut out by Microsoft, in fact made fortunes for themselves, and improved the lives of *their* customers, only because Microsoft had created a stable and widespread computing standard in which their products could operate. And in an age when the American economy is faulted for being dependent on paper shuffling and burger flipping, Gates built his wealth by actually manufacturing something.

So what was Bill's reward for his industry, foresight, and entrepreneurialism? Just like Henry Rearden, the brilliant inventor and industrial titan in Ayn Rand's *Atlas Shrugged*, he was persecuted for his success. He was branded a criminal for not playing soft enough, for not allowing weaker companies a spot on the field, for capitalizing on his opponents' mistakes to score points for his own business—in other words, for succeeding against all odds in a competitive marketplace. Now the market buzzed about possible penalties, including a forced breakup of the firm, confiscation and public dissemination of its intellectual property, or other conditions—like seating government appointees on Microsoft's board—amounting to socialist nationalization of his business.

It's as if Judge Jackson were channeling a passage from *Atlas Shrugged* in support of the "Equalization of Opportunity Bill" reading that "it was society's duty to see that no competitor ever rose beyond the range of anyone who wanted to compete with him." In other words, the best athletes should be hobbled so that the worst can keep up. Gates should play nice, sacrificing himself, his employees, and his shareholders, and leave some room for others.

In turn, *Atlas Shrugged*'s Rearden, like Gates, having dealt only with the clean reality of technology and production all of his life, "had acquired the conviction that one had to concern oneself with the rational, not the insane—that one had to seek that which was right because the right answer always won—that the senseless, the wrong, the monstrously unjust could not work, could not succeed, could do nothing but defeat itself." Gates liked to say, "The business side always seemed simple to me, you know, make great software, figure out a way to get it out there and get people to buy it."[9] But just as Henry Rearden found out in *Atlas Shrugged*, businesspeople who compete on their own merits—naively ignoring the parasites seeking to drain them—do so at their own peril. There is no record to suggest that Gates ever read *Atlas Shrugged*, or ever heard of Rearden. Too bad. It might have helped in the travails to come.

Storming the Gates

In 1988 after a full two years operating as a major public corporation, Microsoft employed just five attorneys on staff (by 2003 Microsoft's legal staff had mushroomed to 300).[10] When his senior executives urged him to boost the company image in mainstream media with a public relations campaign, Gates rejected the idea as distracting the company's focus away from technology. "In the early days of the company I was very proud that we had no lobbyists ever, no PACs [political action committees]," Gates noted. "I had to spend more time in capitals of other countries than our capital. And, what a testament that was to America. You could build a company with great success without involvement in political activities of any kind."[11]

Rearden felt the same way—right up until the government destroyed his business. "He knew that it was necessary to have a man to protect him from the legislature; all industrialists had to employ such men. . . . An inexplicable kind of distaste, part fastidiousness, part boredom, stopped him whenever he tried to consider it."

Now, facing incessant attacks from the very government that was founded to protect his freedom and the products of his individual effort, Gates couldn't comprehend why anyone could begrudge him for selling so much software. What could possibly be wrong with that? And what was he supposed to do instead? Should he *fail* to deliver what the customers demanded? Should he *stop* innovating, *stop* improving his products? In 1999 alone, he had spent $5.3 billion on research and development—more than the entire annual corporate profit of General Motors, Wal-Mart, or Boeing.[12] Why was it his fault that smaller companies couldn't afford to invest as much to benefit their own customers?

As far back as the late 1980s, certain industry players were already plotting against Gates. Instead of focusing their efforts on improving their businesses and doing the hard work needed to take on Microsoft openly, these so-called competitors chose to whine—and conspire—from the shadows. First, complaints against Microsoft were made to the Federal Trade Commission (FTC) along with a road map to help guide the agency to other disaffected companies whose spiteful grumblings might uncover more damaging evidence in support of their spurious claims. The Novell Corporation and its chairman, Ray Noorda, led the opposition, employing two Washington law firms and a well-connected Washington public relations firm in an effort to influence the FTC's evaluation of Microsoft.[13] Despite these poisonous tactics, the FTC found insufficient evidence of any wrongdoing and ceded the investigation over to the U.S. Department of Justice (DOJ).

Then, even more boldly, big names like Oracle, IBM, and Sun Microsystems together spent millions on government lobbying in part to convince the DOJ to take action against Microsoft.[14] Urged on by this angry horde of collectivist interests armed with their quivers of money and political influence, the attacks would persist. As one reporter put it, the government "didn't know what Bill Gates did—but they were sure he must have done something wrong."[15]

Yet his customers clearly didn't share the sentiment. In a poll, 77 percent of Americans believed Microsoft made quality products[16]—and for those who felt otherwise, well, just don't buy them. Microsoft continued to improve its products, cut costs, and offer competitive upgrade options to newer versions—and the marketplace agreed with his approach, rewarding Microsoft with ever greater success.

"The FTC investigation was a lightning rod to bring computer people forward and say that it would be helpful if Microsoft was hobbled in some way," Gates told *Newsweek* in June 1991.[17] In 1994, Microsoft agreed to settle a Department of Justice case by making it easier for personal computer manufacturers to use Microsoft's rivals' software. It signed a consent decree that forbade it from using its operating system dominance that reputedly "choked off competition."[18]

Still, Microsoft's competitors did not let up, claiming that the software titan had achieved and then abused its monopoly status by *forcing others to do business with it*. Who could seriously think that Microsoft really had the power to force someone to buy its goods, as though at the point of some kind of figurative gun—and then argue that the police apparatus of the government ought to force Microsoft to desist at the point of an actual gun? Who, indeed? These were Gates's supposed peers in the computer industry.

Grudgingly, Microsoft finally hired its first lobbyist in Washington in March 1995 to begin countering the political threat to its survival. From now on, Gates wouldn't repeat the same mistake he made in 1994 when his reluctant capitulation signaled weakness to the scavenging hyenas who longed for a bite of the majestic beast. Next time, he would refuse to settle where other custodial-minded CEO pragmatists might cave in. For Gates, it was his company, and it was personal. He would fight any further government intrusions to the bitter end with all of his considerable might and intellect.

When the DOJ brought its antitrust suit against Microsoft in 1998, the case appeared to focus narrowly on a specific Internet browser issue. But it was much more than that. Apparently we like our capitalist system to produce success, just not too much of it. "We have people who think that we are more successful than any company should be," Gates said.[19]

When called into a deposition by the government's hired gun, attorney David Boies, Gates stubbornly made his opponent fight for every inch. Gates said at the time, "I gave totally truthful answers. I have a great memory. When [Boies] would ask imprecise questions

I would simply point out to him the imprecise nature of the question."[20] But Gates did not merely "point out"—he mocked, he argued, he stonewalled—with a chip on his shoulder bigger than a mainframe. To wit:

Boies: *Can you tell me, Mr. Gates, what question you're purporting to answer?*
Gates: *Your last question.*
Boies: *Do you know what it is?*
Gates: *Could I make it as convoluted as you did? No.*

In *Atlas Shrugged*, Henry Rearden finds himself on trial for a regulatory crime as trumped up as the one of which Gates was accused—and stonewalls just like Gates did. Rearden refuses to grant any legitimacy to the court by even answering its questions. Reardon tells the prosecutor,

> "Your law holds that my life, my work and my property may be disposed of without my consent. Very well, you may now dispose of me without my participation in the matter. I will not play the part of defending myself where no defense is possible, and I will not simulate the illusion of dealing with a tribunal of justice."
>
> . . . "Are we to understand," asked the judge, "that you hold your own interests above the interests of the public?"
>
> "I hold that such a question can never arise except in a society of cannibals."

Rearden gets away with it—the court is so flummoxed by his principled resistance that it lets him off with a suspended sentence. But it was only a temporary victory. There was more government intervention to throttle Rearden, and eventually it would destroy his business.

For Gates, there wasn't even a temporary victory. While clearly in the right, his performance had done him no favors in a courtroom more amenable to defendants who show deference to their persecutors, even when it's not deserved. In the end, such intangibles would be the deciding factors. Judge Jackson would decide the case not on objective legal arguments, but on his own whims based on the personalities and theatrics of the various witnesses and counsel in his court. More than once, he was seen to fall asleep at the bench during proceedings. He shouted at Microsoft witnesses and took over questioning from attorneys when frustrated by their approach.[21] He rolled his eyes and shook his head in response to testimony. He held confidential press interviews during the trial in which he likened Microsoft to "drug traffickers" and "gangland killers." His actions would later be declared by an appellate court to be "deliberate, repeated, egregious and flagrant" violations of the judicial code of conduct.[22]

The government, Gates told himself, had no real case. It would get nowhere. He was sure of it. And yet the government persisted. Gates was infuriated—and surprised—that instead of conducting their case purely in the legal arena, the Feds were fighting with PR tactics—"Call me naive," Gates said. And the press, as far as he was concerned, ate it up.[23]

His own hometown paper, the *Seattle Post-Intelligencer*, would refer to Microsoft with the oft-repeated epithet "Evil Empire."[24] *Time* magazine reported on "Demonizing Gates," citing the thousands of diabolical references to him online as "the Great Satan" and "Beelzebub."[25] *Newsweek* ran a story on Gates entitled "The Whiz They Love to Hate."[26] *Business Month* ran a doctored image of Bill's head on a muscle-bound body under the cover heading "Silicon Bully."[27] In the article one unidentified IBM executive said he would "like to put an ice pick in [Gates's] head." The endless water torture of persecution would become too much for even Gates's inner fire to withstand. "It was in the press every single day," says Bill's dad, William Gates Sr. "His own government, suing him, that's not chocolate sundae! He was concerned, he was angry, he was distracted from things he'd rather be doing."[28]

Eventually, Bill Gates would settle with the government. In some sense it was a pragmatic business decision, and mostly a win for Microsoft. But in another sense it was a moral collapse—the victim himself granting a moral sanction to his tormentors—just what Henry Rearden said not to do, warning that "if we value our lives, we must not give it to them." But when it was done, Gates went on strike, just like Henry Rearden finally did when he couldn't take the pain any longer. In 2000, Gates handed over operations to longtime business partner Steve Ballmer, who would shift the company's focus from playing hard to playing nice.

Ultimately in a sad diversion of his productive brainpower, Gates turned aside from creating economic value, and instead began to give away the value he'd created in the past. Gates and his wife endowed the Bill & Melinda Gates Foundation with billions in Microsoft stock, and now the world will just have to wait to see whether it will be better off with Gates donating his wealth to sponsor talk shows on National Public Radio, among other purposes, rather than keeping it at work building Microsoft.

Should Americans aspiring for a better life for themselves, their families, and their nation be proud that their government forced one of the most productive minds in history to stop producing? Here's how Gates would answer that question: "Americans should wish that every business was as competitive as the personal computer business," he says.[29] "This lawsuit is fundamentally about one question: can a successful American company continue to improve its products for the benefit of consumers?"[30]

Ayn Rand would agree, but she'd have another answer as well, operating on a philosophical level, rather than just a pragmatic one. Yes, the unfettered competition of pure capitalism does produce wealth. But even if it didn't, it is still the morally correct way for society to organize economic life. Rand once wrote, "Capitalism is a social system based on the recognition of individual rights . . . the only rational and moral system in mankind's history."[31]

Without it we will all be poorer, no matter how much of his fortune Gates gives away to the poorest. Without it we will be less free, knowing that any of us smart enough and lucky enough to change the world the way Gates did will be targeted for destruction as Gates was.

A Hero from the Start

William Henry Gates III was born on October 28, 1955, to a family that was well off, although certainly not rich by the standards he himself would later set. His parents nicknamed their son "Trey"—a play on his name's suffix. It was a moniker that would stick among his family and close friends for the rest of his life. His father, Bill Gates Jr., was the first member of his own clan to graduate from college, as an honorably discharged Army lieutenant after World War II. Bill Jr. then went on to law school and later became a partner in a Seattle practice. Trey's mother, Mary, came from a socially prominent banking family. While comfortably wealthy, Trey's family disdained pretentious displays of affluence. Instead its focus was on substance, education, making a positive impact on the world, and focusing on creative production as opposed to a lust for money itself. It is a value system that young Bill would carry forward throughout his adult life.

Much has been made—mostly by spiteful critics—of Gates's privileged upbringing and supposed million-dollar trust fund as the origin of his eventual business success. The truth is that he bootstrapped his business endeavors from day one. And even if he hadn't, the world abounds with trust fund kids who created small fortunes by frittering away large ones.

Gates's biggest asset was not an inheritance, but an amazingly powerful mind supercharged by early access to leading-edge technology. Born at the dawn of the computer era, he experienced the synergy of high-octane experience coupled with strong mental horsepower that few could match. Yet while these initial benefits translated into a strong starting position, the race would prove to be long and arduous. Only Bill's sustained efforts of constant work, endurance, competitive drive, and obsessive focus would decide the winner.

Trey was an energetic child who learned to rock his own cradle and spent hours incessantly doing so. Later as an adult, Bill's characteristic rocking back and forth in his office chair and in the boardroom would become legend in the computer industry. While some explain the habit as bleeding off stress or a sign of intense mental focus, the rocking behavior is also associated with conditions along the autism spectrum[32]—a classification that can include highly gifted savants.

The evidence that Bill's brain functions differently than most was apparent very early on. At age 7 he read all 20 volumes of the *World Book Encyclopedia* from beginning to end. At age 11, he could perfectly recite the entire Sermon on the Mount unaided and, according to his flabbergasted youth minister, displayed a deep understanding of its meaning well beyond mere rote memorization.[33]

In the fourth grade, his classmates labeled him "eccentric" for his oddball work habits that bordered on the obsessive. When assigned to write a four-page report, Trey would turn in 30 pages. On the play-ground, he played pickleball as though the fate of the world were at stake. A day at the swimming pool would turn into lap races. A jig-saw puzzle became a contest to see who could place the most pieces. While it may have seemed like eccentric behavior in grade school, looking back we might regard Bill's behavior as indicative of a fiercely competitive spirit and a drive to win. Even leisure activities weren't merely for relaxation—they were opportunities to push the limits of one's potential, to test, stretch, strengthen, and grow.

By the middle of 1968 the United States was retaking the lead in the space race against the Soviet Union. The Apollo moon landing, borne on the wings of newly developed electronic computing power, was tantalizingly close to fruition. Stanley Kubrick's epic *2001: A Space Odyssey* played in theaters nationwide, offering a believable futuris-tic vision featuring a sentient supercomputer named HAL 9000 as a central character. Amid these influences, Gates's high school, Lakeside, vowed to expose its students to this new world of computers. The only question was how to do it.

Early mainframe computers could be owned only by large corpo-rations or government agencies. With footprints measuring in square yards, such systems cost millions of dollars to buy and support. Even with annual tuition at Lakeside at a relatively steep $5,000 per student, these sums were clearly out of reach. Instead, Lakeside purchased a rel-atively inexpensive teletype machine and remotely linked it to one of the several corporate mainframes in the area with spare capacity on a time-share basis—first from General Electric, then from a Seattle start-up called Computer Center Corporation, or C-Cubed. The machine on the other end was a PDP-10 mainframe manufactured by Digital Equipment Corporation and specifically designed with architecture to support multiple remote users.

The first time Gates sat at the Lakeside terminal and typed in a short command, he was thunderstruck. Just think—a hulking silicon-based intelligence formed of transistors and copper wiring, sitting in a building miles away, interpreted the electrical impulses he himself transmitted with his own fingers and then, without any carbon-based human intervention of any sort—*it responded!* This was like an open door to a whole new world of vibrant possibilities, a place where the very nature of physical reality was harnessed and coupled with abstract logic and mathematics to produce something useful and wondrous. He was hooked.

Bill and a handful of like-minded students began spending every minute of their free time in the computer room exploring the system while testing their own reasoning and problem-solving skills. Among these early adherents was an upper-classman named Paul Allen. Despite their age difference, Bill and Paul discovered an affinity in their love of computers and their insatiable appetite for knowledge. They soon became fast friends. It was the beginning of a partnership that, along with several other Lakeside classmates, would become the founding programmers core of the Microsoft empire.

Gates devoured everything he could find about computers, but the field was so new, so undocumented, that he and his fellow computer freaks had to mostly learn by doing. They poked and peeked, observing the results. They posed ad hoc problems to each other that they would then compete to solve. Bill taught the computer to play tic-tac-toe. He created a lunar landing simulation. He programmed the computer to play Monopoly and then had it run thousands of game scenarios to find winning strategies. In the process, he discovered things even the professional computer experts at the time didn't know. Perhaps it's not as romantic as the young Henry Rearden laboring in an iron mine at the birth of his career—but Gates's dedication and efforts as a youth were no less intense, and in any field that's what it takes to launch yourself toward the very top.

The Lakeside kids became such power users that eventually C-Cubed enlisted them to find bugs in its system during off hours in exchange for all the free computer time they could use. In other words, Bill could now try to crash the system by pushing it, and himself, to the limit—for free. All he had to do was report any bugs he discovered to the engineers to find and fix later. As a result, C-Cubed got a robust, crash-resistant commercial product to offer during business hours, while Bill and his friends got to log more computing hours than most NASA engineers of the day.

According to one study, it takes 10,000 hours of deliberate practice to become an expert at almost any task or profession, from playing the violin in Lincoln Center to scoring touchdowns on the National

Football League (NFL) gridiron.[34] By the late 1960s Bill and his night shift at Lakeside were well on their way to vaulting that mark a full half-decade before even the most rudimentary personal computer was introduced, and during a time when the very terms *software* and *hardware* were unknown to most of the population.

It wasn't long before Bill's far-ranging young mind began seeking out ways to profit commercially from his newfound passion. "I was the mover," Gates said. "I was the guy who said, 'Let's call the real world and try to sell something to it.' "[35] In early 1971, he found his first real business opportunity.

A computer time-share company in Portland, Oregon, needed a payroll program written for one of its clients, and had heard through the grapevine about a talented group of students up in Seattle with experience coding for the PDP-10. With legal help from his father, Gates formed the Lakeside Programmers Group with Paul Allen, Richard Weiland, and Kent Evans as partners, then boarded a bus to Oregon to meet their new client. Bill hammered out a creative royalty agreement to guarantee his group a residual income stream instead of a standard fixed price or hourly rate. In a matter of months they had a finished product coded in COBOL. At a mere 16 years of age, Bill had negotiated his first commercial deal with a maturity and foresight beyond his years and then led his team to execute a complex task on a demanding time line.

Paul Allen graduated from Lakeside later that year and enrolled at nearby Washington State to study computer science. By then, he and Gates had already gone on to their next moneymaking venture in the form of a business they dubbed Traf-O-Data. The idea was as obscure as its name—and brilliant.

Municipalities at the time used mechanical punch-tape machines to record traffic volume on main roads in their jurisdictions. These tapes were then tediously hand-transcribed into useful data and presented to city engineers for use in timing stoplights for optimal traffic flow. Paul and Bill built their own elementary computer using an Intel 8008 chip, attached a paper tape reader, and then programmed it to transcribe the data. The process could be done for a fraction of the time and cost of manual transcription, and they successfully pitched it to a series of paying clients. The business reportedly grossed around $20,000,[36] or the equivalent of more than $100,000 today. It's an impressive start for high school kid.

Before Gates graduated from Lakeside, he and Allen completed a series of other commercial ventures. They coded a school scheduling program. They worked a full-time, short-term assignment rescuing a moribund project for defense giant TRW to computerize a regional power grid using PDP-10s. No task was too big or too small as long as it involved solving problems with computers. Bill and Paul talked seriously about forming their own software company, but the idea would have to wait. Mary and Bill Jr. insisted that Trey at least try his hand at college to gain some exposure to other students and the world of higher academics. In the fall of 1973, Bill was off to Harvard.

This was a career detour that Henry Rearden didn't take. But Gates didn't stray for long from the path of Rand's self-made industrialist hero. He would outgrow Harvard in just two years.

Origins of Empire

Officially enrolled in Harvard's prelaw program, Gates was still searching for direction among competing influences. "I was always vague about what I was going to do, but my parents wanted me to go to undergrad school," Gates would recall. "They didn't want me to go start a company or just do graduate work."[37] So he took a respectable class load during his first year at Harvard, including a mix of undergraduate- and graduate-level courses. He scored top marks in one of the university's most difficult math courses, but not *the* top mark. He tended to focus his energy only on subjects that interested him, yet still scored well in other areas simply because of his considerable intellect.

Computers continued to pull on him, and he was often found hacking away in one of several university labs with access to his old friend the PDP-10. Over the summer, he and Allen both landed jobs at Honeywell in Boston. Allen would stay on as an employee that fall while Gates returned to Harvard for his second year. Recharged by his summer months back in the computer industry, Gates became increasingly uninterested in academics and spent more and more time on two passions—one old, programming, and one new, poker. "Bill had a monomaniacal quality," said Andy Braiterman, his roommate at the time. "Perhaps it's silly to compare poker and Microsoft, but in each case, Bill was sort of deciding where he was going to put his energy and to hell with what anyone else thought."[38] It was also during this time when Gates met and became friends with hall-mate Steve Ballmer, whom he'd regale with his poker exploits in a rapid-fire dialogue they'd term "high-bandwidth communication."[39]

Gates was also talking more and more with Allen about starting another business. They were both convinced that the world was on the cusp of a gigantic sea change—the democratization of computing power for the masses—and they believed they could play an important part in that revolution. But how? Hardware was interesting, but ultimately, having tried his hand at building the Traf-O-Data machine, Allen felt it was a "black art."[40] For Bill, software was the soul of the machine and the area of expertise where he and Paul had invested nearly half of their young lives.

Then one December day in 1974, Paul Allen picked up a copy of *Popular Electronics*[41] on his way to visit Bill on Harvard's campus. The issue's cover showed a rectangular box about the size of a small home stereo unit labeled "Altair 8800" under a bold red headline proclaiming, "PROJECT BREAKTHROUGH! World's First Microcomputer Kit to Rival Commercial Models." Inside, the cover story, written by H. Edward Roberts of Albuquerque-based Micro Instrumentation and Telemetry Systems (MITS), began, "The era of the computer in every home—a favorite topic among science-fiction writers—has arrived!"

Billing the Altair 8800 as "the most powerful minicomputer project ever presented" and "a revolutionary development in electronic design and thinking," Roberts went on to describe the unit as a "complete system" that could hold a full 256 bytes in memory (equivalent to the length of his two opening sentences), which would allow its user to input "an extensive and detailed program . . . via switches located on the front panel, providing a LED readout in binary format." The article included sample schematics and a full parts list taking up less than one column of side text. A mailing address was provided along with instructions for ordering an unassembled kit for $397, or a fully assembled unit for $498. MITS would also send along a free set of circuit board etching guides and assembly information for the cost of a 40-cent stamp and an 8½ × 11 envelope. Suggested uses among "thousands of possible applications" included a "digital clock with all time-zone conversion" and a "brain for a robot."

While today the article reads like a spoof of pretechnological naïveté, it fired the imaginations of already eager Gates and Allen by convincing them that the tipping point of the consumer-computer revolution had indeed arrived. When the next month's follow-up article spent two pages of text laying out a detailed nine-step procedure of complicated switch flips merely to enter a program on the Altair for adding two numbers together, Bill and Paul had a brilliant idea. They both were already familiar with the machine's Intel 8080 central processor from their experience with Traf-O-Data, and Bill was a consummate expert in one of the relatively user-friendly programming languages of the day known as BASIC. Why not piggyback off of the Altair's hardware distribution and provide the software that would unlock its potential by bridging the gap between binary machine and human language?

With characteristic entrepreneurial confidence, Gates picked up the phone and dialed Roberts at MITS in New Mexico, offering a version of BASIC that would run on the Altair. Roberts later recalled, "We had at least 50 people approach us saying they had a BASIC, and we just told everyone, including [Gates and Allen], whoever showed up first with a working BASIC had the deal."[42]

For the next eight weeks, Bill abandoned his classes to hunker down with Paul. They spent every waking hour in the computer room working on the project, trying to beat the unknown competition they knew was nipping at their heels to steal the prize.

There is such a moment in the life of every man or woman who succeeds in business—the moment when one decides to win, whatever the personal cost. For Henry Rearden, "He was fourteen years old and it was his first day of work in the iron mines of Minnesota. He was trying to learn to breathe against the scalding pain in his chest. He stood, cursing himself, because he had made up his mind that he would not be tired. . . . [P]ain was not a valid reason for stopping."

Just because writing code ensconced behind ivy-covered walls at Harvard wasn't exactly digging in an iron mine, don't underestimate the vast challenges that faced Gates, or the courage it took for him to take them on. For starters, some experts at Intel didn't even believe that running a high-level programming language on the 8080 chip was possible. In addition, while Roberts provided schematics for the Altair, the only working model at the time was sitting in his offices in Albuquerque, so Gates and Allen had nothing to program or test their work on.

Undeterred, the duo studied the technical specifications of the Intel central processing unit (CPU) and developed an emulator program on the PDP-10 to virtually replicate the functioning of a working Altair. Drawing on all of their reserves built up from long hours on the night shift at C-Cubed, Traf-O-Data, TRW, and Honeywell, Gates and Allen accomplished the seemingly impossible: a working copy of BASIC that Allen flew out to Albuquerque encoded on a paper punch tape.

When Roberts first beheld his box of chips and toggles turned into a useful computer by Gates and Allen's efforts, he remembers, "I was dazzled. It was certainly impressive. The Altair was a complex system, and they had never seen it before. What they had done went a lot further than you could have reasonably expected."[43] After a brief celebration in Boston, Allen headed back to New Mexico to work out the bugs in BASIC and prepare for a coming road show to promote it. Gates joined him during the summer after his sophomore year at Harvard was complete. He would never return to college.

MITS already had preorders for thousands of machines, and the hardware team was struggling to keep up. It must have been this kind of demand for even such a rudimentary machine that confirmed Gates's conviction that the appetite for personal computing was virtually unlimited. Soon thoughts of returning to school in the fall had faded like a sunset over the New Mexico desert. In fact, he would never complete any degree. That summer he and Allen, with legal help from Bill's father and a local attorney, formed Micro-Soft (the hyphen was later removed)—an abbreviation of "microcomputer software"—and struck a licensing agreement with MITS for their version of BASIC. It wasn't just a technology tour de force, but a business one as well. At only 19 years old, Gates helped craft a sophisticated agreement that anticipated many of the key issues in software licensing, including exclusivities, sublicensing, and confidentiality.

BASIC sold briskly at first in tandem with Altair shipments, but soon software volume began to drop in relation to hardware. The reason was simple: Most computer owners at the time viewed hardware as something to buy, but software as a something to copy and share.

In response Gates published "An Open Letter to Hobbyists" in early 1976,[44] accusing his would-be customers of outright theft and laying out a Randian argument for the protection of intellectual property. "Who can afford to do professional work for nothing?" he asked. Without adequate compensation for valuable work done, he argued, "there is very little incentive to make this software available." The moochers who take something for free in the short term are only hurting themselves in the long run. "One thing you do [by stealing] is prevent good software from being written."

Over the next few years as the computer market grew, Gates realized he needed to get out from under an increasingly overwhelmed and inefficiently operated MITS to begin building software for the proliferation of new, competing hardware systems if he ever wanted to realize his dream of Microsoft on every desktop. After relocation from Albuquerque to a new permanent headquarters near his hometown in Washington, the company was beginning to build momentum. Early programmer Steve Wood explains some of the company's early success.

> We were always a year or two ahead of where the demand was really going to be. But we were generally guessing right. A lot of it was Bill's and particularly Paul's ability to see where some of the stuff was going to go. A lot of people are able to see things like that, but we had just an enthusiasm, a real high level of drive and ambition. There wasn't anything we couldn't do. Okay, so no one has done this for a personal computer before, so what? We can do it. No big deal. . . . We overcommitted ourselves. We missed deadlines. We consistently underestimated the time it would take to do a project, and we committed to too many of those projects at a time. But we always got it done.[45]

Gates also began recruiting the talent he needed to keep driving his corporate vision. In 1980, with around 30 employees, he reached out to old Harvard friend Steve Ballmer, who was attending Stanford Business School after a stint at product marketing giant Procter & Gamble. He would become Gates's alter ego, business champion, marketing guru, and eventual heir to the reins of the company. He also took the job of chief recruiting officer from day one and relished the job with entrepreneurial zeal.

"There's a standing policy here," Ballmer said in a 1983 interview. "Whenever you meet a kick-ass guy, get him. Do we have a head-count budget? No way. There are some guys you meet only once in a lifetime; so why screw around?" The interviewer noted that Ballmer's style "hardly complies with standard corporate protocol." Ballmer responded, "I believe in the old cliché, 'rules serve the company; the company doesn't serve the rules.'"[46]

Ballmer's favorite fishing spot for future employees was the under-graduate pond where he liked to spot eager tadpoles full of raw talent who could be nurtured to become stellar producers within the Microsoft ranks. The recipe was simple: Take one brilliant student with drive and initiative coupled with a background in science, math, or computers. Offer scant money up front in exchange for a dynamic, empowered, and lively work environment with the financial potential of long-term equity options. Heat in the crucible of brutal work hours, intense deadlines, and a competitive corporate culture with a drive to win. What comes out is a virtual clone of your company leader—Gates himself—a techie Marine with the killer instincts to take any hill against impossible odds.

The work ethic at Microsoft was indeed legendary. Parking spaces at the office filled from front to back with the earliest arrivals closest to the door. Gates memorized which cars belonged to which program-mers and took note of who came earliest and stayed latest. It was an unwritten rule that nights and weekends were work hours regardless of how much time was spent during the week. Gates even had a contest with his programmers during out-of-town trips to see who could leave the office at the latest possible moment and still catch their flight at SeaTac, the Seattle–Tacoma International Airport.

Act I: DOS Kapital

Although now famous for the nearly ubiquitous DOS and later Windows operating systems, Microsoft nearly missed out on this most fundamental layer of the computer software hierarchy—the intellectual capital on which the Gates fortune, and thanks to Gates so many others as well, is built.

As the 1980s dawned, a company called Digital Research headed by Gary Kildall all but owned the operating system market for Intel 8080-based computers with a product called CP/M (or Control Program for Microcomputers). An *InfoWorld* interview in May 1981 quotes Kildall as claiming "a couple hundred thousand CP/M users out there now," with usage tripling each year.[47] In fact, Gates had partially enabled the standard by actively promoting CP/M while singularly focused on the programming language layer, including BASIC. The advantage seemed obvious at the time. After all, it was easier to code his language for one operating system than hundreds. So, for example, Microsoft licensed CP/M from Digital Research and created a hardware product called SoftCard, allowing Apple users to run CP/M-compatible programs on their otherwise incompatible computers.

Then IBM called. And that call turned out to be one of the most critical moments in the history of American business.

In 1980 Big Blue was engaging in a secretive project to rapidly launch its own personal computer based largely on off-the-shelf components and the new 16-bit Intel 8088 processor. The project was on a fast track and IBM had no time to develop its own software, so it started searching for likely providers. One morning in July, Gates got a call from IBM's Jack Sams asking for an introductory meeting.

"What about next week?" asked Gates.

"What about tomorrow?"[48] responded Sams. Despite Gates's youthful appearance and their seemingly diametrically opposed corporate cultures, the companies quickly found common ground in the language of technology, and the initial meeting went well. Sams returned in August to talk turkey accompanied by a corporate attorney bearing a nondisclosure agreement (NDA), which Gates signed with little fanfare.

With Gates sworn to secrecy, IBM proceeded to unveil the blueprint of the initiative, dubbed "Project Chess." IBM needed high-level languages like BASIC, COBOL, FORTRAN, and Pascal for the new 16-bit platform. Could Microsoft create them? Absolutely, replied Gates with his typical can-do, competitive attitude.

But what about the operating system? Could IBM also sublicense the CP/M source code Gates used in his Apple SoftCard?

Unfortunately, that was going to be a problem. Not only did Microsoft not have the rights to sell or license the CP/M source code to IBM, but Digital Research didn't even have the necessary 16-bit version of the operating system to offer in the first place. If IBM wanted CP/M, it would have to talk to Kildall.

Gates set up a meeting for IBM with Digital Research, and the boys in suits flew out the next day. "The meeting was a fiasco,"[49] recalls Sams. To start with, Kildall didn't even show up. Instead, he left his wife in charge of the proceedings, and she, together with a Digital Research attorney, refused to sign IBM's NDA. IBM badly needed an operating system for its project and was eager to do business. By flying off that night for a Caribbean vacation and by being fussy about an NDA, Kildall turned his back on the opportunity of his lifetime—and left it for Gates to seize.

IBM went back to Microsoft and dumped the problem in Gates's lap. Gates was more than eager to take up the challenge.

Across town, a small CPU board manufacturer called Seattle Computer Products was equally frustrated with Kildall. It had been trying to cajole Digital Research into delivering CP/M in a 16-bit version for the boards it created. Without an operating system, the latest, more powerful hardware was all but useless to users. As a result, sales were slow. Tired of waiting for Kildall, an in-house programmer by the name of Tim Patterson had written his own operating system, which he dubbed 86-QDOS (for Quick & Dirty Operating System), and word of it soon began to spread.

At least it spread to neighboring Microsoft. As fate would have it, apparently IBM was unaware of it. After learning about this ready-made operating system for the 8086 chip, rather than build the OS from scratch, Microsoft struck a deal with Rod Brock at Seattle Computer to license Patterson's program for a one-time fee of $25,000. Around this time, Brock was also approached by software distributor LifeBoat Associates—yet another player tired of trying to coax a 16-bit version of CP/M out of Kildall. He offered Brock $250,000 for the rights to 86-QDOS. Gates and Ballmer countered with an offer to buy, not just license, the code for $50,000 plus sweeteners, including a perpetual license back to Seattle Computer, free OS updates, and favorable pricing on Microsoft computer language products. Brock declined the richer LifeBoat offer and signed with Microsoft because he saw more long-term future benefit from receiving free updates and most-favored-nation status. Besides, he was a hardware guy—software was just an enabler for him to move his CPU boards.

While today it seems like the deal of the century for Gates, at the time it was a substantial risk for a small company like Microsoft in a very crowded field. "We had no idea IBM was going to sell many of these computers," as Tim Patterson, the virtual grandfather of what would become known as MS-DOS, would later summarize. "Somehow, people seem to think we had an inkling it was going to be this big success. I certainly didn't. So buying DOS for fifty thousand dollars was a massive gamble on Microsoft's part."[50] As it turned out, the gamble would pay off in spades and cement Microsoft's place in corporate history.

IBM and its eventual clones exploded onto the scene in the early 1980s. From a starting point of zero in 1981, they accounted for the majority of computers sold by 1986. Microsoft software ran on them all, generating solid revenue from every copy of DOS and BASIC shipped at a minuscule marginal cost. Gates plowed the money back into his business to create new applications and improve the operating system with future versions he'd dub Windows.

Some software industry roadkill, like Seymour Rubinstein, a former TV repairman whose once best-selling WordStar word-processing program would soon join the extinct ranks of the early software dinosaurs,[51] chalked up Gates's success in operating systems to "pure luck." He surely spoke for the legion of second-handers following in the amoral footsteps of Rand's characters like Dave Mitchum in *Atlas Shrugged*, the incompetent railroad superintendent who complained about "injustice," "bad luck," and "the conspiracy of big fellows, who would never give him a chance." According to Rubinstein, "There was no foresight, no imagination, no brilliant maneuvers, just a lucky break caused by a combination of Digital Research screwing up and Seattle Computer Products having something which wasn't very good that could be modified for IBM."

Would he say the same about an Olympic sprinter who invested a lifetime in physical training, only to win gold after the race's leader stumbled? For the moochers, there's no imagination in seeing the future of computing, no foresight in building for multiple platforms, no brilliant maneuvers in striking elegant and creative deals to reach business goals. For the less competent it's easier to chalk it up to lucky breaks than to view their own personal shortcomings in stark contrast to genuine brilliance.

Act II: As Far as Your Mind Will Take You

In John Galt's speech at the climax of *Atlas Shrugged*, he says that "you must drive as far as your mind will take you—with achievement as the goal of your road." Now, from a strong position in operating systems and computer languages, Gates was to set for the world a new distance record of how far a mind can drive.

Gates was eager to capture a share of the third layer in the computer software hierarchy: applications. With the ubiquity of Microsoft products today, such as Word, Excel, PowerPoint, and Outlook, it's easy to forget just what a competitive fight it was in the quickly changing field loaded with frenzied competition from incumbents like WordStar, VisiCorp, Lotus, Symantec, Borland, Ashton-Tate, and MicroPro. Undeterred, Gates set out to beat them at their own game with better products, more features, lower prices, and higher quality.

For example, in 1988 Lotus 1-2-3 had 70 percent of the spreadsheet market, having itself taken the lead from once-dominant VisiCalc some years earlier. Microsoft Excel was seen as an also-ran with a mere 10 percent market share. Less than 10 years later Lotus's share had fallen to 26 percent and Excel's share had increased to 68 percent.[52] It's often assumed that Microsoft applications simply piggybacked off of their huge installed base of operating systems, but the truth is that these applications were separate software packages that had to compete on their own merits in a free market. Good products sold. Bad products died.

Nobody forced anyone to buy anything. Gates struck rigorous deals with computer manufacturers and distributors alike using the full weight of his business leverage to wring the best possible terms from his partners. Gordon Eubanks, one of the industry's pioneers and past president of Symantec, said of Gates, "I do know of instances where he used his influence, but who wouldn't? This isn't a race where there's a handicap. Bill doesn't go around carrying a 100-pound sack on his back. That's what some people think should happen."[53] But that didn't stop resentments from smoldering in the minds of the envious—those willing to bend the police power of the state to the task of putting that 100-pound sack on Gates's back. As Rand put it in *Atlas Shrugged*, those people thought "it was society's duty to see that no competitor ever rose beyond the range of anyone who wanted to compete with him."

To be sure, Gates played hardball. But he played by the rules—and ironically, he fueled resentments by insisting that *others* abide by them as well. In one case, a deal to market Microsoft's OS/2 network software with 3Com was moving too slowly for Gates, so he decided to bypass his partner and sell the product directly to end users—a right he'd carefully built into Microsoft's contract with 3Com. 3Com's Bob Metcalfe viewed it as a double-cross and counter to the spirit of their deal, though clearly within Microsoft's rights under the contract. "The response that I got," said Metcalfe, "was, 'You ought to negotiate your contracts more carefully. You were stupid.'"

Alan Kessler, 3Com general manager, had a more sanguine reaction, saying, "We were adults. We were big boys and girls when we signed the contract. . . . We signed it on the belief that certain things were going to happen to the OS/2 market, they did not happen, and it was not incumbent on Microsoft to give us relief."[54] For Gates, business is war. If you weren't prepared to abide by an agreement, don't expect any quarter from his side.

"It is deep in the [Microsoft] culture that success is never guaranteed,"[55] observed Pam Edstrom, Microsoft's early head of public relations, neatly explaining Gates's drive to win. It was a tough-minded approach at odds with some in the industry who viewed business more like a gentlemanly game of golf than a battle for survival. But you couldn't argue with success. Or could you? By 1994 nine out of 10 computers sold were IBM PC compatibles and Gates was a billionaire many times over. But corporate envy had festered and spawned a government lobbying effort to restrain the juggernaut.

Yet not all competitors bought in. In 1990 a Federal Trade Commission investigator, tipped off by others in the industry, approached Scott Cook, chairman of Intuit, whose flagship Quicken program was facing stiff competition from Microsoft Money after a period of information sharing between the two companies. Cook said he told the FTC it was wasting its time investigating Microsoft. "They are pestering one of the best run companies I've ever seen," he said, "a company that should be the model for American industry. . . . [W]hen you lose to Microsoft, it's because you snooze."[56]

Meanwhile, Gates was flying commercial around the world with no entourage. No pretense. He dined on hamburgers and milkshakes. And unlike a lot of corporate executives, Gates was able to put his ego aside, look at himself honestly, and learn from his errors. "The process of identifying the mistake, figuring out the problem and fixing it is what makes Bill Gates different," wrote one industry observer. "I've watched him do it over and over again."[57] Like a true Randian hero, Gates dealt with objective reality, not wishful thinking. "If he really believed in something, he would have this intense zeal and support it and push it through the organization and talk it up, and whenever he met with people talk about how great it was," said Scott MacGregor, a Xerox manager brought over to guide Windows development. "But if that particular thing was no longer great, he'd walk away from it and it was forgotten. A lot of people have a hard time doing that. It made him incredibly agile in a business sense. . . . People usually fight to the death long beyond when it is the right thing to do."[58]

Oft-quoted industry analyst Esther Dyson said Microsoft was hated because it was so successful. "They've gotten where they are by doing a good job," she said. "Doing a good job isn't illegal."[59] The government, egged on by the cabal of industry whiners, would try to prove otherwise.

Gates through the Looking Glass

No less a personage than Alan Greenspan once wrote that "The world of antitrust is reminiscent of Alice's Wonder-Land: everything seemingly is, and apparently isn't, simultaneously. . . . [T]he entire structure of antitrust statutes in this country is a jumble of economic irrationality and ignorance."[60] This is where Bill Gates—perhaps one of the most supremely and economically rational men who ever lived—found himself transported at the height of his success. At the antitrust trial, Gates must have felt he was dealing not with the American justice system but with Alice's Queen of Hearts proclaiming, "First the sentence, and then the evidence."

The century-old Sherman Antitrust Act passed by Congress in 1890 was designed to protect powerless consumers against huge corporate interests that might use nefarious means to monopolize a market, then artificially raise prices and stop improving their products to the economic detriment of society. The solution, in nineteenth-century logic, was to break up big companies to ensure vigorous competition, which would supposedly result in better products at lower prices thanks to a more efficient marketplace.

One hundred years of subsequent economic thinking calls the whole premise of antitrust law itself into question. In most instances economies of scale achieved only by the largest companies reduce operating costs and benefit consumers, and breaking them into smaller, inefficient pieces would cause more harm than good. In addition, market forces, left to their own devices, will likely displace an overcharging monopolist anyway, since eager upstarts will find ways to cut into the rich profits through creation of substitute products or other innovations. What's worse, antitrust law is inherently subjective—there is no rigorous definition of *monopoly*. Nevertheless, the law is still the law, and such ambiguous legislation will inevitably become fertile soil for collectivist weeds to take root. And for Microsoft, take root they did.

At the heart of the government's case in 1998 was whether Microsoft violated a 1994 consent decree and used monopoly power to stifle competition by giving away its Internet Explorer browser for free as part of its operating system, while competitor Netscape Communications was trying to charge a separate fee for its browser. On the face of it, it's hard to see how consumers are harmed by getting something for free. It's as silly as a bottled water company lodging a complaint against a municipal utility for installing drinking fountains in the public park. And if the water bottler truly had a superior product—or could convince the consumer it did—it would have a willing base of paying customers readily offering value for value.

In the case of Netscape, a ludicrous irony is that, in the beginning, it gave away its browser for free, as a come-on to build an installed base of consumers so that it could sell its server software to corporate clients. In the end Netscape's problem wasn't Microsoft doing the same thing; it was that Netscape behaved incompetently, made bad decisions, missed deadlines, alienated customers, and (most important) failed to create a compelling business model.[61] As Gates once told his own small team working on Internet initiatives in the midst of the dot-com bubble, "What you are doing isn't that hard. This is a feature. This isn't a company. It isn't even a product. It's just a feature."[62] But Netscape apparently missed out on a fundamental lesson of commerce: don't try to sell people something that they can get for free, especially when you yourself conditioned them to expect it for free. If Netscape couldn't muster the strength and insight to create a profitable business on its own, it would play the poor disadvantaged kid beaten up by the big bully, and plead for public sympathy in the name of altruism.

Just like the looting businessmen in *Atlas Shrugged*, Netscape could have hardly been more aggressive in harnessing the power of the state. To start with, CEO Jim Barksdale personally had at least six meetings with trustbusters and sent the agency at least two white papers on the subject of Microsoft's supposedly predatory tactics, urging the government to take action. His company would later circulate an internal document describing the government's resulting antitrust suits against Microsoft as an "opportunity for Netscape."[63] On the witness stand, Barksdale's clever one-liners and folksy banter laced with Mississippi charm would be eagerly received by Judge Jackson over a marathon week on the witness stand, in stark contrast to Gates's independent intransigence.

Judge Jackson himself had little business presiding over a case on free-market commerce in the technology sector—or perhaps any case at all, for that matter. Jackson didn't use e-mail and had little or no familiarity with computer technology. In 1999, he insisted that there was no "best of breed" in browsers and none was likely to emerge "at any time in the immediate future." From his lofty view atop the bench, he acknowledged the exponential growth of the Internet and then fantastically asserted that it "would have no impact on consumers or operating systems for the next few years," and went so far as to argue that many consumers would not even want a browser on their computers.[64]

For Judge Jackson, Microsoft's crime was hubris, not monopoly. Jackson found Gates and his crew "obstinate." "I think he has a Napoleonic concept of himself and his company, and arrogance that derives from power and unalloyed success,"[65] he'd later say of Gates.

The case became one not of legal merit, but of forcing Microsoft and its proud, individualist CEO to submit to the implied guilt thrust forth by the collective, of which Jackson had appointed himself representative.

David Boies, the government's prosecutor, opened the case with excerpts from Gates's videotaped deposition testimony. These "greatest hits" showed Gates's style at it social worst. Slumping in his chair, wearing a baggy earth-toned suit, he appeared sullen and annoyed. He occasionally rocked back and forth broodingly. His responses came across as petulant, arrogant, obstinate, and snippy. "Did you actually *read* what was in there?" he jabbed back when posed a question about the definition of Microsoft's Web browser. "It seems strange that if you're trying to use a dictionary you might as well read what it says," Gates smirked.[66]

Judge Jackson later told Ken Auletta of the *New Yorker* that throughout the trial "he couldn't get out of his mind the group picture he had seen of Bill Gates and Paul Allen and their shaggy-haired first employees at Microsoft." According to Auletta, he went on to say, "[W]hat [I] saw was a smart-mouthed young kid who has extraordinary ability and needs a little discipline. I've often said to colleagues that Gates would be better off if he had finished Harvard."[67]

After 18 grinding months of trial, Jackson released his Findings of Fact using the following analogy about a North Carolina mule trainer to describe his own methods: "How do you train the mule to do all these amazing things? Well, he answered, I'll show you. He took a 2-by-4 and whopped him upside the head. The mule was reeling and fell to his knees, and the trainer said: You just have to get his attention. I hope I've got Microsoft's attention. . . . But we'll see."[68]

In late 1999, Jackson's "Conclusions of Law" were still months from release, hanging like a sword of Damocles ready to deliver the judge's decapitating penalties. Given the damning Findings of Fact, there was a tremendous incentive for Gates to settle. By this point, the struggling Netscape had been gobbled up by America Online in a stock swap valued at a whopping $4.2 billion—not bad for a company supposedly hobbled by Microsoft's unfair practices. The market was sorting things out by itself, but the government was still concerned that Microsoft would continue to bundle new features like voice recognition into its operating system or create deliberate third-party incompatibilities to advantage its own suite of applications.

Earlier proposals suggested forcing Microsoft to bundle rival Netscape's browser along with its own in a remedy Gates equated to "telling Coca-Cola to bundle three cans of Pepsi in every six-pack."[69] Other proposals during the ensuing months of negotiations included signing over Microsoft source code in a move akin to declaring the formula for Henry Rearden's hard-won breakthrough technology, Rearden Metal, a public good—and literally blackmailing him into "giving" it as a "gift" to the nation. Gates was uncharacteristically amenable to certain softer provisions, including a "detachable" Web browser, but ultimately rejected the more extreme technical definitions being proffered. Soon it became impossible to bridge the gap between the stubborn Gates who insisted he had done no wrong and his government persecutors out for blood. The settlement talks fell apart.

Jackson's eventual ruling that Microsoft be broken apart—which when it was announced in April 2000 caused a stock market crash, and was arguably the trigger event that derailed the boom in tech stocks—was later overturned by the D.C. Circuit Court of Appeals. An eventual settlement with the DOJ contained some minor concessions but kept Microsoft intact and largely free to continue its own software development on its own terms.

The same couldn't be said for Gates himself. Years of legal grinding and public persecution had depleted his inner reserves. Gates had gotten into the business to build great software, not defend himself in a war of attrition against an ever-changing landscape of scavenging looters. He had had enough.

Gates Puts His Mind on Strike

In January 2000, Gates relinquished almost all of the operational decision making at Microsoft by turning over the CEO duties to Steve Ballmer. Instead, he would ostensibly focus on strategy and software development in a far less public role. It was at this point of transition that Microsoft stopped playing to win and started playing to be nice.

Ballmer made it clear that an excessive zeal had permeated the culture and gotten the company into one legal tiff after another. The zeal had to be tamed. "Providing value to customers," Gates and Ballmer wrote to shareholders in 2003, "means not only building great products, but also listening carefully to customers, responding quickly, and being more transparent and accountable." It was as if Microsoft's leadership were saying, "We've always thought of ourselves as good guys. We don't think we did anything wrong. But all of you think we're not that great. So now we have to convince you that we truly are good guys."[70]

By 2003, Microsoft's legal staff had mushroomed to 300 to handle the protracted legal avalanche threatening to bury it. In January 2004, Microsoft had 13 lobbyists in the nation's capital and another seven in state capitals. Goldman Sachs analyst Rick Sherlund estimated that the lawsuit lopped off as much as $175 billion from Microsoft's market capitalization. The once singularly focused Gates would become more and more comfortable spending time away from Microsoft pursuits. Where previously he would obsess over computer code or the latest elements of Windows—subjects about which he was the world's foremost expert—his conversations would now turn just as frequently to matters of philanthropy such as infant mortality statistics or malaria in the third world—subjects about which he has no expertise, indeed no experience whatsoever.

His early attitudes toward philanthropy were dismissive at best. Business came first. "He thought the most important thing to do," his father said, "was to have the business succeed."[71] When his mother tried to convince him to be more charitable, he responded that he had employees to pay and deals to do in a very competitive market. He just didn't have the bandwidth to deal with yet another management hassle like a foundation, and certainly not one that didn't produce any economic value.

After the DOJ trial, he did a complete 180. He started the Bill & Melinda Gates Foundation and would join with the likes of Warren Buffett to publicly announce a Giving Pledge that would funnel a huge portion of his wealth to this behemoth charity. Eventually he would be counted among the world's most generous philanthropists. The press that once skewered him in demonizing terms of self-serving greed now lauded his turnaround. They had hated him for making his money, and now they loved him for giving it away—never mind that he had to have made it first.

He had seemingly capitulated to the collectivists. Or had he? Some might say his operational and mental departure from the company

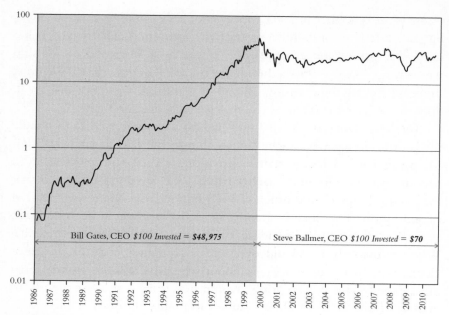

Figure 5.1 Microsoft (MSFT) Stock Price

he founded was his own surreptitious strike of the mind. The high-profile charity would be a misdirection to distract the public from the most salient consequences of Gates's move—he was withdrawing his intellect from the parasites who had sucked value from him through the decades. He walked away in full public view, leaving his creation to stagnate under societal demands of fair play . . . and nobody even realized he did it.

It was nothing so dramatic as Henry Rearden vanishing by dark of night from his ruined steel mills to join John Galt's revolution. Nevertheless, Microsoft investors have already felt it where it counts: in the pocketbook. As Figure 5.1 shows, a $100 investment in Microsoft would have turned into over $48,000 over the 15 years Gates was at the helm. From the day Gates accepted society's demands and became a generous philanthropist instead of a greedy monopolist, that same $48,000 would have shrunk to $33,600 by today.

Bravo, Mr. Gates. Like Henry Rearden, you fought long and hard. Society will miss your contribution—whether or not it ever knows it.

Chapter 6

The Central Planner

Barney Frank as Wesley Mouch, the politician who meddled in the economy and almost destroyed it

> "Fact is," said Mr. Weatherby primly, in a statistical tone of voice, "that in the twelve-month period ending on the first of this year, the rate of business failures has doubled, as compared with the preceding twelve-month period. Since the first of this year, it has trebled."
>
> "Be sure they think it's their own fault," said Dr. Ferris casually.
>
> "Huh?" said Wesley Mouch, his eyes darting to Ferris.
>
> "Whatever you do, don't apologize," said Dr. Ferris. "Make them feel guilty."
>
> "I'm not apologizing!" snapped Mouch. "I'm not to blame. I need wider powers."
>
> —Atlas Shrugged

Who is Wesley Mouch?

Wesley Mouch is one of the key antagonists in *Atlas Shrugged*, a government regulator who destroys the economy while attempting to control it. But he's no super-villain—he is not portrayed

(Continued)

as consciously evil, or even as especially ambitious. He is only a bumbler who ends up almost by accident with extraordinary powers over the economy, which he finds cannot be exercised without unleashing unintended consequences.

Mouch first achieves political power as a pay-off; he is a lobbyist in the employ of industrialist Henry Rearden, one of the central heroes of *Atlas Shrugged*, whom he betrays by not warning him of impending regulatory legislation. But that is the only overtly corrupt or ambitious act Mouch carries out. After that he is shown as a buffoon who nevertheless acquires more and more powers—in a vicious cycle in which additional powers are granted at each stage of the economy's collapse, which his own regulatory powers caused in the first place.

As Top Coordinator of the Bureau of Economic Planning and National Resources, Mouch wields tremendous power. Yet it was only mistakenly "concluded that Wesley Mouch was a man of superlative skill and cunning, since millions aspired to power, but he was the one who had achieved it." He was, in fact, only "the zero at the meeting point of forces unleashed in destruction against each other."

Through Mouch, Ayn Rand shows that while virtue is powerful and requires relentless competence by the virtuous, evil—even very effective evil—is small and impotent. Unlike all the other main characters in *Atlas Shrugged*, heroes or villains, we never hear from Mouch an exposition of his guiding philosophy. It seems he doesn't have one, suggesting that in Rand's view the absence of a philosophy is a form of depravity.

In a December 2006 article from the *Congressional Quarterly Weekly* entitled "A Roof over Every Head," Congressman Barney Frank of the 4th District in Massachusetts is quoted proclaiming, "The problem is that the market is producing too much inequality." The solution? Use government leverage to provide affordable housing as one way to bridge the widening gulf of U.S. income disparity. A new approach to housing policy can be a hallmark of the Democrats' efforts to redistribute wealth, he says.[1]

And redistribute he would. By the time Frank was through, his lifetime quest for ever-increasing political power to promote social equality and universal home ownership would bring a nation to its knees, triggering a banking collapse unparalleled since the Great Depression and plunging millions of productive Americans into unemployment, foreclosure, and financial ruin.

A Czar Is Born

How does one get to have enough control over the economy in order to destroy it? Was Barney Frank smarter, harder working, more honest? No—in the moral universe of Ayn Rand, smart, hardworking, and honest people don't want to control the economy in the first place. They just want to control themselves.

Frank, like Wesley Mouch, the government central planner who destroys the economy in *Atlas Shrugged*, isn't stupid. But of all the not-stupid people in the world, the ones who become economic czars share other key traits. They are people who know they couldn't make it in the private sector, so they turn to politics. They are corrupt, in the sense that they are willing to bend and break even the tainted rules by which the game of politics is played. They are ruthless, willing to let the world go to ruin as long as they can be in control of it. And they are shameless and unapologetic, blaming everybody but themselves when it does.

Barney Frank was named chairman of the House Financial Services Committee in 2006 not through any special expertise or background in the banking sector, but due to the cockroach-like survivability of an entrenched lifelong government bureaucrat. With the exception of some half-stints in academia, Frank has spent his entire career on the government payroll. He has never created a job. He has never had to earn a living on the strength of his contribution to the economy. He has never been responsible for capital investment decisions where he bore personal financial risk. He's never worked on a trading desk or in a bank, brokerage, or corporate finance division. He's never even rung the register at a fast-food restaurant.

Several other congressmen were ahead of Frank in the political pecking order for the high-profile leadership position. But when then-Representative Chuck Schumer, the Democrat of New York, moved from the House to the Senate, Bruce Vento died of cancer, and John LaFalce didn't seek reelection, Frank suddenly found himself enthroned on the committee that oversees insurance, banking, the securities industry, and affordable housing. He said that the role made him "feel like a kid in a candy store," and remarked that "I have more power than knowledge."[2] If only that remark had represented self-awareness rather than a lame attempt at self-deprecating humor, perhaps Frank wouldn't have presided over the worst financial collapse in modern history.

Like Rand's Wesley Mouch, Frank crafted a lifelong career out of patronage and pull, using political power to distort the economy through endless rules and regulations while ignoring their real impact on the nation. Oblivious to the end, he would not only shift blame and shirk responsibility for the destruction he wrought, but would rationalize it as not doing enough—and then clamor for even more power.

Those who have encountered Frank throughout his life invariably come away with certain indelible impressions. The first is that he's smart and verbally acute—if not always intelligible in his fast-talking, marble-mouthed New Jersey accent. His comments are witty, acerbic, and sharp-tongued. He has been known to flay a hearing witness or election challenger with slashing verbal parries, dissect an argument with disarming tongue-in-cheek wordplay, and deflect criticism with blunt-edged insults. "On what planet do you spend most of your time?" Frank tersely cudgeled a constituent at a town hall meeting for the Obama-sponsored health care bill. "Trying to have a conversation with you would be like trying to argue with a dining room table. I have no interest in doing it."[3]

Colleagues from both sides of the aisle give great deference to his debating skills. He can speak extemporaneously on wide-ranging subjects of law and complex bills without reference to notes. His remarks are peppered with clever quips, and his creative positioning of issues makes his arguments both devastating and funny. His aphorisms have made him a bit of a media go-to for irreverent commentary on the public record, like a modern-day legislative Yogi Berra. Even as a junior state rep from Massachusetts, the *New York Times* favored his quotes over more prominent but linguistically guarded figures. "This bill is the legislative equivalent of crack," Frank said in a 1986 debate on a bill funding increased border protection from drug traffickers. "It yields a short-term high but does long-term damage to the system and it's expensive to boot."[4]

While winning verbal jousts and painting colorful metaphors may provide entertaining sound bites that make for great play on the evening news, for Frank it's a diversionary tactic to shunt discussions on substantive issues to a controlled version of reality intended to spare him the need to consider uncomfortable truths. When challenger Richard Jones opposed federal rent subsidies for housing and price controls on energy during a local candidate forum, Frank countered by labeling his position as "cruel" to the elderly.[5] When a Harvard law student asked a straightforward question of how much responsibility, if any, Frank took for the economic crisis as chair of the House Financial Services Committee, Barney struck back defensively. "This is the right-wing attack on liberals' attempt to stop regulation," he spewed as part of an aggressive if not entirely sensible tirade that would have knocked the most seasoned political brawler off balance.[6] He never answered the question, and successfully evaded any hint of culpability by effectively trampling a forum of free speech with verbal jackboots.

Frank used his considerable brainpower and verbal acuity not to create and build, but rather to shift and maneuver. Instead of learning the business of construction and the economics of free-market incentives to create housing, he pushed government subsidies and rent control. Rather than learn about efficient production operations in the face of a globalizing economy to support local manufacturers, he introduced legislation calling for a boycott of products made by a nonunion textile plant that employed over 27,000 American workers across nearly 60 facilities.

Frank is known to read voraciously, often reserving his luggage space on trips for stacks of unread newspapers and legislative documents— even reading while standing at the House urinal. His appetite for words is superseded only by his physical hunger. He has often been seen ravenously gobbling down food at campaign events, and has been heard privately scoring the quality of his hosts by the quantity of their buffets.[7]

At five foot 10 and weighing up to 270 pounds, Frank is frequently seen with food stains on his ill-fitting suits. Thaleia Schlesinger said Barney's shoes looked like "a dog ate them." She later agreed to serve as press secretary for his first congressional campaign only after he agreed to buy three new suits.[8] A 1974 campaign poster promoting his reelection to the Massachusetts Statehouse depicts a rumpled Frank, unshaven and sporting Elvis Costello–style glasses with Coke-bottle lenses under the caption, "Neatness isn't everything."

Born Barnett Frank in Bayonne, New Jersey, in 1940, Frank was reared on a fetid stew of socialistic New Deal politics and outright criminal corruption. His parents, Sam and Elsie, were committed liberals and devoted Roosevelt Democrats. A 1958 photograph shows Barney and his mother posing delightedly next to a seated Eleanor Roosevelt during an Israel Bond drive event in their hometown.

The adulation clearly rubbed off on the young Frank—and then some. In high school, Barney attended a conference at Columbia University for aspiring journalists. Instead of bringing copies of his school newspaper to distribute to his fellow attendees, Barney handed out issues of the Communist paper, the *Daily Worker*.[9]

His myopia seems to have taken hold at an early age as well. One day Barney came home from school with a note that said he needed glasses. When his mother asked, "Why didn't you ever tell me that you couldn't see well?" he replied, "I thought everybody saw things that way." Although Barney got glasses, they seem not to have much clarified his view of the world.[10]

In one early incident while working as an unelected point man for Boston Mayor Kevin White, Barney assigned Colin Diver, who would later become president of Reed College in Portland, Oregon, to work on preparing a rent control proposal. "I had the benefit of some pretty good training in economics and I had the benefit of conversations with some economist friends of mine," Diver said. He told Barney that rent control was bad economics and that it was not going to work, and he predicted that it would have a long-term disastrous impact on the housing market."[11] Barney dismissed Diver's concerns and pushed the initiative forward anyway. The need for popular giveaways to a clamoring constituency, along with Barney's own growing sense of infallibility, outweighed objective economic reality.

When Barney was growing up, his father, Sam, owned a truck stop near the Holland Tunnel entrance in Jersey City called Tooley's. It was a unique full-service facility for its day, with diesel fuel, a weigh station, restaurant, and bunkhouse where weary drivers could spend some horizontal time enjoying a little JC hospitality. Sam also had ties to organized crime. The land behind the stop was a well-known dumping ground for dead bodies and was often searched by New York cops investigating murders and mob hits.[12]

Sam's older brother, Harry, owned a local car dealership. In 1946, he was granted a city contract to supply municipal vehicles in return for kickbacks to members of Frank "Boss" Hague's Jersey City political machine with purported ties to the Mafia, as well as the teamsters and longshoremen's unions. Sam acted as an intermediary of some sort in the deal and spent a year in jail after refusing to testify before a grand jury as a material witness.[13] At the age of only 6, Barney would visit his dad behind bars and later expressed great admiration for his father's strict adherence to the Cosa Nostra's code of *omertà*, or refusal to cooperate with authorities against a known criminal conspiracy.[14]

When Sam died at the age of 53, Barney took a year off from college to help resolve the family's affairs. He reports that members of the Mafia were very supportive during the ordeal. Frank "Funzi" Tieri, who later rose to head the Genovese crime family, attended brother David Frank's bar mitzvah when Barney was 23. It's among these formative influences of socialist-leaning politics and mob-centered criminal activities that Barney had a chance to learn early firsthand lessons on the power of an influential position, and extracting unearned value from it.[15]

In 1966 during an aborted attempt to earn a doctoral degree, Frank received his draft notice. He responded with documentation showing he was a graduate student and received a deferment. The draft board, which was run by local New Jersey politicos, then mysteriously lost or misfiled Frank's record. He was never again called up despite having suspending his studies shortly thereafter.[16]

Abandoning his doctoral studies, Frank cut his political teeth on Boston Mayor Kevin White's staff as his nonelected, de facto deputy. According to White, Barney, like White himself, is a *power collector*— someone who gloms onto everything he can get his hands on, someone who reaches out for more power to do more things—in contrast to a *power user*, someone who wants only the power necessary to do his job.[17] *Boston Globe* reporter Chris Lydon recalled, "Barney was born to be a first-class public man."[18] As we will see, that description is a contradiction in terms.

Frank seemed to thrive on hardball city politics and quickly became known as Mayor White's political troubleshooter. When demonstrators gathered on the Boston Common to protest the city's midnight curfew, Frank showed up at 3:00 A.M. to coordinate the police bust. Barney frequently testified on behalf of the mayor at city council meetings, often fielding hostile questions from the elected representatives. When White ran for governor, Frank ran the city of Boston, making day-to-day decisions.

In 1971 Congressman Michael Harrington offered Barney a job as administrative assistant in his Capitol Hill office. Figuring it was a golden opportunity to learn the inner workings of an even larger power forum, he accepted. "The only legislation that I ever worked on in terms of trying to get something passed was to make sure we got 'three deckers' for the city of Lynn," Barney recalled. "It was a program for one- and two-family houses, a federal loan program. I remember going to a member from Massachusetts on the Banking and Currency Committee, Peggy Heckler, to do it."[19] It was a succulent taste of using political pull to bestow unearned tax dollars on the undeserving in the name of social progress in housing—a taste that would later never seem to be sated.

When State Representative Moe Frye retired from Massachusetts Ward 5, Frank decided to run for the open seat. At the time he looked at it as a stepping-stone to greater political influence in the vein of Michael Dukakis and an opportunity to advance his social causes while honing his political maneuvering skills. Since 1972 was the first year 18-year-olds were eligible to vote, Barney tapped into the mass of young antiwar Boston University students in his ward, winning the general election with a solid 60 percent of the vote.

Loud and controversial, Frank lost no time backing extreme issues in the Statehouse, generating plenty of public notoriety and name recognition in the process. He sponsored bills to legalize marijuana use, to repeal state obscenity laws, to promote gay rights, and to establish adult entertainment zones with legalized prostitution. All were soundly defeated despite some colorful debate.

"Mr. Speaker," Barney pronounced on record during a legislative session in characteristic form, "it is true that I have introduced bills relating to pornography, gambling, prostitution, adultery, marijuana, and homosexuality. But I am going to make a commitment to my colleague from New Bedford. I will keep on trying until I find something he likes to do."[20]

Later, reflecting on his terms in the state legislature, he remarked, "There is no question that the Massachusetts House in those days was a complete dictatorship," adding, "I say benevolent dictatorship, which is the best form of government."[21] It is an odd attitude for someone from the state that threw tea in the waters to protest King George, and one he would carry forward to the U.S. House of Representatives: that the politically powerful have a better, more expansive view of their subjects from the seat of their throne and that they should make the rules for the rest of us, because we don't know what's in our own collective best interest.

Frank's next step up the political ladder was nearly a matter of divine intervention. In 1980 Pope John Paul II got word that one of his Jesuit priests was active and vocal in support of liberalized abortion laws. The kicker was that the priest, Father Robert Drinan, happened to be a five-term Democratic congressman from Massachusetts. The Pope immediately invoked a heretofore unenforced papal law prohibiting priests from holding secular public office, effectively preventing Drinan from seeking reelection and opening up the seat to all comers.

Bored with the state legislature and facing what a biographer called "a mid-life crisis,"[22] Frank threw his hat into the ring and ran in a crowded field as Drinan's handpicked successor. He won the primary, but it proved to be a tough year for Democrats in the general election. Down-home Jimmy Carter was helpless before powerfully charismatic Ronald Reagan and a tide of conservative voters in the wake of high inflation, gasoline shortages, and rampant unemployment. As doomsday pundits decried the end of American prosperity, Reagan's campaign posters exclaimed, "Let's make America great again."

Barney explained to voters that the conservative Reagan position was that government takes care of the basics, such a cleaning the streets and providing police, but that beyond that it is up to private charity to help people in need. The Reagan administration's policy, he said, reflected the credo of David Stockman, director of the Office of Management and Budget: "Nobody is entitled to anything."[23]

Frank was right about Reagan's outlook on the role of government— which matched Ayn Rand's. Rand expressed it through Howard Roark, the hero of *The Fountainhead*, who said, "This our country. The noblest country in the history of men. The country of greatest achievement, greatest prosperity, greatest freedom. This country was not based on selfless service, sacrifice, or renunciation, or any precept of altruism. It was based on a man's right to the pursuit of happiness. . . . Look at the results."

Frank's outlook? Ask *Atlas Shrugged's* Wesley Mouch: ". . . protect the property of the rich and give a greater share to the poor . . . cut down the burden of your taxes and provide you with more government benefits . . . lower prices and raise wages . . . give more freedom to the individual and strengthen the bonds of collective obligations . . . combine the efficiency of free enterprise with the generosity of a planned economy."

But Barney Frank was always more interested in such promises than in founding principles. In a 1991 comment about the document he swore to support and defend against all enemies foreign and domestic, he quipped, "There's too much Constitution worship in this country. It is a good document, but separation of powers is a bad idea. Divided government doesn't work."[24]

Frank's demonization of Reagan's individualist ideals must have resonated just enough in a district with constituents seeking free handouts to sneak past the national conservative bulwark. With an overwhelming advantage, including high-profile endorsements and an historically solid Democratic constituency, Frank eked out a narrow victory against his Republican opponent, winning just five of the 23 cities in the district.

By the time Frank came to Washington, he was leading a conflicted personal life, unable to come to terms with a personal reality that nearly derailed his political career—his homosexuality. Convinced it would quash his national political ambitions, Frank suppressed the truth. He came out of the closet to just a few friends and family members. Staggering under the burden of concealing a double life, he was caustic and belligerent to his colleagues and staff. He comforted himself with an almost manic approach to his work, trying to soothe his private inner turmoil with a public ointment of grandiose rhetoric about helping the less fortunate, including statements about how the "hungry three-year-olds in America bother me a great deal."[25]

On August 23, 1989, the truth broke through Frank's walls of denial. The front-page headline of the *Washington Times* proclaimed, "Sex Sold from Congressman's Apartment," with the subhead, "Frank's

Lover Was 'Call Boy.'" The article ran on the top right side of the page, next to a color photo of the Capitol Hill basement apartment where Barney lived. It began, "A male prostitute provided homosexual and bisexual prostitution services from the apartment of U.S. Rep. Barney Frank on Capitol Hill on a periodic basis from late 1985 through mid-1987, the *Washington Times* has learned."[26]

In the ensuing ethics investigation, Barney acknowledged that in the spring of 1985 he had answered an ad in the *Washington Blade*, the local gay weekly, and paid for sex several times with a male prostitute whom he identified as Stephen Gobie. Barney admitted that he had written letters on congressional stationery to Gobie's probation officer in Virginia stating that he had hired Gobie as a personal aide. Barney also admitted that he allowed Gobie to use his car and his apartment when he was out of town and affirmed that he had used congressional privilege to fix some parking tickets that Gobie had incurred.[27]

Frank acknowledged that he had broken the law by patronizing a prostitute,[28] but maintained that he had not violated any congressional ethics rules.[29] "It turns out that I was being suckered. He was, among other things, a very good con man," he said in his own defense.[30]

The ethics committee concluded that Frank's official memo contained misleading statements in an attempt to reduce Gobie's probation sentence for a previous conviction on cocaine possession and producing child pornography. They also concluded that he improperly used his position for personal purposes to clear Gobie's tickets.[31] The House voted 408 to 18 to accept the ethics panel's recommendation for a reprimand. In the 13 years and seven sessions since Congress established it as an alternative penalty to censure, Frank was just the fifth member of Congress to receive a reprimand from his peers.

While, incredibly, violations of the law do not themselves constitute violations of Congress's ethics code, it's difficult to comprehend how Frank could ever think his conduct reflected creditably on the House, or that he had abided by either the letter or the spirit of the code. In the double-speak world of Barney Frank's relativism, apparently there are no absolutes. The truth is what he wants to believe. It is a theme he'll use again when defending his role in torpedoing the U.S. economy.

Frank's brush with the ethics inquiry did not deter him. As a senior member of the House Banking Committee already rising through the ranks, he wrote a letter to the CEO of Fannie Mae—the giant government-backed housing finance corporation that was under the jurisdiction of his powerful committee for oversight—asking for his help in getting a job for a man named Herb Moses. Moses was subsequently hired by Fannie Mae as a financial analyst.[32]

At the time Barney and Herb were dating.[33]

Frank's "Noble Experiment" in Housing

Barney Frank's story isn't unusual in Washington, but his timing was impressive. He found himself in power at the exact moment when decades of political and philosophical corruption came to a climax that nearly caused the collapse of the American economy.

Ayn Rand's masterpiece, *Atlas Shrugged*, is set in an economic collapse amid such corruption. There are plenty of corrupt government officials like Frank in *Atlas*, first among them Wesley Mouch, the Top Coordinator of the Bureau of Economic Planning and National Resources, who we'd now call an economic czar. A mere congressman, Frank had to confine himself to coordinating just the U.S. housing and financial industries. But he's a match for Mouch when it comes to the economic devastation wrought by his corruption.

In *Atlas*, the cause of the collapse of the economy is "the strike of the men of the mind" led by John Galt. When one by one, the most able businessmen withdraw from the economy and take sanctuary in Galt's Gulch, the economy slides into disaster. Nothing Mouch and his fellow bureaucrats can do will reverse the decline. Galt's strike succeeds in his goal to "extinguish the lights of the world" because a modern economy can't be run based on Mouch's—and Frank's—rotten philosophy.

The core of this philosophical corruption is altruism—or as Frank calls it, "equality." Yes, these words connote noble notions of charity. But to be noble, charity must be voluntary, or else it is simply theft. Mouch and Frank are talking about using the police powers of the state to seize the wealth of some people for the benefit of other people, where *they* get to decide who gets his wealth seized and who gets the benefit. As Rand explained, "Whoever claims the 'right' to 'redistribute' the wealth produced by others is claiming the 'right' to treat human beings as chattel."[34]

We know in great detail Rand's views on government-subsidized housing (Frank's altruistic specialty) because the concept is at the center of the climax of her first major novel, *The Fountainhead*. The individualist architect hero Howard Roark volunteers to design a public housing project without compensation, but only because he thinks he will enjoy the engineering challenge. Roark says at the outset, "I don't believe in government housing. I don't want to hear anything about its noble purposes. I don't think they're noble."

Roark explains,

> "I think it's a worthy undertaking—to provide a decent apartment for a man who earns fifteen dollars a week. But not at the expense of other men. Not if it raises the taxes, raises all the other rents, and makes the man who earns forty live in a rat hole. That's what's happening in New York. Nobody can afford a modern apartment—except the very rich and the paupers."

Ultimately Roark's housing project fails despite his brilliant engineering. When bureaucratic interference destroys his design and thwarts its economies, Roark dynamites the building site. A spectacular blowup to be sure, but it was only one building. The blowup triggered by Frank's bureaucratic interference occurred on a nationwide scale, and the panic it induced spread throughout the global economy. It will take many years for the world to recover from it.

When the end came for Frank's housing bubble, the crowning irony was that the final lethal blow to the system came not from corrupt politicians exploiting the rich, but from corrupt businessmen who became rich beyond the dreams of avarice by figuring out how to exploit corrupt politicians. Just as in *Atlas Shrugged* the corrupt railroad executive James Taggart forged an unholy alliance with bureaucrats like Mouch, corrupt financiers such as Countrywide's Angelo Mozilo (whom we met in Chapter 4, "The Parasite") rode on the easy-money mortgage gravy train made possible by politicians like Barney Frank—and leveraged it up until they drove it straight off the cliff.

Rand once wrote,

> To a . . . primitive socialist mentality—a mentality that clamors for the "redistribution of wealth" without any concern for

the origin of wealth—the enemy is all those who are rich, regardless of the source of their riches. Such mentalities, those aging, graying "liberals," who had been the "idealists" of the 30's, are . . . frantically evading the spectacle of *what kind of rich* are being destroyed and what kind are flourishing under the system they, the "liberals," have established. The grim joke is on them: . . . The collector of their efforts is not the helplessly, brainlessly virtuous "little man" of their flat-footed imagination and shopworn fiction, but the worst type of predatory rich, the rich-by-force, the rich-by-political-privilege, the type who has no chance under capitalism, but who is always there to cash in on every collectivist "noble experiment."[35]

If Frank was the last link in a long, corrupt chain, let's go back to the first link.

Franklin D. Roosevelt created the Federal Housing Administration (FHA) in 1934 as part of his New Deal initiative. During the Great Depression, banks were all but frozen. Mortgage loans, if they were made at all, required 50 percent equity with repayment terms of just three to five years. During this time, less than half of all households owned their homes.

The FHA was born to provide insurance in the form of a government guarantee to give banks confidence in lending on more liberal terms, including significantly lower down payments and 30-year amortization schedules with fixed rates of interest. If a homeowner with an FHA-backed loan defaulted, the federal government would reach into its deep pockets as the ultimate backstop and make the lender whole.

Over time, private mortgage insurance companies came to largely fill this role. Yet despite having outlived its initial usefulness in successfully bridging the scale gap long enough for private enterprise to take hold, the FHA continues to exist in a larger mutated form. As always, once government gets a toehold in the commercial markets, it grows like a fungus. In 1938, the FHA created the Federal National Mortgage Association—now famous by its nickname, Fannie Mae—to sell government-backed bonds and use the proceeds to purchase FHA-guaranteed loans, further institutionalizing the role of government in the private housing market.

From 1968 through 1970, Congress treated the already morphing mass of federal housing programs to a legislative injection of growth hormone. Fannie Mae spawned Ginnie Mae and Freddie Mac, creating an alphabet soup of parallel agencies. Fannie was then spun off as a strange hybrid—a shareholder-owned company trading on the New York Stock Exchange, yet chartered with a "public purpose" and incestuously guided by the department of Housing and Urban Development. To ensure its survival in the savage world of competitive free markets, the enfant terrible also retained special government-sponsored privileges, including tax breaks and an implicit government guarantee of its obligations.

These new so-called government-sponsored enterprises (GSEs) were also given free rein to buy up nongovernment bank mortgages, assuming they met certain standards, including loan limits and credit quality, making them what would henceforth be known as "conforming." Suddenly, commercial banks had a way to offload their mortgages from their books, clearing the way to add new ones and earn new fees. Over a period of years, banks transitioned from lenders who directly retained risks and reaped rewards from their portfolio of investment assets to mere originators of standardized loans passed through to the GSEs for a cut of each transaction. The GSEs, in turn, were permitted to pool conforming loans and package them for further resale to private investors, spawning the first mortgage-backed securities (MBSs), and, in the process, create even more lending capacity.

In its pure form, the MBS is a valuable market innovation. It diversifies away the risk of mortgage default by any individual homeowner, which is inherently difficult to predict. Collect a hundred or so similar loans into a portfolio, and the law of large numbers ensures that whereas any one individual borrower may fall on hard times, the odds that everyone will simultaneously default are small. Investors could buy a share of a mortgage pool and earn a portion of the total profits while spreading the risk of individual default among the entire investor syndicate. To further reduce investor risk, the sponsoring GSE would backstop any losses with a guarantee, making mortgage-backed securities a safe and liquid investment for individuals, institutions, and pension funds alike. Suddenly the housing industry, previously constrained by local lending capacity, was now limited only by the appetite of a gargantuan base of global investors.

And sure enough, during the 1970s as MBSs took hold, home ownership rates rose steadily from 63 percent to 66 percent in 1979. Total national mortgage debt rose modestly as well, from $1.2 trillion in 1970 to $1.9 trillion by the end of the decade. Yet home prices were remarkably stable. The capital markets provided a natural limit to the amount of funding available based on the risk profile of the borrower. As potential homeowners saved responsibly and generated stable income, they could qualify for a mortgage. Others simply rented.

The 1980s ushered in the Reagan era of deregulation, which Frank and his bureaucratic ilk decry as the root of our current mess. The reality is quite different.

In the deregulated world of MBSs, lenders had a larger tool kit of financing options and were able to serve a broader segment of the market with more flexible and customized products while retaining the ability to obtain compensation commensurate to the risks they took. Far from causing a stampede of high-risk loans and a wave of abusive lending practices, the effects were modest at best. Home ownership remained stable during the 1980s, with subprime funding accounting for a tiny fraction of loan volume. So much for the big, bad bugaboo of deregulation. It was the eventual governmental intrusions into that deregulated market under misguided notions of social subsidy— policies originated, pushed, and approved relentlessly by Barney Frank throughout his career—that led us to disaster. (See Figure 6.1.)

It began when new laws in 1986 created a tax asymmetry that caused a wave of debt transfer from consumer loans to mortgages.[36] Mortgage loan volume nearly doubled from a flat-line average of about $1.9 trillion earlier in the decade to $3.5 trillion in 1990. And yet homeowners seemed to have no more trouble than usual making good on their payments. The market ticked along accordingly with modest home price appreciation in line with previous decades. Fannie Mae remained a minor adjunct to the mortgage market during this time, buying primarily bread-and-butter single-family 30-year fixed-rate mortgages and never holding more than 3.5 percent of the nation's total debt outstanding.

Yes, this seemingly subtle change in tax status of debt started a wave. But at first it was only a wave. Frank was about to make it a tsunami.

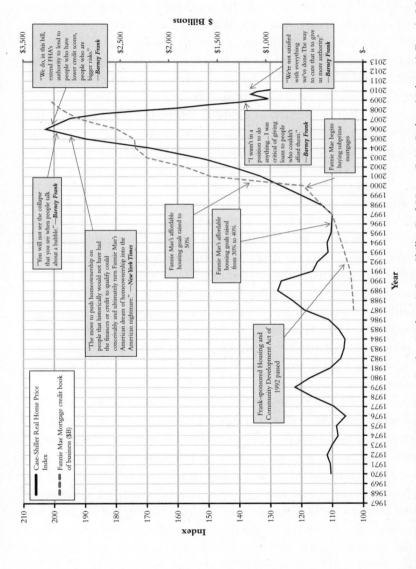

Figure 6.1 Home Prices versus Mortgage Credit. (*Left axis*) Case–Shiller Real Home Price Index; (*right axis*) Fannie Mae Mortgage Credit Book of Business ($ Billions). Under Barney Frank's meddling oversight, government agencies spawned the housing bubble . . . and eventual global economic collapse.

SOURCE: Case–Shiller Real Home Price Index, Fannie Mae 10-Ks, *Congressional Record*

179

Government-Sponsored Booby Prize

Enter the Clinton era and Barney Frank's big chance to spread the nation's productive wealth among the least capable custodians under the banner of social fairness. The Housing and Community Development Act of 1992, co-sponsored by Frank, placed the GSEs, including Fannie Mae, under direct control of the Department of Housing and Urban Development (HUD) and disbanded their advisory board of independent experts in housing finance, actuarial science, and economics. It also authorized the HUD secretary to establish affordable housing goals for the GSEs—putting the fox in charge of the henhouse.

At the time, Herb Moses (Frank's live-in lover and self-proclaimed "only member of the congressional gay spouses caucus") was working at Fannie. Thanks to his relationship with Frank, Moses would rise to become assistant director for product initiatives at the very organization that Frank's committee was charged with overseeing. According to *National Mortgage News*, from his senior-level perch obtained through perks and pull, Moses "helped develop many of Fannie Mae's affordable housing and home improvement lending programs."[37]

There are two ways to make housing affordable. The first is to create fundamental conditions of economic prosperity that encourage productive work and investment. As overall prosperity increases due to core economic growth, more citizens will join the ranks of homeowners with an equity investment in their abodes under rational market economics.

The second is to artificially lower the cost of housing by subsidizing those who can't afford to buy a home priced at a fair market level. Regardless of the terminology used to couch such tactics (government guarantees, lowered down payments, or outright credits), the end result is a redistribution of dollars from people who have earned to people who haven't—and the creation of unsustainable economic distortions that inevitably end in ruin. What Barney Frank and his utopian, quick-fix policies completely miss is that giving someone a house and expecting that person to become economically prosperous is like giving a kid a roomful of books and expecting the child to become literate. Just as literacy breeds book sales, prosperity breeds home ownership—not the other way around.

By 1995, the new law was fully in effect and HUD began jacking up the affordable housing quotas for Fannie from 30 percent to 40 percent, to 50 percent, and eventually to a peak of 56 percent just before the crash. Fannie began buying up mortgages at a furious pace. With so much home-purchasing capacity now open, lenders and mortgage originators couldn't give money away fast enough. Fannie's mortgage credit book ballooned from $254 billion in 1995 to $610 billion in 2000—fully 11 percent of all mortgages in the country—and it hadn't even gotten started.

Frank wanted even more. Barney boldly proclaimed in Congress, "We have an economy that is booming and has helped many people. But it does not help everybody equally, and some people are not helped at all. . . . I think we have an obligation morally, and it makes sense economically, to help with the production of housing."[38]

But there was a problem. It seemed the safe mortgages were already on Fannie's and Freddie's books, so they had to get creative to meet their ever-increasing government lending goals. So in 2000, under Barney Frank's committee's oversight, Fannie and Freddie expanded their mortgage purchases to include Alt-A, A-minus, and subprime mortgages in addition to private-label securities (these are all technical terms for mortgages of less than stellar credit quality, sometimes very much less than stellar).

Alt-A mortgages have little or no borrower income or asset documentation backing them. A-minus and subprime mortgages are made to borrowers with low credit scores and a history of trouble repaying lenders. With a new government-sponsored buyer willing to gobble up these risky loans, the subprime market exploded like Barney Frank's waistline at an all-you-can-eat buffet. What was a minor fringe product in the 1990s accounting for a mere $35 billion in debt outstanding—less than 1 percent of all mortgages—quickly reached critical mass under the GSEs' radioactive funding injection, spawning a mushroom cloud of $1 trillion in new subprime originations during 2006—fully 50 percent of all mortgages issued.[39]

Meanwhile, Barney Frank was reveling in the home ownership rate as it skyrocketed to a historic high, approaching 70 percent of all households. Here was Frank's lifelong vision coming to fruition. "It seems to me," said Wesley Mouch in *Atlas Shrugged*, "that the end justifies the means." But did Frank even understand what means he was employing?

Frank didn't see that by forcing home ownership above 60 percent, you are, by definition, pushing loans on the bottom 40 percent of income earners who probably can't afford to repay them (or even to cover the expenses of home ownership, such as taxes and insurance). In 1995 this represented 20 million households earning less than $27,000 annually. Many earned much less. Is it reasonable to lend the median home value of $120,000 to a family bringing in just a few hundred dollars a week and expect anything less than disaster?

Frank didn't see, because he didn't even look. As Wesley Mouch's fellow bureaucrat Eugene Lawson put it in *Atlas Shrugged*, "We must not let our vulgar difficulties disrupt our feeling that it's a noble plan motivated solely by the public welfare. It's for the good of the people. People need it. Need comes first, so we don't have to consider anything else."

But consider this: With a combination of low rates and easy money available to nearly all comers, buyers began bidding up properties across the nation, exacerbating the affordability gap even further. As prices rose, the GSEs lowered their standards further and bought even more mortgages to achieve their politically forced housing goals. This renewed buying in turn fed the already out-of-control process like a financial Chernobyl. By the end of 2003, Fannie alone held $2.2 trillion in mortgage debt, nearly one in three mortgages in the country. It was a sum larger than the entire housing loan market just 20 years before.

Warning flags began to pop up, followed by signal flares, then alarm bells. Undaunted, Frank ignored the facts, belittled his critics, and pushed for even more. Despite a complete lack of experience in any area outside of politics, he felt he knew better than everyone else on almost any subject he touched upon. "Expertise is sometimes more overrated than the dollar," he once said, delivering another intimidating but logically screwy epigram in a debate.[40]

In 2003, proposals were already being bandied about to increase oversight on the GSEs. When asked by *Mortgage Banking* magazine in November about the odds of mortgage regulatory reform passing his committee by the end of the year, he responded, "Virtually 100 percent negative," adding, "[We] have a lot of other things to deal with."[41] These "other things" included increasing the FHA limits and "doing something about down-payment assistance for low-income people for homeownership."[42]

He went on to defend his opposition to the proposal by the U.S. Treasury—now in Republican hands—to rein in the GSEs by saying that "it interferes with housing. Virtually every entity we deal with in the United States that cares about housing—whether it's low-income housing advocacy groups, community development groups, Realtors, the home builders—they are all opposed to the Treasury proposal as one that would interfere with housing."[43] Since when are Realtors, home builders, and special-interest groups representative of "every entity" in the United States that has an interest in housing? What about 160 million taxpaying households, the majority of whom were doing just fine without Frank's wealth reallocation programs? Isn't invoking the beneficiaries of a housing bubble to justify the government subsidy spigot like citing defense contractors against reducing the size of our military? Apparently, what constitutes "interference" to Barney Frank is what others call laissez-faire capitalism. "Hands off" means not interrupting the flow of money from the producers to the parasites through Barney's hands.

The twisted defense of socialistic policies and denial of economic reality wouldn't stop there. In October 2004, Gretchen Morgenson ran an article in the *New York Times* quoting analyst Josh Rosner, presaging with deadly accuracy the results of Fannie's relaxed underwriting standards. "The move to push homeownership on people that historically would not have had the finances or credit to qualify could conceivably and ultimately turn Fannie Mae's American dream of homeownership into the American nightmare of homeownership where people are trapped in their homes," Mr. Rosner said. "If incomes don't rise or home values don't keep rising, or if interest rates rose considerably, you could quickly end up with significantly more people underwater with their mortgages and unable to pay."[44]

Later that same week in a subcommittee hearing on Fannie Mae, Frank acknowledged that he had read that very article but then dismissed it with a pabulum of blather. "There was an article by Gretchen Morgenson in the *New York Times* on Sunday that said the problem is that they have done too much to bring housing to people who really cannot afford it and should not be given this chance to own the housing. Her article said the problem here has been they have overextended by lending money to people who were below the economic level that should be there," Frank stated for the record. "I think what we need to do is to go forward as we were ready to do with a tougher safety and soundness regulator, but in ways that do not impinge on Fannie's and Freddie's ability to do a better job than they have been doing with affordable housing and to continue to do the job they have been doing with regard to housing in general."[45]

But national integrity of the financial system was not Barney's goal. Later in the same hearing Fannie's chief regulator, Armando Falcon, director of the Office of Federal Housing Enterprise Oversight, seemed desperate to warn the subcommittee of a serious and looming financial crisis before it was too late. During questioning, Frank cut off the witness and refused to hear about the safety and soundness issues that might restrict his ability to continue funneling federal support to an ever-increasing spiral of socially altruistic housing inflation.

> Mr. Frank: *But I have seen nothing in here that suggests that the safety and soundness are at issue, and I think it serves us badly to raise safety and soundness as a kind of a general shibboleth, when it does not seem to be the issue.*
>
> Mr. Falcon: *No, I think our report absolutely does implicate safety and soundness.*
>
> Mr. Frank: *Is the safety and soundness at risk now?*
>
> Mr. Falcon: *Are they at risk of becoming insolvent right now? No. We have an agreement with the board in place that will address these problems, provide an adequate capital cushion. We think we—*
>
> Mr. Frank: *That is the answer. The rest is just rhetoric.*

According to Fannie's annual report, "Determining our loan loss reserves is complex and requires judgment by management about the effect of matters that are inherently uncertain."[46] Even while Frank was busy bludgeoning the prophetic whistle-blowers in his committee hearing, those reserves totaled just $745 million on guaranteed loans of over $2.3 trillion. Put another way, Fannie reserved just 30 cents of every $1,000 to pay for any potential losses due to borrower defaults on loans it guaranteed—just 0.03 percent. Private-sector banks typically hold 8 percent, or $80 per thousand.[47] Residential mortgage delinquencies and outright foreclosure would later top 14 percent, or nearly 500 times higher than accounted for by Fannie's reserves.[48] To borrow Frank's own bombast, "on what planet" is this sound judgment?

The chairman of the subcommittee, Republican Michael Oxley, did hear the warning and in April 2005 introduced H.R. 1461, the Federal Housing Finance Reform Act of 2005. The bill would have effectively removed the GSEs from HUD control and placed them under a new, stronger regulator with the ability to raise capital reserve requirements to ensure safety and soundness, to establish loan limits, and to reduce affordable housing goals. Additional amendments were offered by Republicans to further impose capital strictures on the GSEs, and to dispose of assets or liabilities that pose a risk to the financial system. The amendments were defeated.

The bill itself passed the House, with Barney Frank voting "Nay" on additional regulation. It eventually died in the Senate, where Republicans held the majority but lacked the 60 votes necessary to push the bill past the Wesley Mouch think-alikes Chuck Schumer and Christopher Dodd.

Frank again went on record with some of the most delusional statements of the decade. In front of Congress on June 26, 2005, he made the case for further home ownership subsidies, donning his ephod as an oracle of housing economics.

> Homes that are occupied may see an ebb and flow in the price at a certain percentage level, but you will not see the collapse that you see when people talk about a bubble. So those of us on our committee in particular will continue to push for homeownership. Obviously, the market will take care of a large number of people, but it will not take care of everybody. And if we are going to expand homeownership, there will have to be a sensible set of public policies, such as reducing the down payment in the FHA. . . . There are also a variety of advocacy groups that work with us so that we can make homeownership available to people who might not on their own in a market situation be able to afford it.[49]

Yes, by all means, Comrade Frank, let's make home ownership available to those who can't afford it. Let's reduce the already insignificant 3 percent FHA down payment to zero to make sure we can get even more penniless, financially incapable citizens participating in our socialist vision of free assets for the people at the expense of the rich. Then, when it all blows up, we'll brand the victims as reckless perpetrators of the collapse even as we evict them from their homes, shatter their already fragile credit scores, and put them through the humiliation of bankruptcy or outright financial ruin.

Then, even after housing prices had peaked in late 2005, driven up by government interference in the free market, even as defaults were on the rise and the country's financial system was teetering on the edge of collapse, Frank spoke out in support of H.R. 5121, the Expanding American Homeownership Act of 2006. The bill would further degrade the FHA's already low standards to chase the dragon's tail of home values. It eliminated the measly 3 percent down payment as unaffordable, and raised the government guarantees from 87 percent to 100 percent of the already inflated median home value. Incredibly, he insisted the bill would profit the nation. "This is a money maker bill. This is a bill that expands housing, but it will make money for the Treasury."[50]

With a complete misunderstanding of how free markets manage risk, Frank made the ultimate plunge into collectivism.

> We do, in this bill, extend FHA's authority to lend to people who have lower credit scores, people who are bigger risks. And when that happens, you have to worry about higher defaults. I did not think we, the Federal Government, should be in the position of saying that, as we lend to people who are bigger risks, we should take that risk pool and make those people who are higher risks who meet their obligations pay for the people who are higher risks who don't . . . it is not fair, and we the Federal Government should not set the principle that one low-income person or 10 low-income people who meet their responsibilities are the ones who have to make up for the low-income person who isn't able to.[51]

Democratic California congresswoman Maxine Waters said about the bill's passage that "it certainly could not have happened without my ranking member, Mr. Frank, who has the ability to see things in legislation that no one else sees."[52] Apparently he sees nonexistent profits and views risk through a kaleidoscope created by Karl Marx. In Frank's world, smokers would be charged the same life insurance premium as nonsmokers, while Treasury bonds, stock mutual funds, and slot machines would all pay the same return.

The Money Pit

In 2008, we experienced the full consequences of Frank's collectivist power trip. Bear Stearns failed in March, triggering the collapse of Frank's house of cards. On July 1, Bank of America completed its purchase of Countrywide Financial, one of the largest mortgage lenders on the planet, under severe financial distress from its headlong dash into subprime loans. On July 11, the Federal Deposit Insurance Corporation (FDIC) put IndyMac Bank—a 1997 spin-off from Countrywide—into receivership.

On July 14, a still delusional Frank—the very man supposedly most in the know on the status of the agencies he oversaw on behalf of the American people—said in a CNBC interview, "I think this is a case where Fannie and Freddie are fundamentally sound, that they are not in danger of going under."[53]

On September 8, Fannie Mae and Freddie Mac were placed under conservatorship, a legal status akin to Chapter 11 bankruptcy, sparking a global financial panic. As financial fissures opened worldwide, the Wall Street Journal declared it "the worst financial crisis since the Great Depression."[54]

When Fannie and Freddie were finally taken over by the government in 2008, more than 10 million subprime and other weak loans either were on their books or were in mortgage-backed securities they had guaranteed.[55] An additional 4.5 million were guaranteed by the FHA and sold through Ginnie Mae before 2008, and a further 2.5 million loans were made under the rubric of the Community Reinvestment Act (CRA), which required insured banks to provide mortgage credit to home buyers who were at or below 80 percent of median income. Thus, almost two-thirds of all the bad mortgages in our financial system, many of which are now defaulting at unprecedented rates, were bought by government agencies or required by government regulations.[56]

On September 14, Lehman Brothers collapsed and Merrill Lynch was sold in panic to Bank of America. On September 18, Treasury Secretary Henry Paulson and Federal Reserve Chairman Ben Bernanke met with Barney Frank and other legislators to propose a $700 billion emergency bailout fund to buy toxic assets from financial institutions. Bernanke told them, "If we don't do this, we may not have an economy on Monday."[57]

On September 25, Washington Mutual was seized by the FDIC and its banking assets were sold to JPMorgan Chase for $1.9 billion. Washington Mutual was the biggest bank failure ever in all U.S. history, scuttled by $77 billion in subprime mortgages and billions more in other toxic home loans.[58] Over the next few weeks the stock market would lose over one-third of its value.

After Paulsen and Bernanke's $700 billion Troubled Asset Relief Program (TARP) was approved by Congress, Paulson decided not to buy toxic assets at all as had originally been pitched.[59] Instead, he'd buy equity stakes directly in U.S. banks to make the government a direct owner in private enterprise—a move amounting to a partial socialist-style nationalization.

At the climax of *Atlas Shrugged* when the economy is crashing— economically and physically—Wesley Mouch and the other bureau- crats whose policies had caused it all huddled together in abject fear, thinking only John Galt could save them now. "'He . . . has . . . to . . . save . . . us,' said Mouch slowly, as if straining the last of his mind into blankness and delivering an ultimatum to reality. 'He has to . . . save the system.'"

At the climax of the banking crisis of 2008, it was all in Henry Paulson's hands. Barney Frank personally called the Treasury secretary and didn't exactly beg him to save the system—just one little part of it: a TARP cash infusion for the Boston-based OneUnited Bank.

On November 25, 2008, following Frank's intervention, the Treasury Department awarded $12,063,000 in bailout funds to OneUnited, which is located in Frank's district.[60]

"I Need Wider Powers"

Did Barney Frank admit that his policies to expand home ownership had nearly destroyed the housing market, the mortgage market, the banking system, and the whole world economy? No—and here is the most chilling parallel between the real Barney Frank and the fictional Wesley Mouch.

As the economy is collapsing in *Atlas Shrugged*, a fellow bureaucrat— an especially cynical one—advises Mouch, "Whatever you do, don't apologize. . . . Make them feel guilty." Mouch takes the advice, just as Barney Frank did. "I'm not apologizing! . . . I'm not to blame. I need wider powers."

How did Frank make them feel guilty? Frank's biographer sums up Frank's position this way: "Lenders' ability to package mortgage loans into securities (lend money and sell the loans to passive investors) took away from lenders the incentive to be more careful in making loans."[61]

How did Frank prove he's not to blame? In an interview with Aaron Task in July 2009, Frank denied all responsibility by saying, "I wasn't in a position to do anything . . . even when it did come up as an issue, I was critical of giving loans to people who couldn't afford them. I wanted to help them out with housing, but with rental housing."[62]

Did he really call for broader powers, even when it was his powers that nearly destroyed the world economy? In a speech to young Democrats in June 2010, he said, "You can reach out to your fellow young people and make it clear to them, that when [sic] they may not be satisfied with everything we've done—we're not satisfied with everything we've done. The way to cure that is to give us more authority."[63]

Yes, he really said that. It's almost as though he was *trying* to walk in Wesley Mouch's footsteps. Don't let anyone tell you that life doesn't imitate art.

Did Frank get those wider powers that Wesley Mouch wanted? Yes, at least in a way. In July 2010, President Obama signed into law the Dodd-Frank Wall Street Reform and Consumer Protection Act. It is a massively complex law of 848 pages that creates sweeping new regulatory powers for the federal government over every aspect of the American financial industry, from banking and credit cards to derivatives and monetary policy.

Frank's name is on the bill, which assures that he will go down in history as a noble regulatory reformer, rather than what he actually was: an ignoble regulatory deformer, who used the power of government to destroy rather than to protect.

But maybe the American people aren't as easily gulled as Frank has always expected. Bill or no bill, Frank personally no longer has the power he once enjoyed. In 2010 the Democrats lost majority control of the House of Representatives, which means that Frank is no longer chairman of the Financial Services Committee.

So the real-life Mr. Mouch wants wider powers? The voters have said, "You've done quite enough already, Mr. Mouch."

Chapter 7

The Capitalist Champion

*T. J. Rodgers as Francisco d'Anconia,
the modern Renaissance man and agent
provocateur for capitalism*

*Francisco could do anything he undertook, he could do it better than
anyone else, and he did it without effort. There was no boasting in his
manner and consciousness, no thought of comparison. His attitude was
not: "I can do it better than you," but simply: "I can do it." What
he meant by doing was doing superlatively.*

—Atlas Shrugged

Who is Francisco d'Anconia?
In *Atlas Shrugged*, Francisco d'Anconia is one of John Galt's
inner circle in organizing the "mind on strike"—persuading
men of ability to walk away from an immoral collectivist economic and political system, thus hastening its collapse.

(Continued)

191

D'Anconia is one of the world's wealthiest men, heir to a South American copper-mining business. From childhood he shows extraordinary ability in everything he undertakes, from athletics to academics to business. His ambition is to be worthy of his inheritance by expanding the already enormous d'Anconia Copper empire.

But when Galt persuades d'Anconia to help him with his strike, d'Anconia acts as an intellectual provocateur—brilliantly skewering collectivist politicians and businessmen, and inspiring beleaguered industrialists. In attempting to recruit the nation's leading steel executive for Galt's strike, d'Anconia delivers at a cocktail party an impromptu treatise on the meaning and morality of money that is Rand's most sparklingly compelling writing on the virtues of capitalism.

"Is this the headquarters of a major chip maker in Silicon Valley or the Football Hall of Fame in Canton, Ohio?" we wondered to ourselves as we stood amid a shrine of Green Bay Packers memorabilia in the second-floor Lombardi Conference room on Champion Court in San Jose, California. In front of us, a 15-foot expanse of wall paid tribute to Packers greats through the ages, every inch covered with autographed 8 × 10 framed photos arranged neatly in alphabetical order with an engineer's precision. Behind us, a plaque commemorating Bart Starr's 35–10 victory over the Kansas City Chiefs in Super Bowl I hung next to an engraved homage to the famed 1967 NFL Championship "Ice Bowl" game played against the Dallas Cowboys on rock-hard Lambeau Field during an arctic blast that had stadium thermometers registering 15 below zero. Toward the far window, a Packers lava lamp stood at one end of a vast conference table like a kitschy Buddha overlooking his reverent temple of green and gold.

Suddenly out of nowhere appeared a sandy-haired, compactly athletic figure dressed in a navy blue Dartmouth College jogging suit over a bright yellow T-shirt. He could have been the head coach coming in fresh off the practice field to do a pregame interview with ESPN. "Hi, I'm T. J. Rodgers," he announced. "Let's go to my office."[1]

Dr. Thurman John Rodgers[2]—known universally as T.J.—commands a small but fertile plot of Silicon Valley's vast technology landscape. The company he founded in 1982, Cypress Semiconductor, generates $268 million in cash flow on $850 million in revenues with 3,600 employees worldwide. While its $3.4 billion market cap seems small beside next-door giants like $115 billion Intel, Cypress is world leader in universal serial bus (USB) controllers and maintains a position at the vanguard of technological innovation with the world's only programmable analog and digital embedded design platform, having sold nearly a billion units.

As if on cue, a muffled bark from the reception area prompted a quick explanation from T.J. "It's my dog," he said matter-of-factly. "His name is Dollar. He's a Jack Russell." Why the name? We free-associated to the fact that Ayn Rand wore a golden dollar sign pin on her lapel for decades, and that a golden dollar sign hung high above Galt's Gulch, the hideaway portrayed in *Atlas Shrugged* as the safe haven for the country's greatest industrialists, on strike against collectivism. That dollar sign in Galt's Gulch was a gift of Francisco d'Anconia, the key character in *Atlas Shrugged* of whom T. J. Rodgers is a living embodiment.

D'Anconia was a superb industrialist—as is Rodgers, the founder and longtime CEO of a leading semiconductor manufacturer. D'Anconia was superb at everything he undertook, in a wide variety of fields—as is Rodgers, the double major in chemistry and physics who owns vineyards and makes sublime wine. And d'Anconia was a flamboyant and articulate agent provocateur for capitalism and liberty—as is Rodgers, a fearless and controversial critic of government regulation, corporate welfare, protectionism, and political correctness.

These attributes come together in Rodgers, as they do in d'Anconia, as an integrated whole. He runs his highly successful business in accordance with his philosophy, and his philosophy in turn is informed by the realities of his business, which itself is informed by the realities of the physics of silicon.

This integration is central to all of Rand's greatest heroes. In *Atlas Shrugged*, d'Anconia and his two best friends, John Galt and Ragnar Danneskjöld, went to college together, where they all double-majored in physics and philosophy. As their teacher observed, "It is not a combination of interests one encounters nowadays." But it made sense to d'Anconia. Planning a career in the copper business, he declared, "I'll study electrical engineering, because power companies are the biggest customers of d'Anconia Copper." For similarly practical career reasons, Rodgers would study the same thing; in fact, he earned a PhD in it. Francisco continued, "I'm going to study philosophy because I'll need it to protect d'Anconia Copper." For similarly practical reasons, Rodgers studies the philosophical underpinnings of capitalism, and devotes enormous energies to defending them and evangelizing for them.

This integration can be seen in the short list of Cypress Core Values on display in the headquarters building where Rodgers makes his office. They are an embodiment of Rodgers's personal code.

- We thrive on competing against the world's best.
- We do not tolerate losing.
- We are smart, tough, and work hard.
- We tell the truth and don't make excuses.
- We value knowledge, logic, and reason.
- We admit to solve problems quickly.
- We deplore politicians.
- We choose "Cypress wins" over "looking good."

Rodgers's basic logical premise is the concept that, in his own words, "Freedom is good, period. End of discussion." He doesn't need economic arguments to accept freedom as a fundamental moral good, but he also recognizes that freedom and wealth go hand in hand. He cites empirical studies from the Fraser Institute showing a clear, direct, and universal correlation between objective measures of freedom and economic prosperity among the nations of the world. The freer you are, the wealthier you are as a society. Both are good things, and you can't have the latter without the former. Many of his battles in the arena of public opinion have centered around the misguided notion that somehow money is inherently bad, money corrupts, and money is the root of all evil.

Wearing his signature wire-rimmed owl-round glasses, Rodgers slips easily into his chair—and the conversation. He weaves a complex verbal tapestry from threads of amusing anecdotes and hard facts peppered with mild profanities, including his catchphrase—"bullshit." The experience is as entertaining as it is informative. Assertive but not bullying, persuasive without coming off as salesy, T. J. Rodgers glows with the gravitas found in those who are truly at ease in their own skin. When listening to Rodgers, you get the feeling he's not trying to convince you of anything; he's just calmly reciting the truth for those who choose to hear.

The Bad Boy of Silicon Valley

"If you look at second row up, second one from the right—'The Bad Boy of Silicon Valley,'" begins Rodgers, pointing to an office wall with over a dozen framed magazine covers featuring him, "I got my picture on the cover of *BusinessWeek* for being the bad boy where I said we were losing to the Japanese because we had crappy quality and didn't manage our companies as well, and it had nothing to do with government subsidies, and government subsidies will only make it worse."

Subsidies, or what T.J. refers to as "corporate welfare," are a hot-button annoyance for the 62-year-old CEO. He has testified before Congress against government protectionism and pork-barrel spending. He even wrote and published a "Declaration of Independence" from corporate welfare, decrying a government tax burden totaling 35 percent of gross domestic product (GDP) and supporting major budget cuts, "even if it meant funding cuts for my own company." The proclamation was signed by nearly 100 CEOs, including Jerry Sanders of Advanced Micro Devices (AMD), Wilf Corrigan of LSI Logic, and legendary venture capitalist John Doerr of Kleiner Perkins Caufield & Byers.[3]

"You listen to the CEOs of the really big companies talk blather about free markets and you think okay, I'm CEO, they're CEO, we're brothers, we face the same challenges: government intervention, socialism, in addition to real competitors, and so we ought to be kindred spirits," explains Rodgers. "And yet when you interact on certain things with those CEOs, you see horrible things happening. They're trying to lock Honda out of the United States for chrissake, because they can't make cars well enough. They're going to Washington to get their fair share of the pork."

Over the years Rodgers realized that the vast majority of his fellow CEOs traveled a distinctly different arc to achieve their positions of power. He has very little in common with them. Rodgers built his business through entrepreneurial effort, using his considerable mental power to dissect the very substance of nature down to the atomic structure of silicon itself and then used that knowledge to bring new value into physical creation.

Most other CEOs rose through the ranks of giant bureaucracies by playing politics, currying favor, building a power base, and not rocking the boat. "The statist businessman wins by using the state to gain competitive advantage," Rodgers once wrote. "His perks—corporate jets, limos, lavish expense-account dinners—are the rewards for climbing the ladder."[4] Their primary focus is on holding on to the power and perks of office even at the expense of their own companies.

By contrast, Rodgers flies coach. He has no time for corporate power struggles. He's focused on creating competitive products in the fast-changing world of high technology against a constantly changing field of hungry start-ups and international competitors. "They aren't your buddies and they aren't your kindred spirits," Rodgers finally concluded about many of his fellow CEOs. "They have the same title as you and that's it. And over the years, you find out that there are only a few real free-market capitalists who happen to be CEOs, very few."

Perhaps the sharpest example for T.J., and the one that seems to rankle him the most, was the spawning of a consortium called SEMATECH (Semiconductor Manufacturing Technology). Billed as a "bold experiment in industry-government cooperation,"[5] the very description sounds like socialist propaganda to Rodgers's ears—pure anathema to his core beliefs in free-market competition.

In 1987, the U.S. semiconductor industry was facing tough competition from Japanese chip makers who, according to Rodgers, operated well-run companies in a benign corporate environment with a good tax policy. Instead of upping their game to compete head-on, 14 U.S. technology companies, including big names like Intel, Hewlett-Packard, Motorola, and Texas Instruments, formed SEMATECH and went crying to Washington for help against the supposedly unfair Japanese threat. After the heavyweight consortium played the national security card by claiming that our military would be detrimentally impacted if the U.S. semiconductor industry were harmed, the government eagerly ponied up $100 million a year in subsidies for the group.[6]

It was more than double Cypress Semiconductor's revenues that year. Rodgers wanted nothing to do with it. He likened the group to "General Motors trying to become more efficient by having a centralized fin-design department."[7] His public denouncement and refusal to play along with industry leaders in their conspiracy to sucker the American people earned him an outsider's reputation. Or as he puts it with an air of subdued pride, "Well, 'bad boy' of course is walking away from free government money."

From the Gridiron to Silicon Valley

It's hard to imagine a more genuine American success story. T.J.'s father was literally the son of a sharecropper who farmed cotton in Alabama during the Great Depression. He was in ninth grade before he got his first pair of shoes. He never graduated from high school. The day after Pearl Harbor he left the drudgery of the farm and signed up for World War II and was gone for five consecutive Christmases.

The Army saw fit to make T.J.'s dad a mechanic, and he fought under General Douglas MacArthur in the Pacific. He developed a lifelong hatred of the Japanese, which makes T.J.'s own opposition to government subsidies to fight Japanese competition all the more remarkable. "I remember my dad waking up with nightmares about World War II, as late as the 1960s," recalls Rodgers. "John Kennedy was already president and my dad was still having bad dreams about World War II."

T.J.'s mother graduated from the teaching program at the University of Wisconsin at Oshkosh and began her career in 1940. She and four other single teachers shared a room in a hotel in Sheboygan, Wisconsin. "My mother comes into the hotel and there's this 'cute lieutenant' in the lobby who's recruiting for World War II," relates Rodgers. "So my mother starts flirting with the guy, and talks to him and fills out paperwork and stuff, so she has more face time with him. Then she gets a letter: 'Thank you very much for enlisting. You will report to Truax Air Force base in Madison, Wisconsin.'"

The military tested her and found she had strong intellectual aptitude. With her college degree and teaching background, she was sent to St. Louis University to learn about electronics—the new technology of wireless communications and radar. She spent the rest of the war teaching radio electronics to military technicians.

T.J.'s parents met fortuitously at Camp McCoy in northern Wisconsin when they were both being processed out of the army after World War II. They settled back in Oshkosh, where T.J. grew up in the 1950s and 1960s surrounded by a culture of football—and the Packers were the only game in town.

It was T.J.'s mother who sparked his interest and passion for electronics. "When I was in third grade," remembers Rodgers, "she brought out her books on vacuum tube oscillators and detectors, circuits, and other radios and got me interested in electronics, and that's what I always wanted to do."

He also credits his mother with instilling in him a logical temperament, although as a sort of antimodel. "My mother was smart—excellent verbal skills—and illogical," recounts Rodgers. "If I argued, I'd either get an emotional, screaming response or I'd get some bullshit argument that was ridiculous, so my hackles go up with that kind of treatment."

This is one Silicon Valley titan who was never a geek. T.J. was a high school football star who played in two championship games and was recruited to the Dartmouth gridiron for college. "In football, there's none of the touchy-feely shit," Rodgers explains about his passion for the game, smiling. "You're down on your face in the mud. You know the guy you're supposed to block for has been tackled. The guy who tackled him is laughing at you, and the coach says, 'Pretty shitty job.' . . . You know, I don't know if you can start if you can't turn that around."

Despite a punishing athletic training schedule, he breezed through his chemistry courses, earning a major by his junior year. Then for good measure he tacked on a second major in physics because he was "bored with chemistry." His last term, on what he calls a "lark," he took an electrical engineering course.

"I got a physics degree. I got a chemistry degree. And this electrical engineering stuff has got to be bullshit," he thought. "It wasn't; it was hard," he realized, which is just the kind of challenge that inspires a guy like Rodgers. "It was extremely interesting and it was a course using chips from Silicon Valley to make circuit boards that actually *did* stuff." After building a light organ for his class project that flashed colored Christmas lights based on the various sound frequencies from his home hi-fi, he was hooked.

Graduating second in his class, "back in the days before everybody got A's to make 'em feel good," he was accepted in the graduate physics program at Stanford University prior to rediscovering his true passion for electronics. Switching majors at Stanford, as he would soon find out, was no small feat. At one point T.J. recalls being told by someone in the administration that "they were Stanford and I wasn't, and you didn't just move from one division to another. You're accepted in physics and that was it."

After a persistent networking effort and letter-writing campaign, luck would shine on the budding silicon scientist. The electrical engineering department had just purchased an expensive piece of chip-making equipment to grow semiconductor wafers using exotic gases. The problem was nobody in the double-E department knew anything about the sophisticated chemistry needed to operate the machine. Enter Rodgers, with not only a chemistry degree but a physics undergrad degree to boot. They hired him on the spot. He was in. "I paid my way through college running that machine for that laboratory," he recalls fondly.

Rodgers earned his doctorate among the founding greats of twentieth-century technology. He took courses from William Shockley, co-inventor of the transistor, the device that replaced bulky vacuum tubes of his mother's era and ushered in the microchip and computer revolution. He also studied under J. D. Meindl, who later won the 2006 Institute of Electrical and Electronics Engineers (IEEE) Medal of Honor for pioneering contributions to microelectronics.

It was a heady time to be in Silicon Valley pushing the bleeding edge of technology. The significance wasn't lost on Rodgers. "We knew exactly what was happening," he said about the emergence of microchip technology and integrated circuits. "We knew we were going to conquer the world; we knew it was the revolution."

Rodgers wrote his doctoral dissertation on advanced integrated circuit technology for micro-power integrated circuits. His visionary work correctly predicted the physical needs of futuristic low-power-consumption integrated circuits decades before their modern use in products ranging from powerful, long-life cell phones to military guidance systems.

Planting the Seed of Cypress

With a crisp new Stanford PhD diploma and a fresh idea for a specialized microchip technology he had invented, the now Dr. Rodgers shunned an offer from Intel, opting instead for a role at smaller, more nimble Advanced Microsystems Inc. (AMI). The chip he invented there turned out to be a financial failure and he soon found himself on the street looking for work.

Once again he stiff-armed the giant Intel and took a job with W. J. (Jerry) Sanders at Advanced Micro Devices (AMD) working on a memory chip similar to the one he had created at AMI. Rodgers learned a lot from Sanders about image, marketing, and competing in the rough-and-tumble world of Silicon Valley in the 1970s.[8] He also thought he could do even better than AMD in the memory chip market by striking out on his own.

In 1983 Rodgers scored venture funding and founded Cypress Semiconductor, taking Sanders's vice president of marketing, Lowell Turriff, with him. The move spawned a lawsuit from AMD and a bitter rivalry that lasted for years. The climate of the Valley in those days made it more like a medieval turf battle than a civilized game of country club tennis. Rodgers himself formed "raiding parties" to capture the top engineers from other companies for his own ranks.[9] The competitive experience seems to have cemented his take-no-prisoners business value system and appreciation of hard work.

"All of a sudden, when you are in start-up, and your friends are going to get put on the street if you don't make money and are able to pay them," explains Rodgers about the uniquely entrepreneurial culture of the Valley. "You realize that making the money is good, proper, and moral, and it does good for people."

He adds, "And you look at how hard it is to do that and how hard it is to compete as a start-up against a big, established company, or

Japanese companies as a group, or today the Chinese companies as a group, and you all of a sudden realize that doing that is an accomplishment and it takes all of your skill and all of your energy, and it's the right and proper thing to do."

Despite charging hard for decades, Rodgers still maintains a passion and a work ethic not many match. Aside from a daily lunchtime run, he works every waking hour of the day. He tackles stacks of technical journals in the mornings, saying, "*Transactions on Electron Devices* is not something you read while you are having dinner or a glass of wine." After a brutal day at the office managing his employees and solving problems, he lugs a Pepsi crate of paperwork home to complete in the evenings from a floating desk in his hot tub.

Like Francisco d'Anconia, Rodgers sees money as simply a benchmark, an indicator of value created, not an end to itself. "I like working—working (and learning) is what I like," sums up T.J.'s primary motivation, like a true Rand hero. "It is *the* gratifying thing to me.

"All of a sudden you've got a huge manufacturing problem and the puzzle is multidimensional—extremely complicated—and therefore extremely interesting, and always changing," Rodgers explains eagerly about his inner motivation and source of inherent drive. "What worked two years ago is now obsolete. Either you solve the new set of problems or you're out of there; the whole Valley's that way."

His schedule doesn't leave much time for philosophizing, and Rodgers claims to have never read *Atlas Shrugged* or *The Fountainhead*. Nevertheless, he's an avid fan of Rand's nonfiction work—and has quoted several of her more subtle economic and political ideas in his own writings. He even hired a Randian philosopher named Jason Alexander to conduct presentations on Objectivism to his executive staff. "I got almost all of my knowledge of Rand from him," he relates.

In 1992, Rodgers wrote a book called *No Excuses Management* (Currency/Doubleday) in which he laid out his no-nonsense operating methods in a playbook for like-minded business leaders. His approach to employees seems to be like a hard-charging football coach—or maybe even a bit like a drill sergeant. There is no coddling. The measures of success are objective. Do your job. Solve problems. Understand and admit your mistakes. Rodgers clearly loves doing business, but with his team, it's tough love.

"There are people in the world, those who have been through self-esteem stuff when they were kids and got wrecked that way," sums up Rodgers's perspective on the popular feel-good management culture. "They screw something up and it costs the company a million dollars because they didn't care that much. Then they would like to hear, 'I'm glad that you made that amount of progress, but, you know, we could really improve even further (like lose less than a million dollars) if we did this and that.' I don't do that. To me that's a lie."

Rodgers does tolerate mistakes from his troops; in fact, he welcomes them, saying, "If they don't make mistakes, then we're not pushing them, and if we're not pushing them, we're not going to be competitive." What he won't tolerate are excuses, ignorance, or apathy. "If a guy comes in and doesn't know what's going on, that's bad. If he doesn't *care* that he doesn't know what's going on, that's *real* bad," explains Rodgers. His solution? Displayed in a poster on the wall of his office is a horrifying image of a toothbrush—with stainless-steel bristles. "You bring out the stainless-steel brush and rough the guy up a little bit and if he goes away, congratulations—self-selection."

Rodgers also instills a self-reinforcing culture intolerant of corporate politics. The admonition in Cypress's values statement "We deplore politicians" isn't a reference to public office holders, be they Democrats or Republicans; it's about *office* politicians. "They try their little politics at lunch someday, and they get zapped," T.J. explains of a typical misfit who somehow makes it past his arduous new-employee screening process. "Maybe they undermine somebody and they get zapped again, and then they realize that 'my way of doing business—enhancing my reputation by undercutting others—is not in the interest of the company,' and what happens is the troops eat them up. They go away."

Yet despite his tough management style, Rodgers doesn't see himself as an autocrat. Most of the company's major decisions, from resource allocations to project priorities, are made by a group of talented executive vice presidents together in a room, with no back-room dealing allowed. "It's not because I feel touchy-feely," explains Rodgers, in a rational view of his own limitations. "It's that I know that any time an organization gets bigger than a hundred, the leader can't make all of the decisions. You just don't know enough. Therefore, getting data from layers in the company and chewing on it and letting them think about it, talk to their guys and come back, that's how you make decisions that work."

Yes, there's a pattern emerging here. In his own distinctive style, Rodgers is saying the same things about managing a business as John Allison of BB&T, the Rand-inspired executive we met in Chapter 3, "The Leader." They both learned from Objectivism to be objective, that it's reality that counts; lies and evasion aren't tolerated. They've both learned that complex modern companies depend on the independent decision making of good people throughout the organization. But those people must be united by a robust philosophy that they explicitly agree to hold in common. Those who can't or won't subscribe to the philosophy have to go; the philosophy serves as a filter to select the best people, and to knit the best into a team.

Rodgers's course at the helm of Cypress hasn't always been a straight path upward. The semiconductor businesses is intensely cyclical, not only sensitive to overall economic conditions of growth and contraction, but subject to chip price swings driven by supply, demand, and the inexorable march of new technology under Moore's law.

The dot-com bust and 9/11 attacks dealt Cypress a major loss of $3.28 per share in fiscal year 2002. Its stock plummeted over 90 percent from its all-time high. Then the Great Recession later in the decade sent profits down yet again. But Rodgers retrenched, cut costs, and focused on what he does best: the fundamentals. It's like his beloved Packers—it's all about blocking and tackling.

According to Securities and Exchange Commission (SEC) filings, until just recently the board of directors received no cash compensation for serving the company. Rather, any financial incentives they received were in the form of long-term stock options effectively aligning their decision making to the enduring success of the company. Rodgers himself takes home less than $600,000 in salary—an amount that may seem large, but is modest in the rarefied atmosphere of today's CEO pay—and he lives by his own rules of pay for performance. When the company is cutting costs to weather a downturn, Rodgers and his executive team share in the pain. According to the 2009 Cypress annual report, "Like all other employees, our executive officers were impacted by the Company-wide pay reduction implemented in the second quarter of 2009. As a result, the base salaries of our executive officers were reduced by between 9% and 11%."[10] Furthermore, neither Rodgers nor his executives received any new stock option grants in 2009.

Profits versus Political Correctness

Rodgers's years of slugging it out against domestic and international competition alike also gave him a disdain for noneconomic standards of business success like artificially imposed diversity quotas or so-called social responsibility. In his view, these collectivist benchmarks are based on a faulty moral premise that ultimately does more harm than good for our society and the economy as a whole. "If you go out of college to some big corporation and the first lecture you get from the human resources group is why your company is good because they believe in corporate social responsibility," Rodgers explains, "then all of sudden, you know, you never get put through the test of really making it on your own."

His staunch defense of his business methods—finding the best talent regardless of appearance or background, competing to win rather than maneuvering to look good—has resulted in some now-legendary battles played out on the op-ed pages of our nation's newspapers. Perhaps the most famous was his widely circulated 1996 response letter to a Franciscan nun, Sister Doris Gormley, who criticized Rodgers for the lack of racial and gender diversity on the Cypress board of directors.

Rodgers replied in his letter, which was picked up and reported in a page 1 article by the *Wall Street Journal*:

> Choosing a Board of Directors based on race and gender is a lousy way to run a company. Cypress will never do it. Furthermore, we will never be pressured into it, because bowing to well-meaning, special-interest groups is an immoral way to run a company, given all the people it would hurt. We simply cannot allow arbitrary rules to be forced on us by organizations that lack business expertise. I would rather be labeled as a person who is unkind to religious groups than as a coward who harms his employees and investors by mindlessly following high-sounding but false standards of right and wrong.[11]

The resulting flood of responses was overwhelmingly positive. Ninety-six percent of Cypress shareholders wrote Rodgers in support.

John Allison of BB&T got a similarly positive reaction when his bank announced it would not make loans to develop property acquired under eminent domain. "It seems the liberal-dominated media continue to push us further and further towards the society of Ayn Rand's *Atlas Shrugged*, and your position stands out as one of the few against the downward slide," wrote one individual investor from New Mexico.[12]

A U.S. Congressman from Washington State wrote, "Our educational system is failing in part because it avoids the need to educate young people that capitalism, profits, hard work, and achievement are not bad things." Of the 27 lay Catholics who wrote in supported Rodgers's position, one said, "The Sister Gormleys of the world are neglecting God's work for dilettante socialism."

More than half of all responses argued the philosophical point that capitalism is morally good. Even Nobel Prize-winning economist Milton Friedman sent Rodgers a note along with a copy of a *New York Times* piece he had written in 1970 titled "The Social Responsibility of Business Is to Increase Its Profits." "He made every point I'd made, but 26 years earlier," T.J. quipped. Milton Friedman has inspired many advocates of free markets; we'll meet him again in Chapter 9, "The Economist of Liberty."

The few negative responses were typically emotional—and anonymous—rants. One called Rodgers a "money-grubbing, narrow-minded elitist . . . desperately holding onto [his] white-male bastion of power." One Washington resident wrote, "There are a number of educationally and professionally qualified women and minorities who can excel as board members of Cypress and other male/Anglo-Saxon-dominated companies." The writer didn't provide the names of those qualified women and minorities, nor did she seem to realize that only two of the five Cypress board members were, in fact, Anglo males.

The executive director of the Council of Institutional Investors wondered whether "CEOs who insist on board clones failed to play high school sports or other security-enhancing activities." Apparently Rodgers's two high school football championships and a college career playing for Dartmouth didn't count. The most succinct feedback was submitted to the Cypress web site suggesting simply that T.J. should "pull his head out of his ass."

The Conscience of the Nation

In 1999, one of T.J.'s directors called him to let him know that Jesse Jackson was coming to town. "He's been to New York and called the stock brokerage and the investment banking industry racist," remembers Rodgers. "Then he went to Detroit and called the car industry racist. So he is going to come here and call Silicon Valley racist . . . probably."

"You're not going to say anything, are you?" asked the director. "You understand this guy does this stuff for a living. He's a low-life, but he is going to rip your ass and you're going to embarrass the company, so why don't you just keep your mouth shut?"

"Okay," Rodgers replied. But in the end he just couldn't hold himself back. After the nun incident, news outlets from the *New York Times* to the local television stations knew Rodgers was a reliable source for attention-grabbing sound bites on controversial issues. As Jackson ramped up his rhetoric in Silicon Valley, reporters began beating harder on T.J.'s door. He finally relented.

"Do you have a comment on Jesse Jackson?" asked a reporter from Fox News.

"I said, 'Jesse Jackson reminds me of a seagull,'" Rodgers recounts. "'He flies in, craps all over everything, and then flies out.' And then the guy's looking at me like his jaw drops and he goes, 'Do you really want to say that?' And I go 'Yeah.' He said, 'Well, okay.' Then he didn't ask me another question and he's gone."

After his Fox News television appearance, the *San Jose Mercury News* invited Rodgers to expand on his thoughts in a more reasoned article, which it published on March 14, 1999. The arguments read like one of Francisco d'Anconia's expositions on the virtues of a free-market capitalist meritocracy.

> My company, Cypress Semiconductor, has 35% minority employees—every one a shareholder. And at the top, four of our nine executive vice presidents, or 44 percent, are minorities. Cypress' overall employment statistics are typical for Silicon Valley. I invite the Reverend Jackson to send me the resumes of those disenfranchised people who've received training from "the best universities." With 115 open positions we could use

them. We hire 500 people per year and still never fully meet our needs—just like other Silicon Valley companies.

. . . But why should Silicon Valley companies be forced to deal with Jackson? He is an economic train wreck who recently wrote, according to his Web site: "Deregulated capital markets, free trade, floating currencies—these are simply mechanisms, not measures of virtue." And when the markets aren't free anymore, who will determine what is virtuous—Jackson?

Compare the moral impact of the CEO who says or implies, "Many of you are here because of quotas," to that of a CEO who says, "You are here because you are the best. Period." We should not tolerate any degradation in one basic value that drives Silicon Valley meritocracy—despite Jackson's criticism of it as "an oozing ideology that needs to be addressed."[13]

"We only hire based on merit, period. And right now our company is 64 percent minority," Rodgers reports dismissively—letting the oxymoron "64 percent minority" speak for itself. He's also proud of standing up to Jackson and not cowering in fear from the deliberately charged words "minority" or "prejudice" that Jackson wields to slice his opponents. "Every other CEO just crawls under his desk and waits for it to go away," says Rodgers of the typical corporate reaction when Jesse comes to town to spout off about racism.

Rather than take Rodgers up on his challenge to meet for an open debate, Jackson's camp replied: "We can now officially describe Cypress Semiconductor as a white-supremacist hate group."[14] All we can say about that is that when we visited T.J. on Champion Court, we didn't see any crosses burning outside Cypress's headquarters.

Rodger's in-your-face defense of his moral ground and living a life that simply honors the truth hasn't been without consequences. "These are my lawsuits," Rodgers says pointing to the opposite wall covered with over a dozen black-and-white documents. "I always frame them." And he refuses to settle or be blackmailed into compromising his principles—no matter how drawn-out or expensive the ordeal.

Does he ever end up spending more to fight than to give in to the demands of his extortionists? "It happens all the time," Rodgers says matter-of-factly. "The idea that that decision is a decision about return on investment is bullshit. . . . They're calling you a scumbag and a crook, right? So how much money do you have to save to acknowledge that? Then of course it's 'without admitting guilt'? Bullshit. You gave them a check."

The criticism doesn't seem to faze him much. Not that Rodgers is an unfeeling automaton—in fact, he is an intensely emotional man. But he has a remarkable ability to take a step back from the initial gut reaction to view the situation, and himself, in an objective context. *Fortune* called him up a few years ago for a piece it was running on the world's toughest boss. "Two or three years before, they had issued America's toughest bosses and two of the people that I remember on the list were Jack Welch and Andy Grove," recollects Rodgers. "They were basically good guys who ran great companies that were tough. . . . So I figured it would be the same thing."

What it turned out to be—with Rodgers's face on the cover in extreme close-up, seeming to glower at the reader—was what Rodgers calls a "hit piece on nasty prick bosses . . . and I got real pissed off," he remembers at first. "Then I read it again and the quotes were right, and then I forgot about it. . . . I have this little byline that's in my head: '*Fortune* magazine—yesterday's news tomorrow.' It's like who gives a shit about *Fortune* magazine? Who cares?"

Silicon Always Tells the Truth

Business philosophy is one thing—and Rodgers is one hell of a philosopher. But remember, Francisco d'Anconia was a double major in philosophy *and* physics. And Rodgers is every bit the master of the physics of the business about which he philosophizes so brilliantly.

Listening to T.J. talk about silicon chips, it's easy to be dumbfounded by the breadth and depth of his knowledge. Like a kindly college professor tutoring a couple of school kids, he whipped out a pen and a manila file folder, then illustrated for us the underlying physics of transistors and how they link together to form the ultrafast memory chips his company is famous for. Terms like P-N junction, tetrahedral bonding, and inversion layer conduction as a quantum-mechanical phenomenon rolled off his tongue like an ordinary Joe's barber shop banter on baseball statistics.

Rodgers's latest generation of technology, known as a program-mable system on a chip (PSoC), is a world's first. The design consists of configurable analog and digital peripheral functions, memory, and a microcontroller—essentially an entire computer—on a single chip. Engineers no longer have to hunt down, configure, physically connect, and test individual components to drive electronic products. Using PSoC, they simply drag and drop various modules on a computer-based graphical user interface, hit "go," and the chip configures and programs itself to the designer's specifications. Currently Rodgers's PSoC technology is being used in products as diverse as computer printers, high-definition televisions (HDTVs), touch-screen cell phones, ad even washing machines and coffee makers.

"The big chip we're just now starting to ramp up, it's the size of my little fingernail, and I had 300 engineers working on it for three years," he reveals proudly about his latest project. "When we slice the chip in half to look at a cross section, to look at the transistor profiles and see if the thing's being done right, we literally can see atoms," he said in amazement, laying out a couple of images labeled "High Resolution TEM SiO2." And sure enough, the individual atoms were clearly visible stacked neatly in an organized matrix, "like a rack of pool balls."

All that said, on another level brilliant physics and brilliant philosophy are two sides of the same enterprise. Physics taught T.J. what Aristotle taught Ayn Rand: that A is A, that existence exists, and any philosophy that says it doesn't is a pack of lies. As T.J. puts it, "Silicon always tells the truth."

How did T. J. Rodgers come to such confidently held beliefs, such strong bedrock principles? Was there a primary influence? An Objectivist mentor in college? A libertarian guru leading him through his formative years?

"The fact is there was no one person," he responds thoughtfully. "I really believe it's genetic; I really do. Part of it is the fact that I'm scientist and an engineer and, in that business, Maxwell's equations don't give a shit if you're Republican or Democrat."

He explains, "There are laws of physics and chemistry that allow you to understand and make respectively that chip and then electrical engineering, which allow you to assemble millions of things together and have them work right. And they are what they are. To say, you know, 'It's his fault,' or 'I didn't get enough resources,' or 'If we only had a subsidy.' All that stuff is just crap; it's an excuse. Silicon always tells the truth."

"Man can rearrange the materials that exist in reality, but he cannot violate their identity; he cannot escape the laws of nature,"[15] wrote Leonard Peikoff, Ayn Rand's designated intellectual heir. The political corollary, as Rand herself wrote, is that "To deal with men by force is as impractical as to deal with nature by persuasion."[16]

In the Cypress boardroom hangs a reproduction of Raphael's masterpiece, *The School of Athens*. Rodgers uses it as a metaphor for the concrete reality he so loves and admires. In the picture, Plato and Aristotle walk together in the center of the canvas under a marble archway surrounded by ancient scholars, including Pythagoras, Euclid, Socrates, and Ptolemy. An aged and wise-looking Plato points to the sky with one finger, symbolizing his Theory of Forms, which concludes that abstract ideas, not the material world, are the highest form of reality. Meanwhile a considerably younger-looking and robust Aristotle holds his right hand out facing down as if palming an invisible basketball, silently referencing his philosophy of empiricism, or truth through the study of objective reality.

"We talk about it all the time," Rodgers says of the painting and underlying message. "We just deal with the laws of physics, and there is no interpretation; there are no politics; no crap. We have our own Aristotle built in, and he tells us if we've been competent or not and he *always* tells the truth; he's perfect. One of our core values in the company is that silicon always tells the truth; we are Aristotle, real simple."

Ayn Rand would be proud. She credited Aristotle, who laid out the rules of logic and reason, as the only philosopher from whom she ever learned anything. She considered Plato to be patient zero in a centuries-long epidemic of mysticism and collectivism.

What frustrates Rodgers is that when he takes even a tiny step back from the clean room of science, he starts to see the crazy illogic running unchecked through our social discourse today. "You hear that somehow by taxing ourselves with a carbon tax, we're going to create green jobs . . . that global warming causes snowstorms . . . and how government spending creates wealth. It's just absolute bullshit."

It seems as though Rodgers vents his feelings so frequently to keep from blowing a boiler. His wife has become well practiced at talking him down after a particularly idiotic encounter outside of his corporate safe room. According to Rodgers, "She'll say, 'Remember, T.J., you don't live in the real world. You live in a very special place. It's very different from the real world.' And I really do," he concludes happily. "I really love my job."

Money Is Not Evil

Rodgers supports philanthropy—as long as it's by choice, not by force. "When good works cease to be voluntary and become compulsory, charity becomes confiscation and freedom becomes servitude," he wrote in a *New York Times* response to Bill Clinton's 1997 President's Summit in Philadelphia (a gathering he termed the "wrecking crew"), concluding with what he says is his favorite quote: "Philanthropy is a byproduct of wealth, and wealth is best created in free markets whose workings embody a fundamental and true moral principle long forgotten in Washington. Let's not let the crowd in Philadelphia con us into giving it more than the 40 percent of the economy it already controls."[17]

In early 2010, Cypress and its sister company, SunPower, donated $1.1 million to the Second Harvest Food Bank to install a 322-kilowatt solar power system that is expected to save the nonprofit organization nearly $3 million in electricity costs. Because he's still free to evaluate charities on their own merits, Rodgers gives based on free-market principles of who does the most good with the hard-earned money he donates. "Second Harvest Food Bank is one of the most efficient nonprofit organizations in the country, giving $0.95 out of every dollar it receives back to the community," he said about his choice to fund the group. "Cypress is pleased to help reduce the organization's operating expenses so that it can focus on what it does best—feeding the community."

T.J. also goes on the speaking circuit, when invited, to help the younger generation of aspiring businesspeople. One of his favorite openers is to make the statement "Money can't buy happiness" and then ask the students to react to it as true or false. "Who thinks that is true?" he asks, and 90 percent of the hands go up. Then he says, "Let me speak for a few minutes on variants of the question I just asked you. . . . Money can't buy happiness. Money can never buy happiness for anybody.

Money always buys happiness under every circumstance. In some occasions, money can buy happiness for some people. Money always buys happiness for everybody. Then I pause. Crank and wait and see."

Then he does the poll again and the numbers go to 70 percent true. "Why did you change your vote?" Rodgers then asks of one of the switchers. Once they go through the logical permutations, reports Rodgers, they often reply, "It's clear that at some time money can buy happiness for somebody. Therefore this categorical statement 'money can't buy happiness' is not always true, and therefore, if it's not always true, it's not true." Simple Boolean logic.

Then, to hammer home the point even deeper, T.J. tells a personal story and then repolls the class. "In 1996, my father was diagnosed with Alzheimer's disease, and in 1997, he was so messed up, he couldn't stay in the house anymore," Rodgers begins. "My mother couldn't take care of him. So I flew from California to my home in Wisconsin. I went to the various homes that could take care of him. Some of them were awful. I found a very nice one. It was more expensive than the other ones. I put my dad in it and I just wrote the check to pay for the first quarter. And it was expensive, but I own a company in Silicon Valley and I had enough money that I could just write the check, and being able to take care of my family made me happier. Fact. True story. So now, let me ask you again. Money can't buy happiness. True or false?"

Astonishingly, 15 percent or so of the students still stick to their guns, even when confronted with direct evidence and the fallacy of their illogical conclusion. "So now you have got the real hardcore communists," T.J. chuckles. "Then you get into the real bullshit answers. I mean, it's just insane. 'I don't really understand what happiness is.' The professors hate it—absolutely hate it, because I am pointing out that money is not evil."

T.J. admits, "After my third or fourth appearance at the Stanford Business School, I was never invited back to lecture again." However, he's done his little exercise all over the world. At the University of Hong Kong only two students raised their hands on the very first round. "Okay, well, I guess this drill is not going to work around here," Rodgers said to himself. He reports, "At Santa Clara University—the Jesuit school—they were very good. Stanford Business School is one of the worst. You know, one time I was particularly rankled in this interaction with them and I said, 'If you hate money so much, why are you going to business school?'"

Having never read *Atlas Shrugged*, T.J. may not know that this lecture on the nobility of money is a modern classroom version of a famous epic monologue by Francisco d'Anconia on the same subject, delivered at a cocktail party full of wealthy, guilt-ridden socialites. After one particularly obnoxious heiress declares that "money is the root of all evil," d'Anconia begins, "Money is a tool of exchange, which can't exist unless there are goods produced and men able to produce them. Money is the material shape of the principle that men who wish to deal with one another must deal by trade and give value for value. . . . Money is made possible only by the men who produce. Is this what you consider evil?"

As T.J. might have put it in the same circumstances, "If you hate money so much, why are you going to cocktail parties with all these rich people?"

A Hero on Strike

In 2001 Rodgers helped out Stanford Business School buddy Richard Swanson with a $750,000 investment in his struggling solar cell company, SunPower. It may have seemed like an ironic choice for the financially scrupulous Rodgers: a chummy favor for a friend with a so-called green company in an industry unlikely to exist at all if not for government subsidies.

But the investment actually made quite a bit of sense. Rodgers believes that the market for alternative energy technology will grow in the coming decades, driven by the increasing market price of fossil fuel—government meddling or not. SunPower had technology that was one of the most efficient ways to generate electricity from sunlight on the planet.[18] And the underlying science of photovoltaic cells isn't all that different from memory chips. They both consist of silicon crystals manufactured with similar technology. In the case of solar cells, photons strike the silicon surface, displacing electrons and generating an electrical current under the same physical laws as other semiconductors.

By May 2002, Rodgers had convinced his Cypress board to buy a 44 percent stake in SunPower for $8.8 million.[19] Eventually they invested $168 million in plant, and equipment. SunPower went public in November 2005 at a price of $18 per share—for a total market capitalization of $1.5 billion.[20] Rodgers was named chairman of the board. By the fall of 2010, SunPower earned nearly $2 billion in revenue.[21]

Then along came California Proposition 23, which, if passed, would block a proposed tax on carbon dioxide emissions—a law known as AB32. Carbon taxes would actually be a boon to companies like SunPower. With increased taxes on carbon emissions would come a greater financial incentive for businesses to buy solar panels—sort of a financial shock therapy to encourage clean energy alternatives. Proponents of the tax also talked high-handedly about green job creation.

It did not matter to Rodgers, who would personally stand to benefit from this government manipulation of the private markets. It was just plain wrong—for a number of reasons.

According to Rodgers, "The basic premise of AB32 fails a grade school math test." By using numbers from the Environmental Protection Agency (EPA) and the California Business Roundtable, he discovered that reducing California's tiny contribution to national carbon emissions would barely move the needle from 5.98 gigatons to 5.94 gigatons. For that relatively tiny reduction, 1.1 million Californians would lose their jobs due to the higher tax. "In other words, for almost an unmeasurable change, we're showing 'leadership,'" cracks Rodgers. "California, the 'Green State.' You know, the only thing we've got leadership on is unemployment. It just doesn't work out for all this self-immolation."

So he wrote an op-ed piece in support of Proposition 23 for the *Wall Street Journal* that was published on October 29, 2010, just before the vote.[21] "I got a load of shit from SunPower. . . . They were writing me e-mails; it was clearly a lobbying effort by all but one of the directors—one was a capitalist—writing me these 'What the hell are you doing?' kind of things. And it's real simple. I make shit and pay taxes. I don't take other people's taxes and declare it's good because it's good."

At first Rodgers could tolerate a certain amount of government stimulus into the renewable energy sector to help burgeoning technologies get developed. He figured he could grit his teeth and get through the formative years of the industry, "especially if the company's stated plan is to get through the period and get off the government teat." But then SunPower continued deeper and deeper into becoming what he calls a "ward of the state."

"They started supporting the laws that are clearly bad for where they live, clearly bad for the state that allowed them to have the free market to create their success, and they criticize the chairman of the company because all their little chicken-shit laws are getting passed to get their little chicken-shit subsidies," Rodgers recalls, getting visibly riled and pausing for composure. "I went through a period of intense anger, which I never expressed, and then I just came in the next morning and said, 'I'm out of here.' I resigned. I resigned from the board of SunPower. So even companies that I am a significant contributor to their success, and I pick people that are good people, even then, when it comes to government pork—for me, today, versus saying what's truthful and right—they're whores."

The Laboratory Vineyard

These days, Rodgers is just as likely to deploy his considerable talent, energy, and brainpower to making unique, stunning, and innovative contributions to another of his many interests: winemaking. "You know, I like making things," Rodgers explains. "I have to make things, and when my job became sitting in a chair and talking to people I got vicarious enjoyment, because we are making things here and I was close to it, but I wasn't making anything myself anymore. So now we make wine."

He currently owns three small vineyards in the Santa Cruz Mountains that he uses like his own personal laboratory for the scientific exploration of viniculture. His methods are an extension of the style of his own mind—researching the core sciences developed over hundreds of years of trial and error in the old-world tradition, then melding that with new technology and empirical testing to yield astounding new results.

"Our winery business did 500,000 bucks last year, and within a couple of years we'll cross the million-dollar mark," he reports proudly. "We make a world-class pinot noir." He named his winery Clos de la Tech.

On a 160-acre parcel he named Domaine Lois Louise, after his mother, Rodgers dug three giant caves tiered into the slope under the vineyard. "It turns out that in France in the old days pinot noir was made with a gravity flow process, meaning that they didn't have pumps, and whenever you wanted to move wine from a place to another you had to use a siphon," he explains. The caves are structured so the top of the third cave is lower than the floor of the middle cave. Wine flows by gravity through the process of fermentation, barrel aging, and finally bottling to be trucked off to market four years after harvest.

Rodgers, like Francisco d'Anconia, does everything to the max—and brilliantly. His fermenters are radio-controlled and monitored. He visits France to learn from masters like Aubert de Villaine, the owner of the Domaine de la Romanee-Conti. He grafts a variety of vines to rootstocks, matching them to meticulously documented growing conditions and micro climates on his slopes. Results are then recorded and analyzed to improve his growing methods even further. His French oak barrels are custom ordered from Francois Freres Tonnellerie, which according to T.J. is "the best Burgundy barrel maker. . . . I pay $1,000 for a barrel. You can buy an American barrel for $280."

He personally designed a new type of tractor, perfect for navigating narrow vine rows on exceedingly steep slopes while remaining level in three dimensions through the use of hydraulically telescoping wheeled supports. The tractor is computer controlled and driven by a joystick like a video game. The invention won a gold medal from the European Intervitis Wine Fair for the most innovative new piece of farm equipment in 2001.

T.J. also created and patented a new grape press technology that is efficient and gentle, leaving the grape seeds uncracked to reduce unwanted tannins. The result approximates the ancient art of foot crushing using twenty-first-century technological efficiencies.

Even his failures are technological tours de force. He learned through extensive research that grapes exposed to partial sunlight produce superior wine due to a chemical they produce called quercetin, which acts like a natural sunscreen. But the heat of the sun negates the effect so that, typically, only the small portions of vines exposed to cool morning sun produce the vaunted grapes. T.J. set out to solve the problem by conducting an experiment he called "air-conditioning" a vineyard. He installed custom water misters on a control section of grapes and fitted individual clusters with thermistors to read the real-time temperatures of his subjects. He then linked up a wireless control system using his Cypress PSoC chip, which he custom programmed to monitor and cool the grapes with a series of radio-controlled water valves. In the end, the experiment was a technological marvel—but it didn't make a better grape, or a better wine.

The labels of Rodgers's wine bottles are the joint product of political meddling and technological breakthrough. "Very Burgundian," he says proudly of the label. Of the stylish black and white 1940s portrait on it, Rodgers explains, "That's my mother. That picture was taken in 1946; she's actually holding a cigarette and I had to edit it out." It seems that even in the wine business, Rodgers is bound to run into idiotic governmental regulations and obtuse bureaucracies. "It's illegal to have a cigarette on a wine bottle," Rodgers explains disgustedly. "Some genius passed a law that actually governs that."

Embedded in a red wax seal above the cigarette-free mother rests a silvery mirrorlike square, smaller than a postage stamp. The back label explains, "The silicon chip on the crest of the bottle is a billion-transistor, 144-megabit Static Random Access Memory that can store and retrieve 100 books with 1,000 pages each in one-thousandth of a second."

His hassles with the Bureau of Alcohol, Tobacco, and Firearms (ATF) make him shake his head in frustration almost as much as the California town commissions and zoning boards. "They're such a fucked-up organization that you never can deal with them; they don't answer phones," he says of the ATF when confronting the rolls of red tape standing between his wine and the commercial market. "You're sitting in there trying to sell your wines and it's going to take like nine months. They told us the last time we called them that they were very busy. The time from when they received our letter until they opened it was five months."

Rodgers concludes, "Real people haven't got time for some bullshit government job. It's only the clowns that—you know, you check them out—they were the high school class president; that was their little bit of fame in high school and now they're on the planning commission for some county in California."

A Normal Man

We began our interview with Rodgers hoping to discover the recipe for how he became a success—how he could do so many things so well. After generously giving us more than four hours with him, it was clear that—like Francisco d'Anconia, and in fact like all Ayn Rand's heroes—he simply likes "living on this earth." This means he wants to spend every minute of his life making as much of his life as he can—without wasting a moment on any form of self-deception, and without expecting anyone else to do his living for him.

Hugh Akston, Rand's great philosopher of reason from *Atlas Shrugged*, says it best. He says not to make the mistake of thinking that people like Francisco d'Anconia—and Rodgers—are "some sort of superhuman creatures. They're something much greater and more astounding than that: they're normal men—a thing the world has never seen—and their feat is that they managed to survive as such. It does take an exceptional mind, and a still more exceptional integrity, to remain untouched by the brain-destroying influences of the world's doctrines, the accumulated evil of centuries—to remain human, since the human is the rational."

Chapter 8

The Sellout

Alan Greenspan as Robert Stadler, the libertarian who became an economic czar

"Of any one person, of any single guilt for the evil which is now destroying the world—his was the heaviest guilt. He had the mind to know better. His was the only name of honor and achievement, used to sanction the rule of the looters. He was the man who delivered science into the service of the looters' guns."

—Atlas Shrugged

Who is Robert Stadler?

In *Atlas Shrugged*, Dr. Robert Stadler is a brilliant scientist who sells out to collectivism—and ends up destroying himself.

As a professor of physics at Patrick Henry University, he is mentor to John Galt and two of *Atlas Shrugged*'s other primary heroes, Francisco d'Anconia and Ragnar Danneskjöld. But in his single-minded quest to pursue pure science, he becomes head of the State Science Institute, a government-funded think tank.

(Continued)

Galt abandons his studies with Stadler the moment he endorses the Institute. Galt says, "He's the man who sold his soul. We don't intend to reclaim him."

Throughout *Atlas Shrugged*, the power of the Institute and the prestige of Stadler's name are used to exploit and expropriate the industrialists struggling to keep the economy afloat. Ultimately, scientific theories that Stadler thought were mere abstractions are used by the Institute to create a weapon of mass destruction designed to control the increasingly restive public. At the book's climax, Stadler seizes control of the weapon and inadvertently detonates it, resulting both in widespread destruction of what's left of America's industrial infrastructure, and in Stadler's own agonizing death.

Courtroom scenes figure prominently in two of Ayn Rand's greatest novels, *The Fountainhead* and *Atlas Shrugged*. They are where great men and great ideas are publicly vindicated. It's ironic that the most spectacularly successful of Rand's inner circle, Alan Greenspan, widely hailed as the greatest central banker who ever lived, would be put on trial along with Rand's ideas—and neither would be vindicated.

The trial was a hearing of the House Committee on Oversight and Government Reform, convened in October 2008 to investigate the banking crisis that swept the world in the wake of Lehman Brothers' collapse. The prosecutor was committee chair Henry Waxman, the crusading ultraliberal representative from Beverly Hills. Looking down at Greenspan from an elevated rostrum designed to intimidate witnesses, with his buckteeth, flaring nostrils, jug-handle ears, and bald head, Waxman looked like a cross between Lon Chaney's Phantom of the Opera and Mortimer Snerd.

Waxman pounded Greenspan with pointed questions about the apparent failure of the Federal Reserve under Greenspan's tenure to regulate the banks that collapsed. This was a dangerous matter for Greenspan, for whom there had always been serious tension between the demands of his role as Fed chairman—the most powerful regulator in the world—and his history as an intimate of Ayn Rand, who was so opposed to business regulation that, in *Atlas Shrugged*, she describes a wise judge drafting a constitutional amendment to prohibit it outright.

The toughest moment for Greenspan was surely when Waxman said, "Dr. Greenspan, Paul Krugman, the Princeton professor of economics who just won a Nobel Prize"—and whom we met in Chapter 2, "The Mad Collectivist"—"wrote a column in 2006 as the subprime mortgage crisis started to emerge. He said, 'If anyone is to blame for the current situation, it's Mr. Greenspan. . . .' So do you have any personal responsibility for the financial crisis?"[1]

Looking up at Waxman from the witness table, his enormous, wet, soulful eyes peering through his trademark goggles, looking for all the world like an aging Woody Allen miscast in some great tragic drama, Greenspan said a lot of words but didn't exactly come out and answer "yes." No surprise that. He'd become famous over nearly two decades as Fed chair for his inscrutable oracular comments.

So Waxman just kept at him: "You feel that your ideology pushed you to make decisions that you wish you had not made?" "Do you think that was a mistake on your part?" "My question for you is simple—were you wrong?"

But it didn't matter, really, because Greenspan had already confessed before the hearing even began. In a column for the *Financial Times* seven months earlier, he had written, "Those of us who look to the self-interest of lending institutions to protect shareholder equity have to be in a state of shocked disbelief."[2]

To Waxman, he added, "I found a flaw in the model that I perceived is the critical functioning structure that defines how the world works. . . . That's precisely the reason I was shocked, because I had been going for 40 years or more with very considerable evidence that it was working exceptionally well."[3]

For Greenspan, just as for Rand, self-interest was indeed "the critical functioning structure that defines how the world works," or at least how it ought to work. For Rand, it was embodied in her controversial slogan, "the virtue of selfishness." Greenspan said it decades ago in his own words, in 1963, in an essay for Rand's *Objectivist Newsletter.*[4]

It is precisely the "greed" of the businessman, or, more appropriately, his profit-seeking, which is the unexcelled protector of the consumer.

For Greenspan to repudiate self-interest is tantamount to repudiating Rand—after having been her close friend, colleague, and partner in arms for 22 years, right up until the day she died on Greenspan's birthday in 1982.

To some it seemed that he had repudiated her already, in 1975, when he became chairman of the White House Council of Economic Advisers, betraying her vision of strictly limited government, joining the ranks of the bureaucrats, central planners, and regulators. In that same 1963 essay he had written:[5]

> There is nothing to guarantee the superior judgment, knowledge, and integrity of an inspector or a bureaucrat—and the deadly consequences of trusting him with arbitrary power are obvious.

Those consequences became painfully obvious to Greenspan himself, after years at the very pinnacle of bureaucratic power as chairman of the Federal Reserve, blamed by Waxman and many others for failing to prevent—or perhaps even for causing—a world-historical global banking meltdown.

But Rand didn't feel betrayed when Greenspan went to the White House in 1975. In fact, she went with him, as a photo of Greenspan being sworn in by President Gerald Ford at the White House attests (see Figure 8.1). The little lady with Ford's arm around her is Greenspan's mother, Rose. The little lady next to Greenspan is Ayn Rand.

So apparently Rand, said to be quick to excommunicate acolytes who deviated from her philosophy, didn't object to Greenspan's new role. In fact, she was proud—for Greenspan, and for herself. For the press, she described Greenspan as "my disciple," and "my man in Washington."[6]

So it's difficult for us to say that Greenspan is a Randian villain (Rand didn't think so herself), though it's tempting simply because as Fed chair he became the most prominent and powerful regulator in the world. Perhaps in reality he was a Randian *hero*, a double agent, covertly promoting the ethic of self-interest and its political corollary, laissez-faire capitalism, from within the very center of government power.

If Alan Greenspan were a Randian villain, though, he would be Dr. Robert Stadler from *Atlas Shrugged*. Stadler was a great physicist, and one of the two mentors of Rand's greatest hero, John Galt. He

Figure 8.1 Alan Greenspan Is Sworn In as Chairman of the Counsel of
Economic Advisers, 1975. (*Left to right*) Rose Greenspan, President Gerald
R. Ford, Alan Greenspan, Ayn Rand, Frank O'Connor
Source: Gerald R. Ford Presidential Library and Museum

betrays Galt by doing just what Greenspan did: leaving the private sector and going to work for the government.

Galt calls Stadler "the man who sold his soul." He says of him, and scientists like him who work for the government, that they "sell their intelligence into cynical servitude to force . . . *they* are the damned on this earth, *theirs* is the guilt beyond forgiveness."

At the climax of *Atlas Shrugged*, Stadler's scientific research is co-opted by the government to create a weapon of mass destruction designed to control the civilian population. Amid the chaos of the collapse of the American economy, the weapon is triggered accidentally with Stadler present, and he is killed.

Rand writes, "Nothing remained alive among the ruins—except, for some minutes longer, a huddle of torn flesh and screaming pain that had once been a great mind."

Getting publicly humiliated by Henry Waxman is bad, but it's not *that* bad.

Ayn Rand's Adopted Son

Alan Greenspan first met Ayn Rand in 1952. He was introduced through his new bride Joan Mitchell, who was connected to Rand through their mutual friend Barbara Branden.

Greenspan attended a meeting of "The Collective," the intellectual salon that gathered at Rand's New York apartment to discuss philosophy, politics, and—most important—the ideas of Ayn Rand. Greenspan, who philosophically styled himself a logical positivist, postulated to Rand that there are no moral absolutes. Here's how Greenspan recalls the ensuing debate in his memoirs:[7]

> Ayn Rand pounced. "How can that be?" she asked.
>
> "Because to be truly rational, you can't hold a position without significant empirical evidence," I explained.
>
> "How can that be," she repeated. "Don't *you* exist?"
>
> "I . . . can't be sure," I admitted.
>
> "Would you be willing to say you *don't* exist?"
>
> "I might . . ."
>
> "And by the way, who exactly is making that statement?"

Checkmate! For the young Greenspan, this kind of intellectual jousting was extremely exciting. But at first Rand wasn't sure about Greenspan. She nicknamed him "the undertaker," because of his dark suits and somber demeanor. She asked her protégé Nathaniel Branden, the husband of Joan Mitchell's friend, "How can you stand talking to him? . . . A logical positivist? I'm not even certain it's moral to deal with him at all."[8]

Months later, after relentlessly chipping away at Greenspan's logical positivism, Branden convinced Greenspan that he did, indeed, exist.

He told Rand, "Guess who exists. . . . You'll have to stop calling Alan 'the undertaker' now."[9]

Branden and his wife Barbara took it upon themselves to see to Greenspan's "conversion" to Rand's philosophy. The first step in the conversion would prove to be a fateful one. One day Barbara reported to Branden, "Guess what. I got him to admit that banks should be operated entirely privately. . . . I sold him on the merits of a completely unregulated banking system."[10]

Greenspan became a regular member of Rand's salon, and was granted the privilege of reading *Atlas Shrugged* right as it came off of Rand's typewriter. He was enthralled, finding Rand's arguments "radiantly exact."[11]

The Collective was in some ways a difficult group, full of interpersonal drama, with all members subject from time to time to harsh judgment by Rand for any perceived infraction of her philosophy. Greenspan came in for his share of criticism. Observing Greenspan's relentless networking (which would one day serve him so well in Washington), she asked, "Do you think Alan might basically be a social climber?"[12] She was skeptical of his involvement in the business world, once saying "A.G. is too 'worldly,' too impressed by success. The trouble with A.G. is, he thinks Henry Luce is important."[13]

But Greenspan had a special status in Rand's salon. One member recalls, "He kept somewhat aloof from everybody. He was older and smarter."[14] Another says Greenspan was Rand's "special pet."[15] Contradicting her worries about his being too "worldly," Rand herself said, "What I like about A.G. is basically that he has his feet on the ground. I love his love for life on earth."[16]

After *Atlas Shrugged* was published, Ayn Rand became a full-fledged literary celebrity. Branden franchised Rand and her ideas into a lecture series and a newsletter, and Greenspan participated in both. At what became known as the Nathaniel Branden Institute (NBI), Greenspan taught a course called "The Economics of a Free Society."[17] He contributed to *The Objectivist Newsletter*, and its successor publication, *The Objectivist*, on topics such as business regulation, antitrust, and the gold standard. Some of these writings were eventually republished in a series of anthologies designed to ride on the coattails of Rand's literary popularity, alongside essays by Rand, Branden, and other members of The Collective.

Beyond The Collective

At the same time, Greenspan was becoming a considerable business success. When he first met Rand he was working at the National Industrial Conference Board. Bond trader William Townsend invited Greenspan to join him in forming an independent economics consulting firm. According to Branden, Greenspan hesitated to take the plunge. Branden urged him on, saying, "Take the leap. You can do it. . . . You just don't appreciate how good you are." Townsend Greenspan & Company hit the big time quickly, signing up a glittering constellation of Fortune 500 companies as clients. Several years on, Townsend died, leaving Greenspan in control of the company, and a wealthy man. Again according to Branden, Greenspan later thanked him, saying, "You believed in me."[18] For all that, Greenspan mentions Branden only once in his autobiography, and then only in passing.[19]

Greenspan's involvement in politics began as a spectator in the 1950s, as he watched Arthur Burns, his faculty adviser in the PhD program at Columbia University, become chair of the Council of Economic Advisers (CEA) under President Eisenhower. Rand was suspicious of Greenspan's relationship with Burns. She loathed Eisenhower, seeing him as what we would now call a RINO—a Republican in Name Only.[20]

The path of Burns's career in many ways eerily presages Greenspan's, starting with the CEA and ending with the chairmanship of the Fed. It was also a cautionary tale for Greenspan. In his academic career Burns was a fierce defender of free markets, but when he joined government he seemed to become a Keynesian—following the doctrine of John Maynard Keynes, the British economist—advocating government stimulus and government control. Perhaps it was a pragmatic compromise, accepting the world as it is and sticking up for free markets to the extent possible. But as Fed chief,

Burns is widely regarded as having caved in to political pressures from President Nixon, overly loosening monetary policy, and unleashing the catastrophic inflation of the mid-1970s and early 1980s.

Accounts differ as to exactly how Greenspan's personal participation in politics began. Some biographers attribute his joining Richard M. Nixon's campaign for the presidency in 1967 to a chance meeting with Leonard Garment, an old chum of Greenspan's from his youthful days as a jazz musician, who would several years later become infamous as Nixon's lawyer during the Watergate scandal.[21] Greenspan himself says it started through his friendship with Martin Anderson, a Columbia economics professor whom he had met at an NBI lecture, who at the time was the Nixon campaign's chief domestic policy adviser.[22] Anderson had become a friend of Ayn Rand—he even contributed a book review to an edition of *The Objectivist Newsletter*—but he was never a member of The Collective's inner sanctum.

Greenspan was impressed by Nixon's mind, writing that "he and Bill Clinton were by far the smartest presidents I've worked with."[23] But he saw Nixon's darker side, too: the bigotry, the paranoia, the stream of expletives that "would have made Tony Soprano blush."[24] So Greenspan chose not to accept an offer of a full-time position in the Nixon administration after the election. Smart choice. Not only did he mostly avoid having his reputation damaged by the Watergate scandal, but he also avoided association with a sequence of Nixon's economic policy decisions that utterly flew in the face of free markets—most notorious, Nixon's imposition of wage and price controls and the suspension of gold convertibility in 1971.

Then, in 1974, in the depths of a horrible inflationary recession, during an Arab oil embargo, and at the peak of the Watergate scandal, it all changed.

Ayn Rand's Man in Washington

Greenspan got a call from Treasury Secretary William Simon asking him to become chairman of the Council of Economic Advisers. He said no. He got another call from White House Chief of Staff Alexander Haig.

Again, no. The next call came from Greenspan's old friend Arthur Burns, by then Fed chairman. Greenspan remembers, "My old mentor puffed on his pipe and played to my guilt."[25] This time it was yes. "But I told myself I'd take an apartment on a month-to-month lease, and figuratively, at least, keep my suitcase packed by the door."[26] The same day as Greenspan's Senate confirmation hearing, Nixon announced his resignation.

So Greenspan became CEA chair under new president Gerald Ford, and was sworn in at the White House with his mother, Ayn Rand, and Rand's husband, Frank O'Connor, in attendance (again, see Figure 8.1). Three weeks later, at Greenspan's first CEA meeting, an economist present said that the cure for inflation "applies alike for Bolsheviks and devoted supporters of Ayn Rand, if there are any present." Greenspan chimed in, "There's at least one."[27]

Rand didn't damn Greenspan for going to Washington as John Galt damned Dr. Robert Stadler. She loved it. It was a difficult time in her life—she was beginning a long struggle with lung cancer—and as Barbara Branden put it, "Alan Greenspan's success was one of Ayn's rare sources of pleasure. . . . Ayn was delighted with his accomplishments, and delighted that he spoke openly and proudly of his admiration for her, for her work, for her philosophy."[28]

Sometimes Ayn was outright thrilled with what Greenspan could do in government. While Nixon was still president, Greenspan participated in a commission that led to the abolition of the military draft, a goal near and dear to Rand's libertarian heart. In this effort Greenspan worked closely with Milton Friedman, whom we'll meet in Chapter 9, "The Economist of Liberty."

Rand was over the moon, as it were, when Greenspan arranged for her to attend the blast-off of Apollo 11.[29] But she bickered with him about heading a commission under President Reagan that ended up bolstering Social Security, a program Rand loathed. At a dinner in a New York club, she dressed him down so violently about it that people stopped and stared.[30] But in the end, she said, "I am a philosopher, not an economist. . . . Alan doesn't consult with me on these matters."[31]

The Making of a Maestro

Greenspan got to be both philosopher and economist when he was appointed chairman of the Federal Reserve by President Ronald Reagan in August 1987.

Rand, who died in 1982, didn't live to see it. But it was a moment of supreme irony, and not only because the libertarian Rand-ite Greenspan was assuming the role of the nation's most powerful regulator. More, it was because the Fed is charged with providing the nation with arbitrary amounts of paper money, completely free from the strictures of the gold standard, or any other standard. Yet in a 1963 article for *The Objectivist Newsletter*, Greenspan had written that "gold and economic freedom are inseparable, that the gold standard is an instrument of laissez faire, and that each implies and requires the other."[32]

In the same article, he wrote, "In the absence of the gold standard, there is no way to protect savings from confiscation through inflation."[33] Yet that's just what Greenspan set out to do as Fed chair: to protect savings from inflation in the absence of a gold standard.

Or did he? If you look at the data the right way, it almost seems that Greenspan implemented a covert gold standard for the Fed during the first half of his long tenure as chair.

Consider Figure 8.2. It shows the federal funds rate—the short-term interest rate that is set by the Fed, its major instrument of policy—compared to the price of gold (dashed line). Do you notice anything strange? In the first half of the chart, up through most of 1996, every time the gold price rose, Greenspan raised the interest rate (light gray line). Every time the gold price fell, Greenspan lowered the interest rate. He didn't respond to every little wiggle in the volatile gold price; that's why we show the two-year moving-average price, a way to smooth out the short-term volatility and look at the durable price trend. But when gold made major moves, so did the interest rate.

Why would this be? The reason is simple. When the gold price measured in dollars *rises*, it's telling the central bank that the value of the dollar is *falling*; that is, there is a risk of *inflation*. So *raise* interest

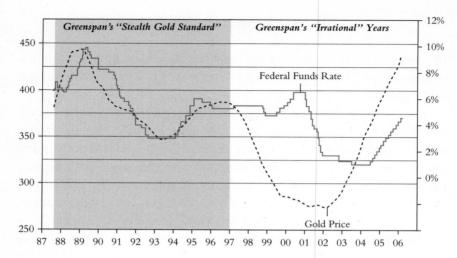

Figure 8.2   Greenspan's Stealth Gold Standard versus His Irrational Years. (*Left axis*) Gold Price, Two-Year Moving Average; (*right axis*) Federal Funds Rate
SOURCE: Federal Reserve, Reuters, author's calculations

rates to stop inflation. When the gold price measured in dollars *falls*, it's telling the central bank that the value of the dollar is *rising*; that is, there is a risk of *deflation*. So *lower* interest rates to stop deflation. There's no gold being physically bought, sold, stored, or moved in this setup. Yet gold is determining monetary policy. It is truly a gold standard, albeit not an overt one.

Why did it have to be only a stealth gold standard? Why not tell the world? Because while for the ordinary man on the street gold is still a superlative symbol of lasting value, in the rarefied air of academic economics it has become a symbol of outmoded and unsophisticated thinking. That epitome of economic snobbery John Maynard Keynes dubbed it "the barbarous relic," and urged the world's nations to abandon the gold standard in the Great Depression. The nickname stuck. While in reality every central bank in the world still hoards gold in its vaults, it's not something respectable economists talk about as a part of modern monetary policy.

Dr. Robert Stadler put it simply enough in *Atlas Shrugged*: "If we want to accomplish anything, we have to deceive them into letting us accomplish it. Or force them."

Greenspan's stealth gold standard worked brilliantly for all the years in which it was applied. They were years of admirable economic stability. Yes, there was a recession in the middle of those years. But it was short and mild, and the stealth gold standard kept the Fed from overreacting to it. Certainly there were none of the bubbles during those years that would come to plague the U.S. economy afterward.

What of the stock market crash in October 1987? You can't blame that on Greenspan or his stealth gold standard—it occurred just two months after he showed up at the Fed. On the contrary, here was another case in which Greenspan admirably didn't overreact, perhaps thanks to the stealth gold standard. The conventional wisdom about the crash is that Greenspan miraculously rescued the world economy from its aftereffects. Some applaud Greenspan as a savior; others criticize him for putting in place after the crash the so-called Greenspan put—the implicit guarantee, the moral hazard, that supposedly led to the bubbles of the late 1990s and the first decade of the 2000s. But the reality is that Greenspan did essentially nothing after the crash. He issued a statement saying, "The Federal Reserve, consistent with its responsibilities as the nation's central bank, affirmed its readiness to serve as a source of liquidity to support the economic and financial system."[34] Just 29 little words. No bailouts. No nationalizations. No bazookas. No helicopter drops of money.

A central banker who does *nothing*—except watch the gold price. Maybe Greenspan was a Randian hero after all, a double agent for libertarianism in the very bastion of regulatory power.

Maybe it was true what Greenspan told U.S. Representative Ron Paul, the only libertarian member of Congress, when Paul asked him whether as Fed chair he would now add a disclaimer to his *Objectivist Newsletter* article on gold and economic freedom. Greenspan told Paul, "I reread this article recently—and I wouldn't change a single word."[35]

The Maestro Untethered

But then something changed in late 1996. For no known reason, Greenspan went off his stealth gold standard. As the price of gold fell, for the first time he didn't lower interest rates. Instead, he raised them.

The stealth gold standard ended at exactly the same moment as Greenspan gave his famous speech warning of "irrational exuberance"— December 5, 1996. Speaking after two excellent years for the stock market, in which the Standard & Poor's 500 had risen 37.6 percent in 1995 and then another 23.5 percent so far in 1996, Greenspan said,

> [H]ow do we know when irrational exuberance has unduly escalated asset values, which then become subject to unexpected and prolonged contractions . . . ? And how do we factor that assessment into monetary policy? . . . the sharp stock market break of 1987 had few negative consequences for the economy. But we should not underestimate or become complacent about the complexity of the interactions of asset markets and the economy.[36]

After that, Greenspan kept rates where he raised them in early 1997. Gold continued to fall, which under the stealth gold standard should have signaled to Greenspan that deflationary pressures were building, and that rates should be lowered to relieve them.

By 1998, those deflationary pressures started to weigh on the world's most fragile debtors: the fast-growing Asian nations that had borrowed vast sums of dollars to build out their commodity-based economies. In the deflation Greenspan had triggered, the prices of commodities fell along with the price of gold, and at the same time debt service in dollars became intolerable. It was much like what happened to debtors around the world in the deflation of the Great Depression of the 1930s. The result was the so-called Asian flu, a contagion of currency devaluations and debt defaults that swept Asia from Thailand to Russia.

In the United States, the highly leveraged hedge fund Long-Term Capital Management (LTCM) got caught in the undertow of Asian and Russian defaults and devaluations. With all the top Wall Street firms exposed to LTCM, it was a systemic crisis. In response, Greenspan finally lowered interest rates—which his stealth gold standard would have had him do years before—and the pressure was relieved.

At the same time, the Fed organized a rescue of Long-Term Capital Management. We say "organized," because that's all the Fed did; it didn't spend a dime of its own money bailing out LTCM. All it did was get all of LTCM's shareholders in one room at the New York branch of the Federal Reserve, and convince them that the only way to save Wall Street was to have all of them kick in extra money to LTCM. It was the opposite of a bailout—it was a bail-in.

When the smoke cleared, Greenspan got credit for expertly averting a global crisis—yes, the same one he himself caused by going off his own stealth gold standard. Greenspan was featured on the cover of *Time* as the chairman of the Committee to Save the World, and people started calling him the maestro.

And the legend of the Greenspan put grew. Ask anyone on Wall Street how the LTCM crisis was resolved, and chances are good you'll be told—wrongly—that the Greenspan Fed bailed it out.

With his laurels polished to the point of gleaming, Greenspan didn't learn from his mistake. As irrational exuberance kicked into high gear and the dot-com stock market went hyperbolic at the end of the decade, Greenspan started raising rates again, taking them to new highs—even as gold kept falling.

He spoke of the "new economy," yet he kept raising rates. It was as though he was now on a stealth Nasdaq standard instead of a stealth gold standard. But try as he might, he couldn't burst the bubble. He says now, in frustration, that he had "raised the spectre of 'irrational exuberance' in 1996—only to watch the dot-com boom, after a one-day stumble, continue to inflate for four more years, unrestrained by a cumulative increase of 350 basis points in the federal funds rate from 1994 to 2000."[37]

From Bust to Bubble

After the dot-com bubble burst in early 2000 (probably more from its own unsustainable silliness than anything Greenspan had done to burst it), the deflationary consequences of abandoning the stealth gold standard took on deadly new dimensions.

Coming out of the brief recession of 2001, inflation fell to the lowest levels in 40 years. It had dipped in mid-1998, and Greenspan had seen the consequences in Asia, Russia, and Wall Street. Now it was lower still. It was not negative—not actual outright deflation. But for Greenspan, knowing in his heart of hearts that he'd been erring versus his own stealth gold standard on the side of deflation, it was scary.

So Greenspan panicked. He went from keeping rates too high for too long to keeping rates too low for too long. He lowered interest rates to a mere 1 percent in mid-2003, a level not seen since the Depression. And he kept them there for an entire year, what the Fed kept announcing to the market, all the while, would be a "considerable period." Then when the Fed finally started raising rates, it announced that its rate-hiking regime would be "measured." Starting in mid-2004, the Fed began a series of regular, timid, 0.25 percent rate hikes at every Federal Open Market Committee (FOMC) meeting. Rates didn't even get back up to a mere 3 percent until mid-2005.

Greenspan denies this,[38] but many scholars now believe that keeping rates so low for so long was what triggered the boom in excessive mortgage lending in the United States and around the world—the boom that became a bubble, the bubble that became a bust, and the bust that became a global banking crisis and the Great Recession.

Among Greenspan's sharpest critics on this is John Taylor, the Stanford University economics professor famed in monetary policy circles for positing the Taylor rule for setting interest rates. Taylor delivered his critique in the summer of 2007, just when the first tremors of the mortgage bust were beginning to be felt—when no one had any idea it would lead to a global crisis. At the Fed's prestigious annual Jackson Hole research symposium, Taylor argued:

> During the period from 2003 to 2006 the federal funds rate was well below what experience during the previous two decades of good economic macroeconomic performance . . . would have predicted. Policy rule guidelines showed this clearly. There have been other periods . . . where the federal funds rate veered off the typical policy rule responses . . . but this was the biggest deviation. . . .
>
> With low money market rates, housing finance was very cheap and attractive—especially variable rate mortgages with the teasers that many lenders offered. Housing starts jumped

to a 25 year high by the end of 2003 and remained high until the sharp decline began in early 2006. . . .

As the short term interest rate returned to normal levels, housing demand rapidly fell bringing down both construction and housing price inflation. Delinquency and foreclosure rates then rose sharply, ultimately leading to the meltdown in the subprime market. . . .[39]

While the Fed's too-low rates fueled the mortgage and housing bubbles, the Fed as banking regulator did little to rein in abusive lending practices or excessively leveraged capital commitments by banks. It's not like Greenspan didn't know there were bad guys out there—and perhaps stupid guys, too. In the wake of Enron and other financial scandals in the early 2000s, he had spoken of "infectious greed"[40]—a phrase that became almost as canonical as "irrational exuberance."

> Why did corporate governance checks and balances that served us reasonably well in the past break down? . . . An infectious greed seemed to grip much of our business community. Our historical guardians of financial information were overwhelmed.

And it's not like he couldn't see housing prices get out of control. As Greenspan now protests, "I expressed my concerns before the Federal Open Market Committee that '. . . our extraordinary housing boom . . . financed by very large increases in mortgage debt—cannot continue indefinitely.'"[41]

Furthermore, it's not like he didn't know that the quasi-government lending agencies Fannie Mae and Freddie Mac were overleveraged and corrupt. He used his bully pulpit as Fed chair to attack them repeatedly and call for sweeping reform.

So when he says now that he is "shocked" by the failure of self-interest to rein in the banks all by itself, one thinks of the police captain in *Casablanca* who was "shocked—shocked!—to find that gambling is going on in here." Yet the Greenspan Fed essentially did nothing about it.

Even if Greenspan were playing the Randian double-agent hero, trying to minimize the Fed's regulatory footprint, there is one huge practical problem that such an idealistic strategy lethally overlooks.

Greenspan forgot that the market expects the Fed to regulate the banking system, whether or not in Rand's moral universe it ought to—especially the Greenspan Fed, in the hands of the maestro, the chairman of the Committee to Save the World, the man who always knows the right thing to do.

So why shouldn't banks take highly leveraged off-balance-sheet risks based on mortgages that nobody in his or her right mind could have expected the borrower to repay? Greenspan's not objecting—and he's regulating this casino, isn't he? Isn't he?

So what's a Randian hero double agent supposed to do? Well, as Dr. Robert Stadler asked in *Atlas Shrugged*, "But what can you do when you deal with people?"

The Maestro's Final Bow

Alan Greenspan politely refused our requests to be interviewed for this book, but he did agree to meet with us.

When we saw him in his Washington, D.C., office, we were struck by how terribly old and small and frail he is, this giant who bestrode the global economy for two decades. His large eyes still bloomed with intelligence at age 84, and his rapid-fire repartee revealed a mind still operating with enormous power. Yet when we grasped his hand to greet him, it seemed for a moment that his whole arm would come off at the shoulder.

It was more than just the physical exhaustion of age. There was also something about him that spoke of resignation, disappointment, even shame. And why not? What must it cost a man, after a record 18-year run as chairman of the Federal Reserve, seeing nearly two decades of unprecedented global growth, able to master every crisis along the way, celebrated as the greatest central banker of all time, and on the cover of *Time* as the chairman of the Committee to Save the World, to be blamed for the banking crisis that triggered the greatest global recession since the 1930s.

For Greenspan, it's more than just having presided over the greatest global boom/bust cycle in history, having gone from adulation as the man who saved the world to vilification as the man who destroyed it.

For Greenspan, this titanic fall from grace is all the more humiliating because it takes place squarely in the long shadow of Ayn Rand.

As Greenspan proudly told us when we met, he spent 30 years as a close friend of Rand, right up until the day she died in 1982. When we asked him whether in his confrontation with Henry Waxman he'd intended to recant his Randian beliefs in the supremacy of free markets, he told us absolutely not.

His despair, he told us, is not that his and Rand's ideas turned out to be wrong. Rather, it's that the world has abandoned them. Coming out of the Great Recession, he sees the United States having crossed a fateful threshold, a point of no return, at which we've taken on too great a government debt, and at the same time made too great a commitment to government control of the economy. He told us that we won't recognize America 20 years from now, and that we won't like what we see.

We asked him to inscribe our copy of Rand's anthology *Capitalism: The Unknown Ideal* (a first edition already bearing Rand's signature), in which is reprinted his article on gold and economic freedom. He told us that he thinks every idea in the book—his own and Rand's—has stood the test of time.

We left feeling that Alan Greenspan is no villain. In his own way, he is indeed a hero—not a Randian hero, but rather a tragic one.

Chapter 9

The Economist of Liberty

*Milton Friedman as Hugh Akston,
the academic who showed the world the
connection between capitalism and freedom*

*"We never make assertions, Miss Taggart," said Hugh Akston. "That
is the moral crime peculiar to our enemies. We do not tell—we show.
We do not claim—we prove. It is not your obedience that we seek to
win, but your rational conviction. You have seen all the elements of our
secret. The conclusion is now yours to draw—we can help you to name
it, but not to accept it—the sight, the knowledge and the acceptance,
must be yours."*

—Atlas Shrugged

Who is Hugh Akston?
In *Atlas Shrugged*, Hugh Akston is an eminent philosopher, an
ardent advocate of reason.

(Continued)

He had been a professor at Patrick Henry University, where he taught three remarkable young students—John Galt, Francisco d'Anconia, and Ragnar Danneskjöld, three of the primary heroes of the book. When John Galt calls for a "strike of the mind," and persuades the men of ability to abandon the economy to collapse in their absence, Akston becomes his first recruit.

When we first meet Akston in *Atlas Shrugged*, he is working as a short-order cook, having left philosophy to whither in the hands of his successor, Simon Pritchett, a nihilistic advocate of unreason. Francisco d'Anconia eloquently describes the difference between the two men's philosophies. When someone says at a party that "Dr. Pritchett was just telling us that nothing is anything," d'Anconia replies that Akston "taught that everything is something."

Throughout *Atlas Shrugged* we see the world gradually collapse in the absence of men of ability. But the most critical collapse is philosophical. Without reason, and without Akston to defend it, there is no limit to the unreasoning depredations of the corrupt businessmen and bureaucrats whom we see bringing ruin to the world.

As the book reaches its explosive conclusion, Akston's former colleague at Patrick Henry—a physicist who allowed himself to be co-opted by government—finds himself being blackmailed into endorsing a horrific weapon of mass destruction. The bureaucrat blackmailing him, a fellow scientist, says, "Who would speak up for us? I believe that some such man as Hugh Akston would have come to our defense—but to think of that is to be guilty of an anachronism."

As Milton Friedman stepped up to the podium in Stockholm, Sweden, on December 10, 1976, he may have felt a mix of emotions. On one hand, it was a great honor to be just the twelfth recipient of the prestigious Prize in Economic Sciences in Memory of Alfred Nobel. On the other hand, perhaps he couldn't help but feel the irony.

Just six years earlier, the very same prize had been awarded to his professional opponent Paul Samuelson, who represented the antithesis of Friedman's ideas. Whereas Friedman was a fervent advocate of the efficiency of free markets, Samuelson argued just as fervently that markets if left to their own devices would invariably spin out of control without preemptive intervention by the government. Their opposing views symbolized the twentieth-century struggle between the forces of collectivism under far-reaching government and individual liberty represented by unhindered free markets. Whereas Samuelson believed government was the solution to a vast array of socioeconomic problems, Friedman's own factual investigations led him to the conclusion that the government itself was the problem.

Friedman wrote in 1962 in his seminal *Capitalism and Freedom*, "The Great Depression, like most other periods of severe unemployment, was produced by government mismanagement rather than by any inherent instability of the private economy."[1] This was no mere political slogan. Friedman and his colleague Anna Schwartz had spent countless years painstakingly assembling data on money, banking, and the economy—ultimately published as the epochal bible of macroeconomic research, *A Monetary History of the United States*. This work had proved beyond doubt that the Federal Reserve's mismanagement of the money supply and the banking system led to the Depression. Revolutionary at the time, this is now so completely accepted that on the occasion of Friedman's 90th birthday, Federal Reserve governor (later chairman) Ben Bernanke publicly apologized on behalf of the Fed. "Regarding the Great Depression. You're right, we did it. We're very sorry. But thanks to you, we won't do it again."[2]

After *Capitalism and Freedom*, Friedman's intellectual rival and fellow Nobelist Samuelson countered in his best-selling textbook *Economics: An Introductory Analysis*, defending the economic benefits of Soviet-style command-and-control economics. In the 1976 10th edition Samuelson wrote that it was a "vulgar mistake to think that most people in Eastern Europe are miserable."[3] In the 1980 11th edition he removed the word "vulgar."[4] Then in the 1989 13th edition, just before the collapse of the Berlin Wall, he wrote, "The Soviet economy is proof that, contrary to what many skeptics had earlier believed, a socialist command economy can function and thrive."[5] Not only did the global collapse of communism—prompted by all those people who weren't miserable, one supposes—prove Samuelson spectacularly wrong, but what followed proved Friedman spectacularly right. As the formerly communist world embraced capitalism, there was an unprecedented surge in global wealth made possible by an unprecedented surge in global economic freedom.

For Friedman, *this*, not the Nobel, was the prize: being right—using economics to make a prediction and see the prediction come true. This was Friedman's way. Start with real-world research. Adduce an economic theory from it that results in a prediction. Then see if the prediction comes true. While this would seem to be little more than the application of the scientific method to economics, Friedman's method stands in stark contrast to that of most economists, which is simply to theorize.

Friedman called his approach "positive economics." Ayn Rand might have simply called it "reason."

In *Atlas Shrugged* Rand symbolized the primacy of reason in the character of Hugh Akston. Milton Friedman was, in many important ways, Hugh Akston come to life. Both were eminent academics—Akston a professor of philosophy, Friedman a professor of economics. Both were influential mentors—Akston to John Galt, and Friedman to a generation of advocates of economic liberty, from Ronald Reagan (who called Friedman's television series *Free to Choose* "a survival kit for you, for the nation, and for freedom"[6]) to Margaret Thatcher (who said Friedman "revived the economics of liberty when it had been all but forgotten"[7]). And both contested with powerful intellectual adversaries representing the dark forces of collectivism—Akston with philosophical imposters who taught students that the mind is impotent, and Friedman with economists like Samuelson who taught students that the government is omnipotent.

Akston's philosophy of reason leads directly to Friedman's positive economics. Akston said, "We never make assertions. . . . That is the moral crime peculiar to our enemies. We do not tell—we show. We do not claim—we prove. It is not your obedience that we seek to win, but your rational conviction."

Former Secretary of State George Shultz put it this way: "I wish I were as sure of anything as Milton is of everything."[8] Such is the power of reason.

There is one very large difference between Friedman and Akston. In *Atlas Shrugged*, Akston walked away from his professional battles, becoming the first recruit to John Galt's strike of the mind. Of his intellectual rivals Akston said, "[M]odern thinkers considered it unnecessary to perceive reality. . . . I could not share my profession with men who claim that the qualification of an intellectual consists of denying the existence of the intellect."

Friedman, in contrast, never gave up his battles on behalf of reason in economics right up to the day he died. And he was great at it. Economist and Reagan intimate Martin Anderson recalls Friedman's technique: "At first he listens quietly, intensely. As long as he totally agrees he listens, but that usually isn't for long. At the first sign of the slightest break in your logic, or your facts, he pounces with a bewildering array of questions, statements, and relentless logic. And it's all done in such a friendly, earnest way that even the intellectually shredded thoroughly enjoy the encounter."[9]

For Friedman, it was always the facts that mattered, not external accolades. So the Nobel Prize was not only ironic, but also faintly absurd, bestowing upon him in the collective mind of society an omniscience that no one deserves. "It is a tribute to the worldwide repute of the Nobel awards that the announcement of an award converts its recipient into an instant expert on all and sundry, and unleashes hordes of ravenous newsmen and photographers from journals and TV stations around the world," he quipped with his characteristic mirthful grin to the crowd at his awards banquet. "I myself have been asked my opinion on everything from a cure for the common cold to the market value of a letter signed by John F. Kennedy."

And then, as if sending forth a cautionary message to the likes of Linus Pauling and Paul Krugman (Samuelson's student at Massachusetts Institute of Technology, by the way, whom we met in Chapter 2, "The Mad Collectivist"), who would later use the imprimatur of their Nobel awards as license to toss around unfounded opinions on everything from the health benefits of Vitamin C to wildly inaccurate predictions on the direction of the stock market, Friedman concluded, "Needless to say, the attention is flattering, but also corrupting. Somehow, we badly need an antidote for both the inflated attention granted a Nobel laureate in areas outside his competence and the inflated ego each of us is in so much danger of acquiring."[10]

Milton Friedman was both a serious academic and a masterful public communicator. During the latter half of the twentieth century he grew to become a well-known and popular voice of reason in an increasingly irrational world. According to George Shultz, "His achievements in professional terms were his work on monetary policy, his work on consumption, and his general impact in terms of professional ideas . . . but then his impact was far greater on the general population and thinking around the world because he was such a good teacher."[11]

Like Hugh Akston, Friedman became a virtual father to legions of student acolytes and, through his work, created a new branch of economic science that came to be called the Chicago school—named for the University of Chicago, where Friedman taught. Friedman's students would eventually fan out across the globe, spreading his economics of reason both as teachers and as technocrats. Dubbed "the Chicago Boys," many of them earned positions of considerable power within the economic policy elites of developing nations, putting to work for the first time Friedman's potent philosophical brew of capitalism and freedom.

In the academic sphere, Friedman wrote many influential treatises, pamphlets, papers, and books, including the magisterial *Monetary History*. In the nonacademic sphere, *Capitalism and Freedom* is his most definitive philosophical statement. But he was best able to reach—and teach—the general public in two other forums. For many years he wrote a column for *Newsweek*, alternating on the magazine's pages with his rival Paul Samuelson. And in 1980, he and his wife Rose produced a 10-part miniseries for public television called *Free to Choose*.

Whether in academia or before the public, his message was unwaveringly in favor of free-market capitalism. But it wasn't political dogma; it was reasoned research discovering the best available system, the one that had proven successful through hard evidence. Or as he told Phil Donohue on television in 1979, "There is no alternative way, so far discovered, of improving the lot of ordinary people that can hold a candle to the productive activities that are unleashed by a free enterprise system."[12]

Friedman was firmly principled, but also pragmatic. He believed that government had a critically important role to play in human affairs—albeit one strictly limited to only those activities that could not be effectively accomplished by the private sector. Referring John F. Kennedy's famous epigram, Friedman wrote, "The free man will ask neither what his country can do for him nor what he can do for his country. He will ask rather 'What can I and my compatriots do through government' to help us discharge our individual responsibilities, to achieve our several goals and purposes, and above all, to protect our freedom?"[13]

Freedom, he believed, was a "rare and delicate plant." So while he was willing to participate in political processes to advance his economic ideas, he always took care to not let himself be used to advance politicians. He once wrote, "The role of the economist in discussions of public policy seems to me to be to prescribe what should be done in the light of what can be done, politics aside, and not to predict what is 'politically feasible' and then to recommend it."[14]

A Young Mind in Training

Milton Friedman was born in 1912, in Brooklyn, the fourth child of immigrants from Austro-Hungary. His mother ran a small retail dry goods store, and his father did odd jobs. "The family income was small and highly uncertain," Milton remembers. "Financial crisis was a constant companion."[15]

Milton was a fast learner from an early age, graduating from Rahway High School in 1928 when he was just 15. His father died during his senior year, leaving his mother and two older sisters supporting the family. He was awarded a scholarship to Rutgers University. He noted that a "class of competitive scholarships for financially needy students which [now] go not to those who score highest in the exams but to underachievers is a nice illustration of how our standards have been corrupted over the years."[16]

Friedman started his college career in mathematics, intending to become an actuary. During his studies, however, he started getting interested in economics. Rather than switching his major, he simply doubled up and earned dual degrees. This combination would serve Friedman very well, as economics was undergoing a transformation from a social science to a mathematical one. It was also at Rutgers that Friedman was introduced to libertarian thought. He credits John Stuart Mill's *Essay on Liberty* as "The most concise and clearest statement of the fundamental libertarian principle, 'The only purpose for which power can be rightfully exercised over any member of a civilized community, against his will, is to prevent harm to others.'"[17]

Another early undergraduate influence was a new professor at Rutgers named Homer Jones. Although only 24 years old at the time, Jones seemed like an elder sage to the teenage Milton as he sat in his introductory classes on insurance and statistics. While these dry subjects hardly seem like fertile ground for intellectual inspiration, Jones's inquiring mind and theoretical bent, combined with the practical sensibilities of an Iowa farm boy, led him to examine the fundamental principles of risk, uncertainty, and profit.

Along the way, according to Friedman, "he put major stress on individual freedom, was cynical and skeptical about attempts to interfere with the exercise of individual freedom in the name of social planning or collective values, yet was by no means a nihilist."[18] He also recalls Jones's "traits that exerted so great an influence on me in my teens: complete intellectual honesty; insistence on rigor of analysis; concern with facts; a drive for practical relevance; and, finally, perpetual questioning and reexamination of conventional wisdom."[19] They were traits Friedman himself would embody for the rest of his career.

With Jones's encouragement, Friedman enrolled in graduate studies at the University of Chicago. He was 20 years old at the time and had never been west of Philadelphia. He remembers in his autobiography, "Though 1932–33, my first year at Chicago, was, financially, my most difficult year, intellectually, it opened new worlds. Jacob Viner, Frank Knight, Henry Schultz, Lloyd Mints, Henry Simons, and, equally important, a brilliant group of graduate students from all over the world exposed me to a cosmopolitan and vibrant intellectual atmosphere of a kind that I had never dreamed existed. I have never recovered."[20]

In his personal life, the most important event that year was meeting fellow economics student Rose Director. They would be married six years later and live the rest of their life together in a "fairy tale"[21] marriage as partners and collaborators.

Friedman earned his master's degree in economics from the University of Chicago in 1933 and decided to attend Columbia University for his second year of graduate studies on a generous fellowship. It was during this year that Friedman reinforced his statistical approach to economics. While Chicago emphasized economic theory, Columbia and the nearby National Bureau of Economic Research (NBER) strove to measure and understand actual economic activity.

Returning to Chicago—and Rose—in 1934, Milton first met lifelong friends Allen Wallis and George Stigler. Both would become leading figures in academia in their own right. Stigler received the Nobel Prize in 1982 and Wallis later rose to the post of chancellor of the University of Rochester, New York. As the academic year ended, Milton needed a job. Wallis had gone to Washington, D.C., earlier, where he landed a role with the newly formed National Resources Committee (NRC), and he arranged for Friedman to join him.

A Detour to the New Deal

The NRC was part of Franklin D. Roosevelt's alphabet soup of new governmental organizations spawned in response to the Great Depression. After years of crushing economic deprivation, people across the globe were beginning to wonder whether strong-arm fascism and authoritarian communism were superior to liberal democracy as forms of government. It was in this climate that the NRC published a report advocating the creation of a National Planning Board[22] akin to the nightmarish central planning bureau of Rand's *Atlas Shrugged*.

At first, the young Friedman was totally on board with the direction Roosevelt was taking the country. New Deal Washington was a lively place. He writes that the "explosion of government, combined with the paucity of academic and business jobs, attracted the best and brightest . . . and enabled them to achieve positions of far greater responsibility than was possible under more static conditions. There was a sense of excitement and achievement in the air. We had the feeling . . . we were in at the birth of a new order that would lead to major changes in society."[23]

Perhaps this is where Friedman started to learn that facts, not feelings, are what count. As his work around Washington progressed, he started to realize that the empirical data he was analyzing just didn't match up with the political rhetoric of collectivist ideas proffered by FDR and his team. He joined the National Bureau of Economic Research in the fall of 1937, where he jointly published a study on professional income with co-author and 1971 Nobel Prize recipient Simon Kuznets, which also served as Friedman's doctoral dissertation at Columbia. That work was finished by 1940, but its publication was effectively censored until after the war because of controversy among some NBER directors about Friedman and Kuznets's observed conclusion that doctors' effective monopoly power had substantially raised the incomes of physicians relative to those of dentists.

From 1941 to 1943 Friedman worked at the U.S. Treasury on wartime tax policy, and then from 1943 to 1945 at Columbia as a mathematical statistician on problems of weapon design, military tactics, and metallurgical experiments. "My capacity as a mathematical statistician undoubtedly reached its zenith on V.E. Day, 1945," he once wisecracked.[24]

Friedman's years in Washington led him to initially support welfare but not the regulatory aspects of Roosevelt's New Deal. While he favored jobs programs for the unemployed, his time at Chicago had taught him the virtues of the price system too well for him to support direct government intervention in markets. Over time, based on additional research and study of the facts, Friedman would temper his support of welfare and move toward a strict framework of capitalism free from interference. But it wouldn't happen overnight.

In 1945, he rejoined colleague George Stigler at the University of Minnesota, where he co-wrote a pamphlet deriding rent control called "Roofs or Ceilings? The Current Housing Problem." "For those, like us, who would like even more equality than there is at present . . . it is surely better to attack directly existing inequalities in income and wealth at their source than to ration each of the hundreds of commodities and services that compose our standard of living."[25] Stigler was impressed by his collaborator and his contribution to the work, saying of Friedman, "It did not take long to recognize Milton's talents: he was logical, perceptive, quick to understand one's arguments—and quick to find their weaknesses."[26]

The pamphlet was widely attacked by both sides of the political spectrum. Some found its message too conservative and squarely at odds with the pro-government and pro-intervention tone of the times. "'Roofs or Ceilings?' outraged the profession," according to Paul Samuelson. "That shows you where we were in our mentality in the immediate postwar period."[27] Robert Bangs wrote in the *American Economic Review* that the work was "a political tract."[28] He later concluded in a popular column,

"Economists who sign their names to drivel of this sort do no service to the profession they represent."[29]

On the opposite end of the political continuum, Ayn Rand herself labeled the pamphlet "collectivist propaganda" and "the most pernicious thing ever issued by an avowedly conservative organization." It wasn't a criticism of the authors' conclusion per se, but a rejection of the approach Friedman and Stigler used to get there. They argued for lifting rent controls on practical, humanitarian grounds, not as Rand would have insisted, in defense of "the inalienable right of landlords and property owners."[30]

A Historic Economic History

In *Atlas Shrugged*, when the reader first meets Hugh Akston, he is laboring as a short-order cook in a diner. When he is recognized by Dagny Taggart, the brilliant railroad executive who is the central protagonist of the book, she asks, "Hugh Akston? . . . The philosopher? . . . The last of the advocates of reason?" Akston replies, "Why, yes. . . . Or the first of their return."

And so it was with Milton Friedman, who would labor deep in a mine of obscure economic data to restore reason to economics.

During the Great Depression, economics had been taken by storm by the British savant John Maynard Keynes. He diagnosed the Depression as a failure of "aggregate demand," and prescribed massive government spending to stimulate it back to life. This became the dominant paradigm that guided the New Deal and captured the economics profession for decades after. For economics, this was a plunge into what amounts to a dark age. It was as though crisis had erased a century and a half of the economics of reason guided by the enlightened thinking of great minds like Adam Smith. Friedman's greatest contribution would be a monumental empirical investigation that would prove—not just argue, but prove—that the Keynesian diagnosis of, and prescription for, the Depression was in error.

In 1936 Keynes bundled his major theories into his magnum opus, called *The General Theory of Employment, Interest and Money*. It is a choppy and poorly structured book, as difficult to plow through as

Finnegans Wake and open to almost as many interpretations. Containing a dearth of objective formulations and no explicit mathematical models, Keynes's book was essentially the product of an armchair sophist arguing against free-market efficiency from the basis of conjecture and philosophical theorizing.

At the core of his argument was the belief that a free-market economy was disastrously inefficient and would not reach an acceptable equilibrium of employment and inflation if left to its own devices. Laissez-faire capitalism, he felt, would inevitably lead to prolonged slumps due to what he termed a "paucity of demand" as the rich saved too much and didn't consume the products of working labor. His solution? Active government intervention on a massive scale that engaged in deficit spending during downturns to stimulate demand, and then raised taxes during upturns to stave off inflation. The goal? To establish perpetual "full employment" and steady economic growth with the government acting like a countercyclical thermostat to the market's boom-bust cycle.

After World War II, Keynes's ideas on economic policy were broadly accepted by leading Western economies. A *Time* cover story from late 1965 entitled "The Economy: We Are All Keynesians Now" trumpeted the success of the 1960s economic expansion, crediting government stimulus as the chief cause. "Basically, Washington's economic managers scaled these heights by their adherence to Keynes's central theme: the modern capitalist economy does not automatically work at top efficiency, but can be raised to that level by the intervention and influence of the government. Keynes was the first to demonstrate convincingly that government has not only the ability but the responsibility to use its powers to increase production, incomes, and jobs."[31] During the postwar period, Keynesian theories were a major factor in spurring the cause of social liberalism, expanded government intervention, and the explosion of government spending.

Then came Friedman.

In 1963, with co-author Anna J. Schwartz, Friedman published the monumental *Monetary History of the United States, 1867–1960*, a vast research project sponsored by the National Bureau of Economic Research and published by Princeton University Press. Instead of Keynesian-style fireside pipe-smoking pontification, Friedman dug into the data. Using meticulous research methods unearthing for the first time a comprehensive history of money in America, he demonstrated how the United States Federal Reserve allowed the money supply to contract by a third during the period 1929 to 1933. His statistical work gave powerful credence to the idea that it was government mismanagement, not free-enterprise capitalism, that had in fact caused the Great Depression. What made the Depression so bad wasn't the Keynesians' lack of demand; it was the government's efforts to save the gold standard that kept interest rates artificially high. This government meddling overwhelmed the economy's normal recovery mechanisms. By way of empirical proof, once countries left the gold standard (Britain in 1931, the United States in 1933), recoveries began. Between 1933 and 1936, U.S. unemployment dropped from 25 to 17 percent.

Despite Keynes's lack of mathematical rigor in his theories, many models were later developed by Keynesian-inspired economists like Paul Samuelson to fill the credibility gap. A famous example was the Phillips curve, which posited an inverse relationship between unemployment and inflation. It implied that unemployment could be reduced by government stimulus, which would then lead to inflation. Conversely, low inflation meant high unemployment.

With the Phillips curve, statist economists were able to concede to Friedman that monetary policy was more effective than government spending to smooth out business cycles. But at the same time, they could now anoint the Federal Reserve—responsible for monetary policy—as their agent for government control of the economy. For the neo-Keynesians armed and dangerous with the Phillips curve, if Congress couldn't control the economy, then the Fed would. The new mantra: If you can't spend your way to prosperity, inflate your way there.

Then came Friedman. Again.

In 1968 he published a paper arguing that the fixed relationship implied by the Phillips curve did not exist.[32] Friedman suggested that sustained Keynesian policies of easy money could lead to both unemployment and inflation rising at once. That was his prediction—and the proof of it came just a few years later in the 1970s, when the world saw the phenomenon that soon became known as stagflation, when double-digit unemployment accompanied skyrocketing inflation. If predictive ability is the hallmark of sound science, then Friedman transcended and demolished the theoretical philosophizing of his Keynesian colleagues in one fell swoop.

The Keynesians were stunned by the apparent contradiction. The Phillips curve told them that stagflation was impossible. Yet there it was. Hugh Akston could have told them what to do: "By the essence and nature of existence, contradictions cannot exist. . . . [C]heck your premises. You will find that one of them is wrong." In this case, Akston's axiom was too modest. *All* of the Keynesians' premises were wrong.

Then Friedman delivered the coup de grâce. If monetary policy couldn't be used proactively to artificially create prosperity—in other words, if the best it could do was avoid catastrophes like the Great Depression—then who needs a Federal Reserve with policies controlled by political appointees? Instead, Friedman said that "central banks could profitably be replaced by computers geared to provide a steady rate of growth in the quantity of money."[33] No, Friedman never got all the way to the radical libertarianism of Congressman Ron Paul, who has called for outright abolition of the Fed. But this was a classic Friedman finesse, and it shows why he was so effective: accept the reality that there is a Federal Reserve, and find an elegant way to deprive it of its powers to interfere with economic liberty.

From Academia to Main Street

When Ayn Rand was once asked to very briefly describe Objectivism, she reduced her philosophy of politics to a single word: capitalism. Friedman was making the same philosophical journey at the same time—understanding that a society's economics was inexorably linked to the political structure it chose. It was only a short step from trumpeting economic freedom to championing individual liberty as an integrated cornerstone of a successful socioeconomic system.

Friedman put it all together in his 1962 book *Capitalism and Freedom*. In just 200 pages of succinct and engaging prose, he covered a vast range of topics on the role of government in a free society—international trade, social welfare, fiscal policy, distribution of income, education, and discrimination. He laid out the case for free-market capitalism as both a means to achieve economic freedom and a fundamental requirement of political freedom.

Throughout the book, Friedman dove deep into a raging sea of complex social and economic questions and recovered from them exactly how free-market solutions are superior to the force of government. But he was no extremist, no anarchist. Government, he believed, was a valuable instrument with a critical role to play. That role, however, was that of an umpire, not a dictator or even a paternalistic provider. The umpire enforces the rules, mediates disputes, and maintains a free field of play; the umpire doesn't dictate outcomes or advantage one team over another.

"The need for government in these respects arises because absolute freedom is impossible. However attractive anarchy may be as a philosophy, it is impossible in a world of imperfect men," Friedman wrote. "Men's freedoms can conflict, and when they do, one man's freedom must be limited to preserve another's—as a Supreme Court Justice once put it, 'My freedom to move my fist must be limited by the proximity of your chin.'"[34]

When *Capitalism and Freedom* was first published at the dawn of the 1960s, not a single mainstream U.S. newspaper or magazine would review it; not the *New York Times*, the *Chicago Tribune*, *Newsweek*, or *Time*. Since then, *Capitalism and Freedom* has sold over half a million copies in English and has been translated into 18 languages. *Atlas Shrugged* had received the same treatment—or worse—when it had debuted five years before. It, too, enjoyed a brilliant future despite having been ignored or maligned by the mainstream media.

Starting in the 1960s, Friedman became more active in public affairs. He served as an informal economic adviser to Barry Goldwater in his unsuccessful campaign for the presidency in 1964, to Richard Nixon in his successful 1968 campaign, and to Ronald Reagan in his 1980 campaign (Ayn Rand supported the first two, opposed the third). Friedman recalls his friend Stigler as fond of saying later, "Milton wants to change the world; I only want to understand it."[35]

In 1969, Friedman was appointed as a member of the Gates Commission, a presidentially appointed panel assigned to consider replacing the draft with an all-volunteer military. This was a challenge worthy of Friedman's great mind—putting the burden to show that voluntary market forces could take the place of involuntary government coercion that virtually everyone had come to think of automatically as utterly necessary to wage war.

General William Westmoreland, the U.S. commander in Vietnam, strongly supported involuntary conscription, and told the commission that he didn't want to command an army of mercenaries. "General," Friedman interrupted, "would you rather command an army of slaves?"

Replied Westmoreland indignantly, "I don't like to hear our patriotic draftees referred to as slaves." Friedman shot back: "I don't like to hear our patriotic volunteers referred to as mercenaries." Friedman moved in for the kill. "If they are mercenaries," he told Westmoreland, "then I, sir, am a mercenary professor, and you, sir, are a mercenary general; we are served by mercenary physicians, we use a mercenary lawyer, and we get our meat from a mercenary butcher."[36]

With this kind of persuasion from Friedman—and similar efforts from his fellow Gates Commission member and Ayn Rand acolyte Alan Greenspan, whom we met in Chapter 8, "The Sellout"—the Gates Commission ended up recommending the abolition of the draft, and President Nixon ultimately signed it into law. Libertarians like Friedman and Greenspan—and Rand—were able to claim at least one spectacular victory for liberty under the otherwise dismal reign of Richard Nixon. Nowadays we falsely remember the antidraft movement coming from the political left, but conservatives/libertarians like Friedman and Greenspan—and Rand—are the ones who made abolition of the draft happen.

At the close of the 1970s, fresh on the heels of his Nobel award, Friedman began to gain a wider audience. He wrote a regular column for *Newsweek* (remember, the magazine that 15 years earlier hadn't deigned to review *Capitalism and Freedom*), dueling alternately with Paul Samuelson using opposing philosophical swords: Friedman's light rapier honed by the Chicago school's brand of free-market monetarism versus Samuelson's blunt claymore of Keynesian government intervention. The columns were extremely popular. Friedman's message, it seemed, resonated somewhere deep within the American psyche well outside the hallowed halls of academia and banquet rooms of Stockholm.

It was clear that Friedman had arrived right in the middle of Main Street when he was invited to appear in 1979 on the popular daytime talk show hosted by Phil Donohue. The show's limousine-liberal host whined to Friedman about "mal-distribution of wealth" and "the

desperate plight of millions of people in underdeveloped countries."
He then asked Friedman, with arms flailing, "When you see the greed
and the concentration of power, did you ever have a moment of doubt
about capitalism?" Friedman's response was calm and masterful, literally
stunning the unflappable Donohue into dumbfounded silence.

> "Is there some society you know that doesn't run on greed?"
> Friedman challenged. "Do you think Russia doesn't run on
> greed? Do you think China doesn't run on greed? What is
> greed? Of course none of us are greedy—it's only the other
> fellow who is greedy. The world runs on individuals pursuing
> their separate interests. The greatest achievements in civiliza-
> tion have not come from government bureaus. Einstein didn't
> construct his theory under order from a bureaucrat. Henry
> Ford didn't revolutionize the automobile industry that way. In
> the only cases in which the masses have escaped the grinding
> poverty that you're talking about—the only cases in recorded
> history—are where they have had capitalism and largely free
> trade. If you want to know where the masses are worst off, it's
> in exactly the kinds of systems that depart from that. So that
> the record of history is absolutely crystal clear: that there is no
> alternative way, so far discovered, of improving the lot of ordi-
> nary people that can hold a candle to the productive activities
> that are unleashed by a free enterprise system. Is it really
> true that political self-interest is nobler somehow than eco-
> nomic self-interest? Just tell me where in the world you find
> these angels who are going to organize society for us. I don't
> even trust *you* to do that."[37]

This was not Gordon Gekko proclaiming that "greed is good." It
was classic Friedman. He made his point with supreme effectiveness, but
there was not a hint of rancor in it, nor a trace of self-aggrandizement.
It was all delivered with good cheer and an impish smile. Here was
Rand's Hugh Akston come to life, delivering not a deathblow in a
debate, but more of a prayer—what Akston described as "a full, confident, affirming self-dedication to my love of the right, to the certainty
that the right would win."

Helping People Learn
(Because Governments Don't)

While Friedman's 1962 classic *Capitalism and Freedom* got Friedman's ideas to Main Street, they were soon to go further, potentially to every television set in the United States. With his wife Rose he created *Free to Choose*, a 10-part PBS miniseries and accompanying book. Here Milton and Rose, in homespun style and sparkly-eyed humor, led the viewer on a journey around the world, seen through the prism of their free-market philosophy. Using you-are-there real-world examples and personal interviews, the Friedmans made abstract ideas such as equality, freedom, and the power of the markets intensely accessible to the general public—even those with no formal training in economics or philosophy.

Using popular vernacular, they translated complicated principles into understandable examples. "The strongest argument for free enterprise is that it prevents anybody from having too much power, whether that person is a government official, a trade union official, or a business executive. It forces them to put up or shut up. They either have to deliver the goods [and] produce something that people are willing to pay for [and] are willing to buy, or else they have to go into a different business,"[38] he said in episode 2, "The Tyranny of Control." It was perhaps the first time in history that a Noble laureate publicly uttered the phrase "put up or shut up." He also provided pithy maxims that were easy to recall in response to the collectivist claptrap of the day, including: "A society that puts equality before freedom will get neither. A society that puts freedom before equality will get a high degree of both."[39] "The most important single central fact about a free market is that no exchange takes place unless both parties benefit," and "Governments never learn. Only people learn."

The Prophet of Profit

In *Atlas Shrugged*, John Galt stopped the engine of the world by persuading its most brilliant minds to go on strike. His first recruit was the philosopher of reason, Hugh Akston. In *Atlas*, we read the question: "Isn't it odd? When a politician or a movie star retires, we read front page stories about it. When a philosopher retires, people do not even notice it." Rand's answer, in the voice of Francisco d'Anconia: "They do, eventually."

That's because ideas move the world—they can save it, or they can destroy it. The *absence* of ideas can enable the world to destroy itself. So it was when Hugh Akston went on strike—and so it was when Milton Friedman died, in November 2006. The timing was almost too perfect. The financial crisis that swept the globe and became the Great Recession started within months of his death, with the first wave of defaults on subprime mortgages. The Obama administration and a radical leftist Congress used the turmoil—under the doctrine of White House Chief of Staff Rahm Emanuel, who said, "You never want a serious crisis to go to waste"[40]—to implement a new New Deal.

Up to his last breath, Friedman had been a stunningly effective agent in dismantling the New Deal leviathan that he had once served. He always saw the unintended consequences of government meddling in the economy and in our lives, and warned us of the dangers we were inadvertently creating for ourselves. Often we listened, and often we didn't.

In the case of the mortgage credit crisis that erupted shortly after his death, he had been on the case a full 16 years before. Anticipating the government's role in the debacle through expanding Fannie Mae and Freddie Mac, he described in a 1992 pamphlet entitled *Why Government Is the Problem* exactly why the differences in private versus public ownership yield dramatically different results to society. "If a private enterprise is a failure, it closes down—unless it can get a government subsidy to keep it going; if a government enterprise fails, it is expanded. I challenge you to find exceptions. . . . If the initial reason for undertaking an activity disappears, they have a strong incentive to find another justification for its continued existence."[41]

In the same pamphlet he went on to sum up the first decade of the twenty-first century as if he had mentally time-traveled forward almost two decades. "The problem is not that government is spending too little, but that it is spending too much. The problem in schooling is that the government is spending too much on the wrong things. The problem in health care is that the government is spending too much on the wrong things. The end result has been that government has become a self-generating monstrosity. . . . What we now have is a government of the people, by the bureaucrats, including the legislators who have become bureaucrats, for the bureaucrats."[42]

In the case of artificially imposed diversity quotas for faculty and staff at his university, he would tell the administration as early as 1974, "Balance and diversity have been and will continue to be valuable by-products of an undeviating emphasis on quality alone. They are not objectives to be sought directly."[43] Friedman would keep sounding his trumpet as the voice of reason and freedom until the day he died.

As late as 2004, at the age of 92 when most economists have long since retired or passed on, Friedman's voice of reason and liberty was as loud and articulate as ever, distilling difficult ideas and coating them with charm to be deliciously palatable to a mass audience. In a Fox News interview in May of that year, he explained the basic construct of government spending.

> There are four ways in which you can spend money. You can spend your own money on yourself. When you do that, why then you really watch out what you're doing, and you try to get the most for your money. Then you can spend your own money on somebody else. For example, I buy a birthday present for someone. Well, then I'm not so careful about the content of the present, but I'm very careful about the cost. Then, I can spend somebody else's money on myself. And if I spend somebody else's money on myself, then I'm sure going to have a good lunch! Finally, I can spend somebody else's money on somebody else. And if I spend somebody else's money on somebody else, I'm not concerned about how much it is, and I'm not concerned about what I get. And that's government. And that's close to 40% of our national income.[44]

The only thing that Friedman failed to anticipate was the enormity of his own influence. He had guessed that *Free to Choose* would be received by the country about as well as Barry Goldwater in the early 1960s. Yet by the early 1980s he and Rose not only had generous sponsorship for their television show and an avid viewership, but they had a conservative Goldwater sound-alike in the White House after Ronald Reagan's landslide victory over Jimmy Carter.

On December 19, 1969, Friedman would appear on the cover of *Time*—another publication that had snubbed him and Rose earlier in the decade. The magazine grudgingly gave him credit for his emerging influence, saying, "Friedman, a 57-year-old economics professor at the University of Chicago, is still regarded by critics as a pixie or a pest, but he has reached the scholar's pinnacle: leadership of a whole school of economic thought. It is called the 'Chicago school.' . . . Milton Friedman has done much to revive faith in the competitive market and to change the theories by which nations guide their commercial destinies."[45]

In 1962, Friedman had compiled a list of 14 unjustified government activities that included agricultural subsidies, trade tariffs, rent control, minimum wages, control of radio and television by the Federal Communications Commission (FCC), Social Security, public housing, the post office, and compulsory military conscription. So far, only the draft has been entirely eliminated. Yet there have been significant inroads into some areas, including fewer international trade restrictions under the North American Free Trade Agreement (NAFTA) and elimination of the price controls of the early 1970s. However, during the latter half of the 1980s spending by government had grown to 45 percent of national income. "By that test, government owns 45 percent of the means of production that produce the national income. The U.S. is now 45 percent socialist,"[46] he would opine in a 1989 *New York Times* piece.

By 2002—40 years after *Capitalism and Freedom*—Friedman had started to take a more global view and would credit a number of world developments as evidence that, ironically, capitalism was making greater gains outside of the United States, the very birthplace of modern democracy. The collapse of the Berlin Wall and the dissolution of the Soviet Union ushered in a wave of increased economic opportunity in Eastern Europe. Prosperity in China was exploding under freer economic—if not political—policies. Success stories like the East Asian "Tigers" of Taiwan, Singapore, and South Korea (all of which had followed in the footsteps of Hong Kong, which Friedman had long celebrated as an exemplary free economy) showed that largely unfettered, market-oriented systems not only worked, but thrived.

For himself, Friedman refused to take credit for any modest advancement in liberty. He felt it was a function of individual choice and people's gradual recognition that the creep of collectivism ran directly counter to our rational need to pursue our own interests. He wasn't driving the change; he was only describing and presaging the inevitable. "The change in the climate of opinion was produced by experience, not by theory or philosophy,"[47] he wrote in 1982. Then, echoing Hugh Akston, he advised, "The only person who can truly persuade you is yourself. You must turn the issues over in your mind at leisure, consider the many arguments, let them simmer, and after a long time turn your preferences into convictions."[48]

Before his death in 2006, Friedman would sum up his work in the humblest of terms: "My contribution to the libertarian cause has not come on the level of values or the like but rather by empirical demonstration . . . by advancing the science of economics and showing the relevance of those advances to the policy of economics."[49]

Hugh Akston might have quibbled with Friedman's phrasing; he would have said that empirical demonstration itself is the result of one's values—the value of reason. But we expect Akston would have been pleased when Friedman said in a 1975 interview, "One of the great mistakes is to judge policies and programs by their intentions rather than their results."[50]

Akston might also have quibbled with Friedman's generosity with his intellectual enemies. Akston blasted philosophers of unreason as using "the prestige of philosophy to purchase the enslavement of thought." Friedman was gentler: "When I come to the question of the dispute and difference I have made with modern liberals, the conclusion that I always reach is that the problem with the modern liberal is not that their hearts are soft, but that their heads are."[51]

Now with Friedman gone, recall what George Shultz once said of him: "Everybody loves to argue with Milton, particularly when he isn't there."[52] Sadly, he isn't there. And the arguments against reason and liberty seem louder than ever. But Friedman showed us all how to defend those values; now it's up to us.

Afterword

Learn from Ayn Rand's heroes—don't be intimidated by their exceptional achievements.

Yes, they are steel tycoons who invent new metals, architects who build the tallest buildings in New York, and rebels who save the world by stopping its engine. And today's real-life Rand heroes are titans of technology and finance, among the wealthiest people who ever lived. But these heroes are exceptional only in their epic scale, not in their intrinsic nature. Rand's books—like life itself—are full of characters who build exceptional lives by following Rand's philosophy, even though they do not become world-famous industrialists.

From *The Fountainhead*, think of Mike, the humble but superlatively competent construction worker who works with the brilliant architect Howard Roark. From *Atlas Shrugged*, think of Eddie Willers, the unassuming but—again—superlatively competent assistant to the high-powered railroad executive Dagny Taggart. Or how about Quentin Daniels, the young but—are we seeing a pattern here?—superlatively competent student who strives to reproduce John Galt's technology breakthrough? The most unforgettable may be Jeff, merely a tramp who bums a ride on one of Dagny's trains. It turns out he was once a factory worker—superlatively competent, no doubt—who reveals to Dagny the true identity of John Galt. He then masterfully takes charge for Dagny when the train they're on is abandoned by its crew.

Rand herself summed it up perfectly. Speaking in *Atlas Shrugged* through the voice of Ellis Wyatt, a brilliant oilman who has abandoned his fields to join Galt's strike: "There's no such thing as a lousy job—only lousy men who don't care to do it."

Whether or not you'll ever be a titan of industry, there are two core lessons that can be learned from each and every one of our real-life Rand heroes.

First, they teach us how much is possible—more than we ever would have thought without them to show us the way. Before there was a Bill Gates, we just didn't know that anyone could get that rich anymore. Gates's self-made wealth hasn't been seen in this world for a century, since the days of men like Cornelius Vanderbilt. Gates proved it can still be done.

Yes, there's that old joke (repeated by envious cynics like Paul Krugman[1]) that when Bill Gates walks into a bar the average income for everyone there goes up but no one is actually richer. That is patently untrue. First, everyone in the world is richer because of the value created by Bill Gates; if they weren't, he wouldn't have been able to get so rich in the first place. But separately, and more importantly, everyone is made richer by the *example* of Bill Gates—the fact that he is living proof that great things are possible, things greater than you ever would have imagined if Gates hadn't proved it in his own life.

Second, our real-life Rand heroes teach us that Rand's value system works. Follow her precepts (she once condensed them into just four words: self-interest, reason, objective reality, and capitalism[2]) and you will succeed.

At the same time, our real-life Rand villains show what happens if you reject those precepts. Whether or not you achieve ostensible success in your life, you will be a parasite and a thief who brings ruin to everyone you deal with. Look at the case of Alan Greenspan. By following Rand's precepts he took himself to the height of fame and power, and the U.S. economy benefited from his steady hand. But by violating them once he had that power, he helped usher in a global banking crisis and the Great Recession, and now lives his twilight years in bitter regret.

John Allison is the clearest case in point. He proves that there is much you can learn from Rand's heroes, because he built a spectacular career and one of America's strongest banks by formally analyzing the virtues that made Rand's heroes great, and consciously emulating them. Then look at Angelo Mozilo, a banker of Allison's generation who took the path of Rand's villains. Today Mozilo clings to the remnants of the fortune he built by corrupting politicians and government agencies to aid and abet his house of subprime cards, but he is a ruined shell of a man who nearly ruined the entire global banking system.

So yes, you can learn from Rand's heroes—the fictional ones and the real-life ones.

From John Allison you can learn not only to live your own life in accordance with Rand's values, but to teach them to others you work with. At Allison's bank, BB&T, every one of the 30,000 employees has been trained in Rand's value system—from the executive suite to the teller line. Self-evidently, it works.

Are you looking for a concrete plan to put the value system of Rand's heroes to work in your own life? Allison has written one for you, by identifying and articulating BB&T's 10 core values. You don't have to work there to put those values to work in your life. Do it on your own, and then put yourself through the ongoing process that all BB&T employees experience: Every six months, give yourself a rigorous self-evaluation based on how you've measured up to the values.

From Bill Gates you learn that you must love your work and devote yourself to it fully. When fate offered the opportunity to build the operating system that would underlie almost every personal computer in the world, Gates's competitor, who was in a much better position to grab the opportunity, was on vacation. Gates wasn't. You might say he became the richest man in the world simply because he didn't take a vacation on one particular day.

You can also learn from Gates that you must not only be consecrated to your work, but always be on the alert to protect yourself from the envious parasites who will seek to bring you down. It's not enough to build. You must defend. Gates came within inches of losing everything because he didn't know that until it was far too late. But you know it now.

From Steve Jobs you learn that your work is your own in every sense. Do the work you love, and love the work you do. Don't think about the money—follow your passion, give it everything you've got, do it your way, and money will come. If it doesn't, it surely wouldn't have if you'd spent the same energies compromising. And don't think about all the other people; ignore the bureaucrats and the naysayers, and shrug off the critics who think you're a single-minded monster. If you have passion for something, there will be enough other people out there who will share that passion if you just wait for them to find you.

From T. J. Rodgers you learn that the passion and excellence you bring to your work can infuse your whole life. If you can do *one* thing well, then you're the kind of person who can do things well—so you can do *lots* of things well. Do so, and don't settle for less. Work only with people who are the same way. Don't waste too much time being nice to incompetents—move on; surround yourself with people who care as much as you do, and who will work as hard as you will.

You can also learn from Rodgers not to be afraid to speak out. Sure, in today's culture dominated by media all too eager to tear down people of achievement and fame, and in a political environment soaked in implicit and explicit obeisance to principles of collectivism, you can feel like a pariah if you speak up for freedom, for individualism, or even for achievement. But Rodgers gets away with speaking his mind, and so can you. His secret weapon? It's the utterly guilt-free and fear-free confidence that he is right. That can be your secret weapon, too. Just don't feel guilty about believing what you believe.

What can you learn from real-life Rand villains?

From Angelo Mozilo you can learn that you can make some quick bucks by conniving with politicians, lying to stockholders, and tricking suckers into buying homes they can't afford with mortgage debt they can't repay, and then get a government agency to take all the risk. Want to be responsible for a worldwide banking collapse and live out the rest of your days as a discredited scumbag? Want to destroy countless lives—many of those you purported to help? Then you know just what to do.

From Barney Frank you can learn to act like a big guy by pretending you care about the little guys, many of whom will vote for you in return. Then when it turns out that you destroy the U.S. housing market—and cause irreparable harm to the little guys whose votes you were courting—because your idea of using taxpayer risk to buy off your electorate blew up, just blame Wall Street and demand to be made an even bigger guy. It's easy.

From Paul Krugman you can learn that all it takes to be a media celebrity is to say anything, whether or not it's true—as long as you make sure to tell the collectivist stories the media wants to hear. Never admit error. Never admit fault. If anyone disagrees with you, accuse him or her of being partisan, dishonest, an ideological racist, or—better yet—a stalker. Creating a political atmosphere steeped in hate is a small price to pay for your fame. Go for it.

And what can we learn from Alan Greenspan, the man who knew better—the man who started as a Rand hero and then, seemingly with the best of intentions, ended up living the life of one of her most pathetic villains? Learn that no matter how smart you are, no matter how right you are, you can't save the world by using the police power of the state to carry out your brilliant ideas. Might makes wrong. Always.

So with all this to fortify you, go forth and be a Rand hero. All you really have to do is take John Galt's oath—and mean it.

"I swear by my life and my love of it that I will never live for the sake of another man, or ask another man to live for mine."

Notes

Introduction

1. David Burger, "Longhorns 17, Badgers 1," Iowahawk blog, March 2, 2011.
2. Modern Library 100 Best Novels, www.randomhouse.com/modernlibrary/100bestnovels.html.
3. Library of Congress Center for the Book, www.englishcompanion.com/Readings/booklists/loclist.html.
4. *Chicago Tribune*, October 13, 1957, B1.
5. Ayn Rand, "The Goal of My Writing," in *The Romantic Manifesto* (New York: New American Library, 1969; 2nd ed. 1975).
6. Anne Heller, *Ayn Rand and the World She Made* (New York: Knopf, 2009).
7. Whittaker Chambers, "Big Sister Is Watching You," *National Review*, December 18, 1957.
8. Ayn Rand, "A Last Survey," *Ayn Rand Letter* 4, no. 2 (1975).
9. Ayn Rand, "Of Living Death," *Objectivist*, October 1968.
10. Ayn Rand, "The War in Vietnam," in *Ayn Rand Answers* (New York: New American Library, 2005).

11. Ayn Rand, "Miscellaneous," in *Ayn Rand Answers* (New York: New American Library, 2005).

12. Ibid.

13. Ayn Rand, "On Racism and Feminism," in *Ayn Rand Answers* (New York: New American Library, 2005).

14. Heller, *Ayn Rand and the World She Made*.

15. Ibid.

16. "Reds' Program Tints Platform of Wallaceites," *Chicago Daily Tribune*, July 23, 1948, 3.

17. Tom Junod, "Steve Jobs and the Portal to the Invisible," *Esquire*, October 2008.

18. Paul Krugman, "Fannie, Freddie and You," *New York Times*, July 14, 2008.

19. Deroy Murdock, "Jesse Jackson's Corporate Cash Cow," *Chief Executive*, July 2001.

Chapter 1   The Individualist

1. John Markoff, "Company Reports: Apple's First Annual Profit since 1995," *New York Times*, October 15, 1998.

2. Press release, "Apple Announces New Board of Directors," August 6, 1997.

3. Michael R. Lawrence, "Memory and Imagination: New Pathways to the Library of Congress," film for Library of Congress, 1990.

4. Tom Junod, "Steve Jobs and the Portal to the Invisible," *Esquire*, October 2008.

5. Peter Elkind and Doris Burke, "The Trouble with Steve," *Fortune*, March 17, 2008.

6. Brent Schlender, "The Three Faces of Steve," *Fortune*, November 9, 1998, 96–104.

7. Leander Kahney, "Being Steve Jobs' Boss," *Bloomberg Businessweek*, October 24, 2010.

8. Ibid.

9. Jeffrey S. Young and William L. Simon, *iCon Steve Jobs: The Greatest Second Act in the History of Business* (Hoboken, NJ: John Wiley & Sons, 2006).

10. Kahney, "Being Steve Jobs' Boss."

11. Steve Jobs, Stanford commencement speech, 2005, www.youtube
    .com/watch?feature=player_embedded&v=UF8uR6Z6KLc.

12. Young and Simon, *iCon Steve Jobs*.

13. Daniel Alef, *Steve Jobs: The Apple of Our i* (Meta4 Publishing, 2009),
    Location 54. www.amazon.com/Steve-Jobs-Apple-Our-ebook/dp/
    B00359FCCE.

14. Young and Simon, *iCon Steve Jobs*.

15. Anthony Imbimbo, *Steve Jobs: The Brilliant Mind Behind Apple*
    (Gareth Stevens Publishing, 2009).

16. Ibid., 42.

17. Phil Patton, "Steve Jobs: Out for Revenge," *New York Times*,
    August 6, 1989.

18. Andrew Pollack, "Next, a Computer on Every Desk," *New York
    Times*, August 23, 1981.

19. Company brochure, reproduced in *Interface Age*, October 1976.

20. Young and Simon, *iCon Steve Jobs*.

21. Pilar Quezzaire, *Steve Jobs* (Great Neck Publishing, 2006).

22. Imbimbo, *Steve Jobs*.

23. Robert Metz, "Market Place: I.B.M. Threat to Apple," *New York
    Times*, September 2, 1981.

24. Robert J. Cole, "An 'Orderly' Debut for Apple," *New York Times*,
    December 13, 1980.

25. Young and Simon, *iCon Steve Jobs*.

26. Kahney, "Being Steve Jobs' Boss."

27. John Sculley and John Byrne, *Odyssey: Pepsi to Apple—A Journey of
    Adventure, Ideas and the Future* (New York: HarperCollins, 1989).

28. Elkind and Burke, "Trouble with Steve," 88–160.

29. Andrew Pollack, "Apple Computer Entrepreneur's Rise and Fall,"
    New York Times, September 19, 1985.

30. Mark Alpert and Sally Solo, "The Ultimate Computer Factory:
    Steve Jobs Has Built a NeXT Workstation Plant with Just about
    Everything: Lasers, Robots, Speed, and Remarkably Few Defects,"
    Fortune, February 26, 1990.

31. Pete Mortensen, "NeXT Fans Give Up the Ghost," *Wired*, December
    21, 2005.

32. Young and Simon, *iCon Steve Jobs*.

33. Cathy Booth and David S. Jackson, "Steve's Job: Restart Apple," *Time*, August 18, 1997.

34. PR Newswire, "Pixar to Sell Image Computer Operations to Vicom Systems; Pixar and Vicom Systems Sign Image Computer Agreement," www.highbeam.com/doc/1G1-8389470.html.

35. www.w3.org/People/Berners-Lee/Overview.html.

36. Planet Rome.ro, "Apple-NeXT Merger Birthday," December 20, 2006, http://rome.ro/2006/12/apple-next-merger-birthday.html.

37. John Markoff, "Apple Computer Co-Founder Strikes Gold with New Stock," *New York Times*, November 30, 1995.

38. Young and Simon, *iCon Steve Jobs*.

39. Ibid.

40. John Markoff, "Apple to Take Big Write-Off on Acquisition," *New York Times*, February 11, 1997.

41. Kahney, "Being Steve Jobs' Boss."

42. Markoff, "Company Reports: Apple's First Annual Profit since 1995."

43. Schlender, "Three Faces of Steve."

44. Jeff Goodell, "Steve Jobs: The *Rolling Stone* Interview," *Rolling Stone*, December 2003.

45. Ibid.

Chapter 2 The Mad Collectivist

1. *This Week*, ABC News, November 14, 2010.

2. Paul Krugman, "Incidents from My Career," Princeton University web site.

3. Ibid.

4. *The NewsHour with Jim Lehrer*, PBS, October 13, 2008; and Allisa Macfarquar, "The Deflationist," *New Yorker*, March 1, 2010.

5. Paul Krugman, "Games Nations Play," *New York Times*, January 3, 2003.

6. Paul Krugman, "Rule by the Ridiculous," *New York Times* web site Conscience of a Liberal blog, December 28, 2010.

7. Krugman, "Incidents from My Career."

8. "Interview with Paul Krugman," *Die Weltwoche*, December 24, 1998.

9. Paul Krugman, "The Sons Also Rise," *New York Times*, November 22, 2002.

10. Ibid.

11. Daniel Okrent, "13 Things I Meant to Write About but Never Did," *New York Times*, May 22, 2005.

12. Paul Krugman, "How I Work," Krugman's web site.

13. Michael Hirsh, "The Great Debunker," *Newsweek*, March 4, 1996.

14. Paul Krugman, "Stimulus for Lawyers," *New York Times*, January 14, 2003.

15. Sigmund Freud, *Collected Writings* (London: Hogarth Press, 1924).

16. Macfarquar, " Deflationist."

17. Paul Krugman, "Taking on China," *New York Times*, March 14, 2010.

18. *Tim Russert*, CNBC, August 7, 2004.

19. Krugman, "Incidents from My Career."

20. Paul Krugman and Lawrence Summers, "Inflation During the 1983 Recovery," Council of Economic Advisers, September 9, 1982.

21. Paul Krugman, "An Economic Legend," *New York Times*, June 11, 2004.

22. Paul Krugman, "Dow Wow, Dow Ow," *New York Times*, February 27, 2000.

23. Paul Krugman, "No Relief in Sight," *New York Times*, February 28, 2003.

24. Paul Krugman, "Still Blowing Bubbles," *New York Times*, June 20, 2003.

25. Paul Krugman, "A Fiscal Train Wreck," *New York Times*, March 11, 2003.

26. Paul Krugman, "Mistakes," Conscience of a Liberal blog, *New York Times* web site, September 1, 2010.

27. Paul Krugman, "For Richer," *New York Times Magazine*, October 20, 2002.

28. Author interview with Princeton Township officials.

29. Macfarquar, "Deflationist."

30. Macfarquar, " Deflationist"; and Alex Kowalski, "Krugman Buys Manhattan Apartment for $1.7 Million," *Bloomberg*, August 12, 2009.

31. *The Haraka*, September 1999.

32. Paul Krugman, "Capital Control Freaks," *Slate*, September 27, 1999.

33. Ibid.

34. Paul Krugman, "Listening to Mahathir," *New York Times*, October 21, 2003.

35. Glen Tobias, "ADL Letter to the *New York Times*," Anti-Defamation League, October 21, 2003.

36. Paul Krugman, "The Smear Machine Cranks Up Again," Krugman's web site, October 24, 2003.

37. Paul Krugman, "The Great Divide," *New York Times*, January 29, 2002.

38. Paul Krugman, "The Ascent of E-Man," *Fortune*, May 29, 1999.

39. Mark Tran, "Enron 'Sting' Used Fake Command Center," *The Guardian*, February 21, 2002.

40. Paul Krugman, "My Connection with Enron, One More Time," Krugman's web site, February 8, 2002.

41. Paul Krugman, "Power and Profits," *New York Times*, January 24, 2001.

42. Paul Krugman, "Crony Capitalism, U.S.A.," *New York Times*, January 15, 2002.

43. Paul Krugman, "Death by Guru," *New York Times*, December 18, 2001.

44. Paul Krugman, "On the Second Day, Atlas Waffled," *New York Times*, February 14, 2003.

45. Donald Luskin, "Krugman, Greenspan and Ayn Rand," Conspiracy to Keep You Poor and Stupid blog, February 16, 2003.

46. Donald Luskin, "Paul Krugman: Party Animal," Conspiracy to Keep You Poor and Stupid blog, November 8, 2002.

47. Paul Krugman, "Into the Wilderness," *New York Times*, November 8, 2002.

48. Paul Krugman, "Let Them Hate as Long as They Fear," *New York Times*, March 7, 2003; "Off the Wagon," *New York Times*, January 17, 2003; "Steps to Wealth," *New York Times*, July 16, 2002; and "Liberal Oasis Interview with Paul Krugman," *Liberal Oasis*, August 29, 2003.

49. "What Greg Mankiw Really Thinks about Paul Krugman," Curious Capitalist blog, *Time* web site, October 14, 2008.

50. Donald Luskin, "Meet the Krugman Truth Squad," *National Review Online*, March 20, 2009.

51. Donald Luskin, "Krugman's Job-Robbing Calculus," *National Review Online*, April 23, 2003.

52. Paul Krugman, "Jobs, Jobs, Jobs," *New York Times*, April 22, 2003.

53. *Wall Street Week*, PBS, January 31, 2003.

54. Paul Krugman, "Jobs, Jobs, Jobs: A Follow Up," Krugman's web site, April 24, 2003; "Fiscal Policy and Employment: Simple Analytics," Krugman's web site, April 28, 2003; "Even More on Jobs," Krugman's web site, April 29, 2003; "Zero Is Not Enough," Krugman's web site, May 4, 2003; and "Elephant Shit," Krugman's web site, May 5, 2003.

55. Paul Krugman, "Tax Cuts and Jobs: A Summary of the Debate," Krugman's web site, May 8, 2003.

56. Krugman, "Elephant Shit."

57. Revelle Forum, University of California at San Diego, October 6, 2003.

58. Author's contemporaneous notes.

59. Author's contemporaneous notes.

60. Donald Luskin, "Face to Face with Evil," Conspiracy to Keep You Poor and Stupid blog, October 7, 2003.

61. Atrios, "Diary of a Stalker," Eschaton blog, October 7, 2003.

62. *Hannity & Colmes*, Fox News, October 17, 2003.

63. Ben McGrath, "Balking," *New Yorker*, November 17, 2003.

64. Author's contemporaneous notes.

65. Daniel Okrent, "Okrent Responds," Public Editor's Journal blog, *New York Times*, May 31, 2005.

66. Daniel Okrent, "The Privileges of Opinion, the Obligations of Fact," *New York Times*, March 28, 2004.

67. Ibid.

68. Okrent, "13 Things I Meant to Write About."

69. Paul Krugman, "What They Did Last Fall," *New York Times*, August 19, 2005.

70. Donald Luskin, "*This* Again?" Conspiracy to Keep You Poor and Stupid blog, August 19, 2005.

71. Ford Fessendon and John M. Broder, "Study of Disputed Florida Ballots Finds Justices Did Not Cast the Deciding Vote," *New York Times*, November 12, 2001.

72. Paul Krugman, "Don't Prettify Our History," *New York Times*, August 22, 2005.

73. Byron Calame, "The Story of a Correction," Public Editor's Journal blog, *New York Times*, September 2, 2005.

74. Paul Krugman, "Summer of Our Discontent," *New York Times*, August 26, 2005.

75. Calame, "Story of a Correction."

76. Paul Krugman, "Correction: From Paul Krugman," *New York Times* web site, October 2, 2005.

77. Byron Calame, "Columnist Correction Policy Isn't Being Applied to Krugman," Public Editor's Journal blog, *New York Times*, September 16, 2005.

78. Byron Calame, "Columnist Correction Policy to Be Addressed," Public Editor's Journal blog, *New York Times*, September 28, 2005.

79. Gail Collins, "A Letter from the Editor: It All Goes on the Permanent Record," *New York Times*, October 2, 2005.

80. "For the Record," *New York Times*, October 2, 2005.

81. Paul Krugman, "Assassination Attempt in Arizona," Conscience of a Liberal blog, *New York Times* web site, January 8, 2011.

82. James Taranto, "'It Did Not,'" Best of the Web Today blog, *Wall Street Journal* web site, January 13, 2011.

Chapter 3 The Leader

1. This and all quotations in this chapter, unless otherwise noted, are from December 2009 author interviews with the person quoted.

2. This and all other quotations of BB&T's philosophy, mission, and values are from BB&T: *The BB&T Philosophy*, 1998.

3. John Allison, "The Financial Crisis, Causes and Possible Cures," speech at the Ayn Rand Center for Individual Rights, January 29, 2009.

4. Ibid.

5. Ibid.

6. John Allison, "Allison on Strategy, Profits and Self-Interest," interviewed by Russell Roberts on Econtalk podcast at the Library of Economics and Liberty web site, May 7, 2007.

7. Allison, "Financial Crisis."

8. Ibid.

9. Ibid.

10. Allison, "Allison on Strategy."

11. Allison, "Financial Crisis."

12. Ibid.

13. Ibid.

14. Ibid.

15. Ibid.

16. Allison, "Allison on Strategy."

17. Ibid.

18. Aristotle, *The Nicomachean Ethics*, trans. James Alexander, Kerr Thomson, Hugh Tredennick, and Jonathan Barnes (New York: Penguin Classics, 1955).

19. Aristotle, *Rhetoric*, ed. James H. Freese (Tufts University, Perseus Project web site), 1378b.

20. Allison, "Allison on Strategy."

21. Ayn Rand, *The Virtue of Selfishness* (New York: Signet, 1964).

22. Allison, "Allison on Strategy."

23. Ibid.

24. Ibid.

25. Ibid.

26. Allison, "Financial Crisis."

Chapter 4   The Parasite

1. Jeff Bailey, "The Mortgage Maker vs. the World," *New York Times*, October 16, 2005.

2. Shawn Tully, "Meet the 23,000% Stock," *Fortune*, September 15, 2003.

3. Angelo Mozilo, "From the Bronx to the Boardroom," *Directorship*, September 2007.

4. Federal National Mortgage Association Annual Report, 2003.

5. Bethany McLean and Joe Nocera, *All the Devils Are Here* (New York: Penguin, 2010).

6. John Tierney, "Privileged Life in Peril for 2 Mortgage Giants," *New York Times*, June 17, 2003.

7. Ibid.

8. "Friends of Angelo: Countrywide's Systematic and Successful Effort to Buy Influence and Block Reform," Staff Report, U.S. House of Representatives, 111th Congress, Committee on Oversight and Government Reform, March 19, 2009.

9. Mozilo, "From the Bronx."

10. Tierney, "Privileged Life."

11. McLean and Nocera, *All the Devils.*

12. *Securities and Exchange Commission v. Angelo Mozilo, David Sambol, and Eric Sieracki*, Case No. CV09-03994, United States District Court, Central District of California, June 4, 2009.

13. United States Securities and Exchange Commission, Excerpts of E-Mails from Angelo Mozilo.

14. *SEC v. Mozilo et al.*

15. *SEC v. Mozilo*, Case 2:09-cv-03994-JFW-MAN, Document 301, filed August 16, 2010, page 17 of 47.

16. Countrywide Financial Corporation Q2 2007 earnings call, July 24, 2007.

17. Ibid.

18. Liz Moyer, "Countrywide, Markets on the Ropes," *Forbes*, August 16, 2007.

19. Liz Moyer, "Countrywide Is on Its Side," *Forbes*, August 16, 2007.

20. Ibid.

21. Federal Reserve press release, August 17, 2007.

22. McLean and Nocera, *All the Devils.*

23. Mozilo, "From the Bronx."

24. Bailey, "Mortgage Maker."

25. Gretchen Morgenson and Geraldine Fabrikant, "Countrywide's Chief Salesman and Defender," *New York Times*, November 11, 2007.

26. David Stix, "Naive, Egotistical, but Smart," *Forbes*, October 1, 1990.

27. McLean and Nocera, *All the Devils*.

28. Paul Muolo and Matthew Padilla, *Chain of Blame: How Wall Street Caused the Mortgage and Credit Crisis* (Hoboken, NJ: John Wiley & Sons, 2008).

29. Ibid.

30. Ibid.

31. Ibid.

32. Letter from Representative Darrell Issa to Alfred M. Pollard, General Counsel, FHFA, July 20, 2010.

33. Albert Crenshaw, "High Pay at Fannie Mae for the Well-Connected," *Washington Post*, December 23, 2004.

34. Annys Shin, "Examining Fannie Mae," *Washington Post*, May 4, 2006.

35. Crenshaw, "High Pay."

36. Morgenson and Fabrikant, "Countrywide's Chief Salesman."

37. Federal National Mortgage Association Annual Report, 2003.

38. U.S. Census Bureau, Current Population Reports, August 2008.

39. Angelo Mozilo, "Act Now to Make Every Month National Homeownership Month," *Mortgage Banking*, June 2004, 16–18.

40. Steven A. Holmes, "Fannie Mae Eases Credit to Aid Mortgage Lending," *New York Times*, September 30, 1999.

41. Jonah Goldberg, "Wall Street Fat Cats Aren't at Fault This Time," *National Review*, September 19, 2008.

42. Gretchen Morgenson, "Inside the Countrywide Lending Spree," *New York Times*, August 26, 2007.

43. "Friends of Angelo," op. cit.; Glenn R. Simpson and James R. Hagerty, "Countrywide Friends Got Good Loans," *Wall Street Journal*, June 7, 2008.

44. "Friends of Angelo," op. cit.

45. Ibid.

46. Ibid.

47. Ibid.

48. Daniel Golden, "Countrywide's Many Friends," *Condé Nast Portfolio*, June 12, 2008.

49. "Friends of Angelo," op cit.

50. Dan Golden, "Angelo's Many 'Friends,'" *Condé Nast Portfolio*, July 16, 2008.

51. Ibid.

52. "Friends of Angelo," op. cit.

53. Glenn R. Simpson and James R. Hagerty, "Countrywide Friends Got Good Loans—Mozilo Sought, Received Better Rates for Some: Problems for Fannie Mae?" *Wall Street Journal*, June 6, 2008.

54. "Friends of Angelo," op cit.

55. Morgenson, "Inside Countrywide Lending Spree."

56. Jody Shenn, "ARMed—Not 'Stuck': Bank Making Countrywide Less Rate Sensitive," *American Banker*, June 21, 2004.

57. Bailey, "Mortgage Maker."

58. McLean and Nocera, *All the Devils*.

59. Morgenson, "Inside Countrywide Lending Spree."

60. Ibid.

61. McLean and Nocera, *All the Devils*.

62. Ibid.

63. United States District Court Central District of California, Civil Minutes—General, *Securities and Exchange Commission -v- Angelo Mozilo, et al.*, Case 2:09-cv-03994-JFW-MAN, Document 351, filed September 16, 2010.

64. *Mortgage Guaranty Insurance Corporation v. Countrywide Home Loans, Inc., and BAC Home Loans Servicing, LP (Formerly Countrywide Home Loans Servicing, LP)*, February 24, 2010.

65. Jody Shenn, "Fannie, Freddie Subprime Sprees May Add to Bailout," *Bloomberg*, September 22, 2008.

66. Ibid.

67. Ibid.

68. "Friends of Angelo," op. cit.

69. Gretchen Morgenson, "How Countrywide Covered the Cracks," *New York Times*, June 27, 2006.

70. *Mortgage Guaranty Insurance Corporation v. Countrywide Home Loans, Inc., et al.*, op. cit.

71. Countrywide Financial Corporation Q2 2007 earnings call, July 24, 2007.

72. *Mortgage Guaranty Insurance Corporation v. Countrywide Home Loans, Inc., et al.*, op. cit.

73. Ibid.

74. RealtyTrac, "U.S. Foreclosure Activity Increases 75 Percent in 2007," January 29, 2008.

75. Glenn Setzer, "SEC Turns Spotlight on Countrywide CEO Mozilo," *Mortgage News Daily*, October 18, 2007.

76. "Countrywide CEO Angelo Mozilo Awarded $22.1 Million in Compensation," *New York Times*, April 25, 2008.

77. "Bank of America to Acquire Countrywide: Deal for Country's Largest Mortgage Lender Valued at $4.1 Billion," Associated Press, January 11, 2008.

78. Claire Suddath, "Biggest Golden Parachutes," *Time*, October 8, 2008.

79. Peter J. Wallison and Charles W. Calomiris, "The Last Trillion-Dollar Commitment: The Destruction of Fannie Mae and Freddie Mac," American Enterprise Institute, September 2008.

80. Fannie Mae 2008 Q2 10Q Investor Summary Presentation, August 8, 2008.

81. "Timeline: Events Leading to the Fannie, Freddie Rescue," Reuters, July 26, 2008.

82. Dawn Kopecki, "Fannie, Freddie 'Insolvent' after Losses, Poole Says," *Bloomberg*, July 10, 2008.

83. David Bogoslaw, "Fannie Mae and Freddie Mac: A Damage Report," *BusinessWeek*, August 29, 2008.

84. Andrew Ross Sorkin, "Paulson's Itchy Finger, on the Trigger of a Bazooka," *New York Times*, September 8, 2008.

85. Nick Timiraos, "Views Conflict on Fannie Meltdown," *Wall Street Journal*, April 14, 2010.

86. Ibid.

87. *SEC v. Mozilo*, op. cit.

88. United States District Court, Central District of California, Civil Minutes—General, *Securities and Exchange Commission -v- Angelo Mozilo, et al.*, Case 2:09-cv-03994-JFW-MAN, Document 351, filed September 16, 2010.

89. United States District Court, Central District of California, Civil Minutes—General, *Securities and Exchange Commission -v- Angelo Mozilo, et al.*, Case 2:09-cv-03994-JFW-MAN, Document 301, filed August 16, 2010.

90. Walter Hamilton and E. Scott Reckard, "Angelo Mozilo, Other Former Countrywide Execs Settle Fraud Charges," *Los Angeles Times*, October 16, 2010.

Chapter 5   The Persecuted Titan

1. Joel Brinkley, "U.S. versus Microsoft: The Overview; U.S. Judge Declares Microsoft Is a Market-Stifling Monopoly; Gates Retains Defiant Stance," *New York Times*, November 6, 1999.

2. *United States of America v. Microsoft Corporation*, Civil Action No. 98-1232 (TPJ) Court's Findings of Fact, November 5, 1999.

3. Robert Slater, *Microsoft Rebooted: How Bill Gates and Steve Ballmer Reinvented Their Company* (New York: Penguin, 2004).

4. Stephen Manes and Paul Andrews, *Gates: How Microsoft's Mogul Reinvented an Industry and Made Himself the Richest Man in America* (New York: Simon & Schuster, 1993).

5. James Glassman, "A Right to an Internet Connection?" *American Enterprise*, April/May 2000.

6. GartnerGroup, "GartnerGroup's Dataquest Says Worldwide PC Market Topped 21 Percent Growth in 1999," press release, January 24, 2000.

7. Peter Newcomb et al., "The Forbes 400 America's Richest People," *Forbes*, October 22, 1999.

8. *CIA World Factbook*, 1999.

9. Chris Long, "Gates Opens Up (Cover Story)," *The Director*, April 1999.

10. Slater, *Microsoft Rebooted*.

11. Ibid.

12. Fortune 500, 1999, and Edward Rothstein, "Wronging Microsoft," *Commentary*, September 2001.

13. John Markoff, "For Microsoft's Rivals, It's a Question of Fairness," *New York Times*, July 19, 1993.

14. Rothstein, "Wronging Microsoft," and United States Senate, Lobbying & Disclosure Act Database.

15. Mark Lewyn, "Going After Microsoft," *National Review*, January 24, 1994.

16. Rothstein, "Wronging Microsoft."

17. M. Rogers and J. Stone, "The Whiz They Love to Hate," *Newsweek*, June 24, 1991.

18. U.S. Department of Justice, press release: "Microsoft Agrees to End Unfair Monopolistic Practices," July 16, 1994.

19. Slater, *Microsoft Rebooted*.

20. Steven Levy, "Behind the Gates Myth," *Newsweek*, August 30, 1999.

21. Adam Cohen, "Microsoft Enjoys Monopoly Power," *Time*, November 15, 1999, 46.

22. United States Court of Appeals for the District of Columbia Circuit, Argued February 26 and 27, 2001. Decided June 28, 2001. No. 00-5212: *United States of America, Appellee v. Microsoft Corporation, Appellant*. Consolidated with 00-5213 Appeals from the United States District Court for the District of Columbia (No. 98cv01232) (No. 98cv01233).

23. Levy, "Behind the Gates Myth."

24. Todd Bishop, "Software Notebook: 'Evil Empire' Microsoft Warms to Open Source," *Seattle Post-Intelligencer*, August 15, 2005.

25. Adam Cohen and Declan McCullagh, "Demonizing Gates," *Time*, November 2, 1998.

26. Rogers and Stone, "Whiz They Love to Hate."

27. James Henry, "Silicon Bully: How Long Can Bill Gates Kick Sand in the Face of the Computer Industry?" *Business Month*, November 1990.

28. Levy, "Behind the Gates Myth."

29. Michael Paulson and Dan Richman, "Microsoft Ruled a Monopoly: Company's Conduct Has Hurt Consumers, Judge Says," *Seattle Post-Intelligencer*, November 6, 1999.

30. Tom Stein, "Microsoft Ruled a Monopoly: Court Finds Firm Abused Its Power," report from MSFT Press Conference, November 6, 1999.

31. Ayn Rand, "What Is Capitalism?" in *Capitalism: The Unknown Ideal* (New York: New American Library, 1966).

32. Harvey S. Singer, MD, "Motor Stereotypes," *Seminars in Pediatric Neurology, Johns Hopkins University* 16 (2009): 77–81.

33. James Wallace and Jim Erickson, *Hard Drive: Bill Gates and the Making of the Microsoft Empire* (New York: John Wiley & Sons, 1992).

34. K. Anders Ericsson, Ralf Th. Krampe, and Clemens Tesch-Romer, "The Role of Deliberate Practice in the Acquisition of Expert Performance," *Psychological Review*, 1993.

35. Wallace and Erickson, *Hard Drive*.

36. Ibid.

37. Ibid.

38. Ibid.

39. Ibid.

40. Ibid.

41. H. Edward Roberts and William Yates, "Altair 8800 Minicomputer Part I," *Popular Electronics*, January 1975, 33.

42. Wallace and Erickson, *Hard Drive*.

43. Ibid.

44. Bill Gates, "An Open Letter to Hobbyists," *Homebrew Computer Club Newsletter*, January 31, 1976.

45. Wallace and Erickson, *Hard Drive*.

46. John Markoff and Paul Freiberger, "In Focus—Making the Most of Opportunities at Microsoft," *InfoWorld*, August 29, 1983.

47. Maggie Cole, "Gary Kildall and the Digital Research Success Story—The Man Behind CP/M," *InfoWorld*, May 25, 1981.

48. Wallace and Erickson, *Hard Drive*.

49. Ibid.

50. Ibid.

51. Jeffrey R. Yost, "An Interview with Seymour Rubinstein," *Oral History* 391, Charles Babbage Institute, May 7, 2004.

52. Stan J. Liebowitz and Stephen E. Margolis, *Winners, Losers, and Microsoft: Competition and Antitrust in High Technology* (Independent Institute, 1999).

53. James Wallace and Jim Erickson, "Computer Kid Grows into a Formidable Foe," *Seattle Post-Intelligencer*, May 9, 1991.

54. Wallace and Erickson, *Hard Drive*.

55. Slater, *Microsoft Rebooted*.

56. Ibid.

57. Ibid.

58. Ibid.

59. Ibid.

60. Alan Greenspan, "Antitrust," in *Capitalism, the Unknown Ideal* (New York: New American Library, 1966).

61. Michael A. Cusumano and David B. Yoffie, *Competing on Internet Time: Lessons from Netscape and Its Battle with Microsoft* (New York: Free Press, 1998).

62. Slater, *Microsoft Rebooted*.

63. Steve Lohr and Joel Brinkley, "Microsoft Defiant in First Response to Antitrust Case," *New York Times*, October 21, 1998.

64. Rothstein, "Wronging Microsoft."

65. Ken Auletta, "Final Offer—What Kept Microsoft from Settling Its Case?" *New Yorker*, January 15, 2001.

66. Bill Gates, deposition testimony, August 27, 1998.

67. Auletta, "Final Offer."

68. Ibid.

69. Cohen, "Microsoft Enjoys Monopoly Power."

70. Slater, *Microsoft Rebooted*.

71. Ibid., 121.

Chapter 6 The Central Planner

1. Michael R. Crittenden, "A Roof over Every Head: Longtime Advocate of Affordable Housing Brings His Passion to Helm of House Financial Services," *CQ Weekly*, December 11, 2006, 3262, www.cq.com.

2. Stuart E. Weisberg, *Barney Frank: The Story of America's Only Left-Handed, Gay, Jewish Congressman* (Amherst, MA: University of Massachusetts Press, 2009).

3. Town hall meeting, Dartmouth, MA, August 18, 2009.

4. "A Way with Words," *New York Times*, May 13, 2008.

5. Weisberg, *Barney Frank*.

6. Speech at Harvard University Kennedy School of Government, April 7, 2009.

7. Weisberg, *Barney Frank*.

8. Ibid.

9. Ibid.

10. Ibid.

11. Ibid.

12. Ibid.

13. Jeffrey Toobin, "Barney's Great Adventure: The Most Outspoken Man in the House Gets Some Real Power," *New Yorker*, January 12, 2009.

14. Weisberg, *Barney Frank*.

15. Ibid.; and Toobin, "Barney's Great Adventure."

16. Ibid.

17. Ibid.

18. Ibid.

19. Ibid.

20. Ibid.

21. Ibid.

22. Ibid.

23. Ibid.

24. R. Wilkinson, "Frank Talk," *Mother Jones*, January/February 1991.

25. Weisberg, *Barney Frank*.

26. George Archibald and Paul M. Rodriguez, "Sex Sold from Congressman's Apartment," *Washington Times*, August 23, 1989.

27. Weisberg, *Barney Frank*; and Margaret Carlson, Robert Ajemian, and Hays Gorey, "A Skeleton in Barney's Closet," *Time*, September 25, 1989.

28. Allan R. Gold, "Rep. Frank Acknowledges Hiring Male Prostitute as Personal Aide," *New York Times*, August 26, 1989.

29. Charles P. Pierce, "To Be Frank," *Boston Globe*, October 2, 2005.

30. Gold, "Rep. Frank."

31. Frank Phillips, "Frank Tells of His Despair during '89 Sex Scandal," *Boston Globe*, August 14, 2004.

32. Weisberg, *Barney Frank*.

33. Sally Quinn, "Rep. Barney Frank, Minority Wit," *Washington Post*, December 18, 1998.

34. Ayn Rand, "The Monument Builders," in *The Virtue of Selfishness* (New York: New American Library, 1964).

35. Ayn Rand, "The New Fascism: Rule by Consensus," in *Capitalism, The Unknown Ideal* (New York: New American Library, 1966).

36. Souphala Chomsisengphet and Anthony Pennington-Cross, "The Evolution of the Subprime Mortgage Market," *Federal Reserve Bank of St. Louis Review*, January/February 2006.

37. Bill Sammon, "Lawmaker Accused of Fannie Mae Conflict of Interest," Fox News, October 3, 2008.

38. Congressional Record, October 24, 2000.

39. Theresa R. DiVenti, "Fannie Mae and Freddie Mac: Past, Present, and Future," *Cityscape*, U.S. Department of Housing and Urban Development, 2009.

40. Weisberg, *Barney Frank*.

41. "Two Views: Barney Frank," *Mortgage Banking*, January 2004, 53–57.

42. Ibid.

43. Ibid.

44. Gretchen Morgenson, "A Coming Nightmare of Homeownership?" *New York Times*, October 3, 2004.

45. The OFHEO Report: Allegations of Accounting and Management Failure at Fannie Mae Hearing Before the Subcommittee on Capital Markets, Insurance and Government Sponsored Enterprises of the Committee on Financial Services, U.S. House of Representatives, One Hundred Eighth Congress, Second Session, October 6, 2004.

46. Federal National Mortgage Association Annual Report, 2007.

47. Morgenson, "Coming Nightmare of Homeownership?"

48. Press release: "Delinquencies Continue to Climb in Latest MBA National Delinquency Survey," Mortgage Bankers Association, November 19, 2009.

49. *Congressional Record*, June 27, 2005.

50. *Congressional Record*, July 25, 2006.

51. Ibid.

52. Ibid.

53. CNBC, July 14, 2008.

54. Jon Hilsenrath, Serena Ng, and Damian Paletta, "Worst Crisis Since '30s, with No End Yet in Sight," *Wall Street Journal*, September 18, 2008.

55. Peter J. Wallison, "Barney Frank, Predatory Lender," *Wall Street Journal*, October 15, 2009.

56. Ibid.

57. Joe Nocera, "As Credit Crisis Spiraled, Alarm Led to Action," *New York Times*, October 1, 2008.

58. Carrie Bay, "Probe Finds WaMu's Demise in Subprime Lending, Regulatory Turf War," *DS News*, April 16, 2010.

59. Edmund L. Andrews, "U.S. Shifts Focus in Credit Bailout to the Consumer," *New York Times*, November 12, 2008, www.nytimes.com/2008/11/13/business/economy/13bailout.html? _r=1&hp&oref=slogin.

60. Press release: "Treasury Emails Suggest Rep. Barney Frank Called Former Treasury Secretary Paulson to Obtain TARP Cash for OneUnited Bank," *Judicial Watch*, March 31, 2010.

61. Weisberg, *Barney Frank*.

62. Aaron Task interview, July 20, 2009, http://finance.yahoo.com/tech-ticker/article/285683/Barney-Frank-Don't-Blame-Me-for-the-Housing-Bubble?tickers=len,fnm,fre,kbh,tol,xhb,hd.

63. Massachusetts Democratic State Convention Kickoff Party hosted by Young Democrats of Massachusetts and Worcester County Young Democrats, June 4, 2010.

Chapter 7   The Capitalist Champion

1. This and all Rodgers quotations in this chapter, and recollections by Rodgers of statements of others, unless otherwise noted, are from a January 2011 author interview.

2. Richard Brandt, "The Bad Boy of Silicon Valley," *Business Week*, December 9, 1991, 64–69.

3. T. J. Rodgers, "Statement of Dr. T. J. Rodgers," Senate Committee on Governmental Affairs, Subcommittee on Oversight, June 3, 1997.

4. T. J. Rodgers, "Why Silicon Valley Should Not Normalize Relations with Washington D.C.," Cato Institute, November 19, 1998.

5. "SEMATECH History," SEMATECH web site.

6. United States General Accounting Office, "Report to Congressional Requestors: Assessment of the Financial Audit for SEMATECH's Activities in 1991," December 1992.

7. Brandt, "Bad Boy of Silicon Valley."

8. Ibid.

9. T. J. Rodgers, *No Excuses Management* (New York: Doubleday, 1992).

10. Cypress Semiconductor Corporation, Annual Report, 2009.

11. T. J. Rodgers, "Profits vs. PC," *Reason*, October 1996, 36.

12. Ibid.

13. T. J. Rodgers, "Valley Should Stand Up to Jackson's Divisive Tactics," *San Jose Mercury News*, March 14, 1999.

14. Deroy Murdock, "Jesse Jackson's Corporate Cash Cow," *Chief Executive*, July 2001.

15. Leonard Peikoff, "The Analytic-Synthetic Dichotomy," in Ayn Rand, *Introduction to Objectivist Epistemology*, ed. Harry Binswanger and Leonard Peikoff (New York: Penguin, 1990).

16. Ayn Rand, "The Metaphysical versus the Man-Made," in *Philosophy: Who Needs It* (New York: Signet, 1984).

17. T. J. Rodgers, "Holding Up the Shareholder," *New York Times*, April 29, 1997.

18. SunPower Corporate History.

19. "Cypress Announces Investment in Designer and Manufacturer of Ultra-High-Efficiency Silicon Solar Cells," SunPower Press Release, May 31, 2002.

20. www.fool.com/investing/high-growth/2005/11/17/sunpower -shines.aspx.

21. http://finance.yahoo.com/q/ks?s=SPWRA+Key+Statistics.

22. T. J. Rodgers, "Prop 23 and the Green Jobs Myth," *Wall Street Journal*, October 29, 2010.

Chapter 8 The Sellout

1. House Committee on Oversight and Government Reform, Hearing on the Financial Crisis and the Role of Federal Regulators, October 23, 2008.

2. Alan Greenspan, "We Will Never Have a Perfect Model of Risk," *Financial Times*, March 16, 2008.

3. House Committee Hearing, October 23, 2008.

4. Alan Greenspan, "The Assault on Integrity," *Objectivist Newsletter*, August 1963.

5. Ibid.

6. William Bonner with Addison Wiggin, *Financial Reckoning Day* (Hoboken, NJ: John Wiley & Sons, 2003).

7. Alan Greenspan, *The Age of Turbulence* (New York: Penguin Books, 2007).

8. Nathaniel Branden, *My Years with Ayn Rand* (San Francisco: Jossey-Bass Publishers, 1999).

9. Ibid.

10. Ibid.

11. Anne Heller, *Ayn Rand and the World She Made* (New York: Doubleday, 2009).

12. Branden, *My Years with Ayn Rand*.

13. Ibid.

14. Ibid.

15. R. W. Bradford, "Alan Greenspan—Cultist? The Fascinating Personal History of Mr. Pinstripe," *American Enterprise*, September/October 1997.

16. Branden, *My Years with Ayn Rand*.

17. Barbara Branden, *The Passion of Ayn Rand* (New York: Doubleday, 1986).

18. Branden, *My Years with Ayn Rand*.

19. Greenspan, *Age of Turbulence*.

20. Bonner with Wiggin, *Financial Reckoning Day*.

21. Jerome Tucille, *Alan Shrugged* (Hoboken, NJ: John Wiley & Sons, 2002).

22. Greenspan, *Age of Turbulence*.

23. Ibid.

24. Ibid.

25. Ibid.

26. Ibid.

27. Heller, *Ayn Rand*.

28. Branden, *Passion of Ayn Rand*.

29. Heller, *Ayn Rand*.

30. Ibid.

31. Ibid.

32. Alan Greenspan, "Gold and Economic Freedom," *Objectivist Newsletter*, July 1963.

33. Ibid.

34. Greenspan, *Age of Turbulence*.

35. Bonner with Wiggin, *Financial Reckoning Day*.

36. Alan Greenspan, "The Challenge of Central Banking in a *Democratic* Society," at the Annual Dinner and Francis Boyer Lecture of the American Enterprise Institute for Public Policy Research, Washington, D.C., December 5, 1996.

37. Alan Greenspan, "The Crisis," at the Brookings Institution, April 15, 2010.

38. Ibid.

39. John Taylor, "Housing and Monetary Policy," at the Kansas City Federal Reserve Bank Economic Symposium, Jackson Hole, Wyoming, August 2007.

40. Alan Greenspan, Federal Reserve Board's semiannual monetary policy report to the Congress, before the Committee on Banking, Housing, and Urban Affairs, U.S. Senate, July 16, 2002.

41. Greenspan, "Crisis."

Chapter 9   The Economist of Liberty

1. Milton Friedman, *Capitalism and Freedom* (Chicago: University of Chicago Press, 1962).

2. Ben Bernanke, "Remarks by Governor Ben S. Bernanke at the Conference to Honor Milton Friedman," November 8, 2002.

3. Arnold Beichman, "Letters to the Editor: How Wrong Can You Get?" *Wall Street Journal* (Eastern edition), November 17, 1994, A.25.

4. Ibid.

5. Ibid.

6. Introduction to PBS's *Free to Choose*.

7. Rupert Cornwell, "Milton Friedman, Free-Market Economist Who Inspired Reagan and Thatcher, Dies Aged 94," *The Independent*, November 17, 2006.

8. "The Intellectual Provocateur," *Time*, December 19, 1969.

9. Brian Doherty, *Radicals for Capitalism* (Cambridge, MA: PublicAffairs, 2007).

10. Milton Friedman, "Banquet Speech" at the Nobel banquet, December 10, 1976.

11. PBS, "The Commanding Heights," October 2, 2000, www.pbs .org/wgbh/commandingheights/shared/pdf/int_georgeshultz.pdf.

12. *Phil Donohue Show*, 1979.

13. Friedman, *Capitalism and Freedom*.

14. Milton Friedman, *Essays in Positive Economics* (Chicago: University of Chicago Press, 1953).

15. Milton Friedman, "Friedman—Autobiography," Nobelprize.org, March 1, 2011.

16. Lanny Ebenstein, *Milton Friedman: A Biography* (New York: Palgrave Macmillan, 2007).

17. Milton Friedman, "My Favorite Libertarian Books," Foundation for Economic Education, April 2002.

18. Milton Friedman, "Homer Jones: A Personal Reminiscence," *Journal of Monetary Economics* 2, 1976.

19. Ibid.

20. Friedman, "Friedman—Autobiography."

21. Ibid.

22. Matthew J. Dickinson, *Bitter Harvest: FDR, Presidential Power and the Growth of the Presidential Branch* (New York: Cambridge University Press, 1996).

23. Milton and Rose Friedman, *Two Lucky People: Memoirs* (Chicago: University of Chicago Press, 1998).

24. Friedman, "Friedman—Autobiography."

25. Milton Friedman and George J. Stigler, "Roofs or Ceilings? The Current Housing Problem," *Popular Essays on Current Problems*, September 1946.

26. William Breit and Barry T. Hirsch, *Lives of the Laureates: Twenty-Three Nobel Economists* (Cambridge, MA: MIT Press, 2009).

27. Leonard Silk, *The Economists* (New York: Avon Books, 1978).

28. Robert Bangs, "Reviewed Work: 'Roofs or Ceilings? The Current Housing Problem' by Milton Friedman, George J. Stigler," *American Economic Review*, June 1947.

29. Milton Friedman, "George Stigler: A Personal Reminiscence," *Journal of Political Economy* 101, no. 5 (October 1993): 768–773.

30. Ayn Rand, *Letters of Ayn Rand*, ed. Michael S. Berliner (New York: Dutton, 1995).

31. "The Economy: We Are All Keynesians Now," *Time*, December 31, 1965.

32. Milton Friedman, "The Role of Monetary Policy," *American Economic Review*, March 1968.

33. Friedman, Nobel banquet speech.

34. Friedman, *Capitalism and Freedom*.

35. Friedman, "George Stigler."

36. Milton and Rose Friedman, *Two Lucky People*.

37. *Phil Donohue Show*, 1979.

38. *Free to Choose* (1980), PBS segment 2 of 10, "The Tyranny of Control."

39. *Free to Choose* (1980), PBS segment 5 of 10, "Created Equal."

40. Editorial: "A 40-Year Wish List," *Wall Street Journal*, January 28, 2009.

41. Milton Friedman, *Why Government Is the Problem* (Stanford, CA: Hoover Press, 1993).

42. Ibid.

43. Milton Friedman, "Schools at Chicago," *University of Chicago Record*, 1974.

44. Fox News interview, May 2004.

45. "Business: The Rising Risk of Recession," *Time*, December 19, 1969.

46. Milton Friedman, "We Have Socialism, Q.E.D.," *New York Times*, December 31, 1989.

47. Friedman, *Capitalism and Freedom* (20th anniversary ed., 1982).

48. Friedman, *Free to Choose*.

49. Ebenstein, *Milton Friedman*.

50. Interview with Richard Heffner on *The Open Mind*, WNET, December 7, 1975.

51. Ebenstein, *Milton Friedman*.

52. PBS, "The Commanding Heights."

Afterword

1. "New York Times Columnist Paul Krugman," *Fresh Air*, WHYY, February 25, 2003.

2. Anne Heller, *Ayn Rand and the World She Made* (New York: Knopf, 2009).

Acknowledgments

Thanks to Pamela van Giessen at John Wiley & Sons, who patiently waited eight years for this book and put together the team that made it possible. We couldn't have done it without Emilie Herman, who set the deadlines and almost made us meet them—and the production team at Wiley, who tried their best to meet all theirs under extraordinary circumstances. And special thanks to Peter Canelias, a lawyer who should be an editor if he'd take a cut in pay.

Thanks to the wonderful people at BB&T who allowed us to interview them about the role of Ayn Rand's philosophy in their lives—John A. Allison, Kelly S. King, Christopher L. Henson, Edward D. Vest, Carla Fox, Timothy R. Davis, and Gena Reiswig. And thanks to the tireless Bob Denham, who made the interviews possible.

Thanks to T. J. Rodgers for an inspiring and exhausting four hour-plus interview—and the wine.

Thanks to Alan Greenspan, who did not agree to an interview, but who met with us and shared his enduring belief in Rand's ideas.

In addition, Don thanks Amanda Urban, who is not his agent, but who set us on the path of writing about Rand in today's world. And thanks to David Duval, who introduced Don to Ellsworth Toohey.

Andrew thanks Dave Kansas, a fellow TheStreet.com alum, for the introduction to Pamela. And thanks to the Aurora Public Library for its speedy and responsive research assistance.

About the Authors

Donald L. Luskin is chief investment officer of TrendMacro, an investment strategy and economics research firm. He is formerly vice chairman and co–chief investment officer of Barclays Global Investors. After a decade building Wells Fargo Investment Advisors into the world's largest and most innovative investment manager—where indexing, tactical asset allocation, and quant-active investing were invented and popularized—Don was a member of the three-man management team that sold the firm to Barclays Bank PLC in 1995. The firm was acquired by BlackRock in 2009.

While at Barclays, Don invented and patented target-date mutual funds, which have become a standard for retirement investment. Don was the inventor of the POSIT electronic communication network (ECN), and founder of the Investment Technology Group. He was CEO of MetaMarkets.com. He has been a hedge fund manager and an options market maker on the Chicago Board Options Exchange, the Pacific Stock Exchange, and the New York Stock Exchange.

Don appears weekly on CNBC's *Kudlow & Company*. He contributes frequently to the op-ed page of the *Wall Street Journal*. His articles and commentaries have been published in *Reason*, the *Harvard Business*

Review, *National Review*, *Pensions & Investments*, *Townhall*, the *American Spectator*, the *San Jose Mercury News*, and the *Detroit News*. He was formerly a columnist for TheStreet.com, Business 2.0 (now FastCompany), and SmartMoney.com.

He is the author of *Index Options and Futures: The Complete Guide*, and editor of *Portfolio Insurance: The Guide to Dynamic Hedging*, both published by John Wiley & Sons.

Andrew Greta is an author and business executive with more than fifteen years of experience in the financial markets. He currently holds an appointment with the College of Business at the University of Illinois in Champaign-Urbana. Previously, Andrew led corporate and business development at CME Group in Chicago—the world's largest and most diverse financial exchange. Andrew also served as Director, Global Business Development for General Electric, where he led global mergers and acquisitions, divestitures, and strategic partnership deals for one of GE's financial services divisions.

Andrew is a former contributing editor for TheStreet.com. His articles on finance and investing topics have appeared in numerous national publications, including *Stocks, Futures & Options*, *DS News*, ABCNews.com, *Online Investor*, and *Individual Investor*.

Andrew began his career as a financial adviser with Prudential Securities and holds an MBA from the Krannert Graduate School of Management at Purdue University. He currently lives in the Midwest with his wife Emily and daughter Lucy.

Index